INTERDISCIPLINARY CULTURAL PRODUCTION IN PRACTICE

Combining history, theory, case studies and practical guidance, this book offers a critical introduction to interdisciplinary production in the arts and cultural industries.

Taking a production studies approach, the book examines how arts and cultural organisations produce and present new work that integrates knowledge and working methods from different disciplines, while accounting for cultural policy, funding and audiences. It provides rich and detailed case studies of interdisciplinary production in practice across a range of international contexts. Rather than taking a specific art form as a starting point, the author focuses on the strategic act of conjunction and considers examples across multiple art forms including the visual and performing arts and beyond. Whilst providing historical and theoretical contextualisation, this book primarily focuses on new, accessible ways to both understand the promise of interdisciplinarity and execute its creation.

As the first text to examine the working process of creating complex interdisciplinary cultural projects, this book will be of interest to advanced students in various creative disciplines, including media production, cultural industries and arts management, and curating.

Peter Merrington is a Lecturer in the Business of the Creative and Cultural Industries at the School of Arts and Creative Technologies, University of York, UK.

INTERDISCIPLINARY CULTURAL PRODUCTION IN PRACTICE

Peter Merrington

Routledge
Taylor & Francis Group
LONDON AND NEW YORK

Designed cover image: Amalia Pica, *Venn Diagrams (Under the Spotlight)*, 2011.

First published 2026
by Routledge
4 Park Square, Milton Park, Abingdon, Oxon OX14 4RN

and by Routledge
605 Third Avenue, New York, NY 10158

Routledge is an imprint of the Taylor & Francis Group, an informa business

For Product Safety Concerns and Information please contact our EU representative GPSR@taylorandfrancis.com. Taylor & Francis Verlag GmbH, Kaufingerstraße 24, 80331 München, Germany.

British Library Cataloguing-in-Publication Data
A catalogue record for this book is available from the British Library

Library of Congress Cataloging-in-Publication Data
Names: Merrington, Peter author
Title: Interdisciplinary cultural production in practice / Peter Merrington.
Description: London ; New York : Routledge, 2026. |
Includes bibliographical references and index.
Identifiers: LCCN 2025053139 (print) | LCCN 2025053140 (ebook) |
ISBN 9781032847801 hardback | ISBN 9781032847788 paperback |
ISBN 9781003514947 ebook
Subjects: LCSH: Cultural industries | Arts and society |
Interdisciplinary research | LCGFT: Case studies
Classification: LCC HD9999.C9472 M47 2026 (print) | LCC HD9999.C9472 (ebook)
LC record available at https://lccn.loc.gov/2025053139
LC ebook record available at https://lccn.loc.gov/2025053140

ISBN: 9781032847801 (hbk)
ISBN: 9781032847788 (pbk)
ISBN: 9781003514947 (ebk)

DOI: 10.4324/9781003514947

Typeset in Galliard
by Newgen Publishing UK

CONTENTS

ACKNOWLEDGEMENTS

This work has a long genesis, tracing back to my time as part of the team at AV Festival in Newcastle, I am particularly grateful for the dedicated curators and producers I worked with there including Rebecca Shatwell, Diana Stevenson, Rebecca Morrill and Paul Smith, whose work sparked many of the questions that run as undercurrents through the topics explored here. My thanks also extend to collaborators and mentors from my time at Newcastle University, including Prof Venda Louise Pollock, and the Surface group (Tijana Stevanović, Elodie Roy, Sophie Yarker, and Ko-Le Chen) – all invaluable interlocutors where the initial seeds of this thinking were first tested. The students on the MA Management in the Creative and Cultural Industries at the University of York also deserve recognition. They were the first to encounter, and endure, the interdisciplinary live briefs I developed with external arts organisations as part of their collaborative teaching. Their constructive responses and insights were invaluable in developing an understanding of several key issues in this book. Crucially, the substance of this book would not have been possible without the generosity of those I interviewed and who I have had rich and detailed conversations with in the process of developing this work. Notably, these included Che Onejoon, Kate Farrell, Tom Higham, Ruhi Jhunjhunwala, Bronwyn Lace, Claudia Lastra, Sooyoung Leam, Katy Merrington, Ilana Mitchell, Sun A Moon, Anna Santomauro and Clara Vaughan. I am deeply grateful to all those who have kindly given their time to share their insights into their professional experience and the working practices of their organisations. Thanks to those who contributed anonymously. I extend further thanks to colleagues in the Cultural and Creative Industries Research Cluster at the University of York for comments on early work, as well as to Prof Duncan Petrie for his valuable insights into the book proposal. I am also grateful for the travel and research funds from the School of Arts and Creative Technologies at the University of York. This funding, alongside a research leave over a semester in 2025, enabled me to undertake much of the writing for this book. Additionally, I would like to thank colleagues at ENCATC (the European Network on Cultural Management and Policy) and The Association for Interdisciplinary Studies for their valuable questions, comments, and insights on early drafts of two chapters. I am also very grateful to Amalia Pica and Herald St, London, for their generous permission to use an image of *Venn Diagrams (Under the Spotlight)*, 2011 on the cover of the book. Finally, and most importantly, I owe special thanks to Laura, the boys, and my family for their constant support and patience.

1

INTRODUCTION

Interdisciplinary cultural production in practice

This book is about how and why arts and cultural organisations seek to connect, reorganise and integrate art forms and knowledge disciplines into new configurations and conjunctions as part of their work. It is about what this activity promises in terms of breaking conventions, of innovation, of novelty, of reaching new audiences and how the spaces built by arts organisations to hold and support such practices achieve these objectives. While interdisciplinarity may be predominantly associated with academic research and is common jargon in academic discourse, it is also increasingly prevalent in arts management, where cultural managers, producers and curators may regularly deploy interdisciplinarity as a particular ethos, although it is rarely interrogated in a rigorous way. At worst, this usage can become performative, verging on quasi-intellectualism and pretension. This book addresses that gap by offering a rigorous consideration of interdisciplinarity as a concept and a mode of cultural production, with a particular emphasis on the creation of new work by arts organisations.

If we take the 'inter' element of interdisciplinarity to simply mean 'between', this offers a valuable sense of flexibility and indeterminacy; its nature is determined by what, exactly, it seeks to bring together and how. As Moran (2010:14) notes, to fix the meaning of interdisciplinarity would be to 'discipline' it and set it within confined conventions. This book broadly defines interdisciplinary cultural production as any form of dialogue, synthesis, or interaction between two or more distinct disciplines where the interaction's mode, form, purpose and effect must be considered. Generally, it is a process where components from multiple art forms or disciplines, ones that do not conventionally collaborate, come together to create something new that is not reducible to the single components involved. This approach

DOI: 10.4324/9781003514947-1

aligns with Moran's (2010:13) view of interdisciplinarity as the reorganisation of knowledge out of established disciplines 'into new configurations and alliances,' often in reaction to ways of thinking that appear 'stale, irrelevant, inflexible or exclusory.' At this stage it is important to distinguish this from multidisciplinarity, which represents juxtaposition and proximity without direct attempts at collaboration or integration (Klein, 1990). While some art forms, like filmmaking or performing arts, are inherently collaborative, involving specialists in defined roles (directing, writing, lighting, sound etc.), this is not the focus here. Instead, this book is concerned with arts organisations that demonstrate a commitment to working in an interdisciplinary mode to actively challenge conventions through the conjunction of divergent practices and knowledge. The focus is on non-profit arts organisations operating outside of the academy that commission or create new interdisciplinary work where a central approach is to integrate knowledge from divergent disciplines, work that is not easily assimilated into existing institutional forms. This framing raises a core question, similar to that posed by sociologist Howard Becker (1982:28): 'how do non standard works ever get exhibited, performed, or distributed?' Since disciplinarity is the default, and novelty and complexity increase the financial and aesthetic risk of failure, this book investigates how this non-standard work gets made. We explore the role of arts organisations, and the cultural managers and producers who lead them, in simultaneously supporting, establishing, controlling disciplinary boundaries and seeking to challenge them through interdisciplinary means. Furthermore, we seek to understand why interdisciplinarity is assumed to be a necessary or important ambition in the context of arts production.

The impetus for this book is multifaceted. While there is a substantial, wide-ranging body of existing scholarship on interdisciplinary work, it remains fragmented. This includes significant work on interdisciplinary art (Cecchetto et al, 2008; Augsburg, 2017); literature on the convergence of art, science, and technology (Rogers et al, 2021); and a broad, if disjointed, field of study covering the historic and contemporary integration of art forms, such as music and visual art (Shaw-Miller, 2004), within visual arts (Hughes and Lafortune, 2001), expanded practices like post-dramatic theatre (Lehmann, 2006), and reconfigured social relations (Kester, 2004; Bishop, 2012). There are also practical guides for collaborative contexts (Morrison, 2022) and valuable reflections from practitioners and curators who have extensively worked in interdisciplinary contexts (Triscott, 2017; Triscott and Santomauro, 2021).

Despite this existing landscape, there has been limited focused scholarship into the organisations operating outside of the academy that privilege interdisciplinarity in their work. Specifically, there has been limited in-depth examination of the complex questions and negotiations that arts and cultural organisations face when amalgamating arts and non-arts disciplines. This focus is particularly crucial for smaller arts organisations, where experimentation and risk are central to their development of new work. This study seeks to account for this as well as the cultural policy context in which they operate, how they sustain themselves financially, and how they seek to connect with or engage particular publics and audiences. This practical, organisational perspective is important because it is frequently arts and cultural managers, leaders, and producers who instigate this kind of work, bring practitioners from different disciplines into conjunction, and take on key facilitation and mediation roles in the process of collaboration. It is to this gap, the lack of rigorous examination into the how and why of organisational practice in interdisciplinary arts management, that this book seeks to contribute.

Secondly, a better understanding of this work in practice is prompted by the increasing privilege afforded to interdisciplinary methods by arts funding agencies, cultural policymakers, and cultural institutions. In this context, there is often an underlying assumption that interdisciplinary approaches are inherently superior to conventional, discipline-specific work, on the grounds that traditional disciplines and established art forms are siloed and outmoded. There is a sense that conventional forms hinder, rather than enable, effective engagement with the complexity of the contemporary world. Consequently, interdisciplinary practice is presented as a mechanism to yield a broad range of valuable outcomes, primarily in the domains of innovation and the capacity to effectively engage with complex problems. This mandate is clearly evident in the promotion of interdisciplinarity as the vital route to address major crises such as climate change, to foster the social understanding of science, and to generate innovation through the adoption of new technologies. The prioritisation of interdisciplinary research as a strategy for understanding and tackling major crises has been mirrored, to a certain degree, within the arts and cultural sector. However, as is clear from the academic literature, the concept has at times been mistakenly championed as a panacea – a kind of shortcut or quick-fix route to novelty and innovation, or as the default way to engage with complex issues (Klein and Philipp, 2023). As Barry and Born (2013) observe, interdisciplinarity has emerged as a key political preoccupation, yet the term often tends to obscure as much as it illuminates.

This strategic framing is exemplified at the level of international cultural policy by the EU-funded Cultural Relations Platform. Seeking to 'strengthen the EU's ability to engage meaningfully with different audiences and stakeholders,' the Platform employs its Global Cultural Relations Programme as a primary mode of achieving these aims (Cultural Relations Platform, 2025). This short, intense professional training event, which began in 2016, originally focused on network building among cultural professionals. However, in 2023, it shifted to an explicit interdisciplinary approach, directly connecting cultural professionals with a non-arts discipline, focusing on climate change in 2023 and 'safer societies' in 2024. The intention, as articulated by the platform, is to provide 'a unique opportunity and space for innovative discussions and exchanging ideas with peers who have a strong willingness to contribute to a more interdisciplinary and sustainable world' (Cultural Relations Platform, 2023). Through intense dialogue and exchange, the programme strategically seeks to form social bonds and educate practitioners from different disciplines, thus building a professional network that links cultural producers with the potential for future collaboration. While no formal outputs are required, the underlying logic is that these new relationships will lead to future action, positioning the programme as both a driver of innovation and a form of cultural diplomacy. This is just one recent instance where interdisciplinarity is employed as a key route to innovation, and various others are examined throughout this book. The urgency to address issues that are too complex for any single field has thus positioned interdisciplinarity as the presumptive approach for arts organisations seeking to move beyond conventional forms of practice and address challenging global concerns, including systemic injustices, the climate crisis and digital transformation. While this framework has been used to justify the synthesis of tools, methods, and concepts from other fields, this thinking has been adopted by cultural policymakers and arts organisations with limited critical consideration of what interdisciplinarity entails or how it can be effectively developed in practice. This lack of scrutiny highlights a significant gap: there has been little empirical research or scholarship in arts management examining how and why organisations successfully, or unsuccessfully, work through these modes of interdisciplinary practice. This book begins to address that deficiency by seeking to better understand the practical production and outcomes of these complex projects.

Another motivating factor for this book is the need to understand the wider appeal of interdisciplinary work for artists, curators, cultural managers, and producers. As interviews with cultural producers undertaken for this research suggest, one of the primary draws is that working in this mode is perceived as exciting, cutting-edge, and risky, embodying a sense of inherent progressiveness. This stands in contrast to the perception of rigid, often market-oriented replication of practice associated with disciplinary art forms. One of the other fundamental appeals of interdisciplinarity is that it can be utilised as a strategic means for status mobility, allowing individuals and organisations to elevate their standing through association with higher-status bodies of knowledge and powerful institutional actors. The high demand for such interdisciplinary opportunities underscores this appeal. For instance, the Arts at CERN programme recently reported it received 718 applications from 91 countries for its Collide Copenhagen residency, celebrating the 'outstanding quality and daring with bold and innovative ideas' in every proposal (Arts at CERN, 2024). This demand raises questions not only about the precarity of artists and the general dearth of opportunities, but also about why interdisciplinarity is considered essential to artistic self-conception in contemporary society. Ultimately, this appeal points to a danger – that interdisciplinarity is viewed as a shortcut, a quick route to innovation and novelty, or that curiosity, nothing in itself to be discouraged, leads to forms of disciplinary tourism. This assumption often obscures the wider questions surrounding the practical management of these complex relationships: What, precisely, are the rigorous modes of interdisciplinary collaboration needed to develop new cultural work, and what are the considerable risks and hazards of working outside one's established discipline?

My own experience, both producing new interdisciplinary projects in arts management contexts and teaching cultural management students through live interdisciplinary briefs with cultural partners, confirms that collaboration in this mode is far from an easy route; in fact, the opposite is often true. It is a fraught process with uncertain outcomes. The inherent danger is that cultural production lacking valid justifications or rigorous methods simply produces an indistinct medley, a dull miscellany, or an odd, unexamined juxtaposition. This book is therefore driven by the need to work through the gap between the idealised rhetoric of innovation and the challenging reality of effective interdisciplinary practice.

The overarching methodological approach for this book is developed from production studies, a framework originally developed within media and cultural studies (Mayer et al., 2009). This choice is central to the book's aim – to move beyond an aesthetic or critical reading of interdisciplinary cultural projects and instead to provide a rigorous, practical, and systemic understanding of why this practice occurs, how it is accomplished, and what the strategic implications are for cultural managers and organisations. Traditionally, production studies focus on the context, process, and politics surrounding the creation and distribution of media artifacts. It is an explicitly holistic approach that seeks to understand the myriad factors that shape cultural output, from the initial conceptualisation through to its final distribution and reception. This framework systematically examines the step-by-step creation process across multiple analytical scales, which include – the practicalities of production, technical factors, questions of collaborative labour, and the realities of work and conflict in practice at the micro-level. As well as the meso-level management decision-making processes, resource allocation, internal management structures, and organisational culture. And the macro-level context of wider industry standards, policy and regulatory frameworks, questions of funding and financing, and the political economy of culture.

In this book, the production studies methodology is strategically deployed to address the unique complexities of interdisciplinary creative projects. In practice, this means shifting the analytical focus from the individual project outcome to the institutional and relational dynamics required to realise it. This approach requires paying granular attention to the lived experiences of the individuals involved, artists, producers, and managers, and understanding their decision-making processes, experiences of collaboration, negotiation, and conflict inherent in working with distinct fields. This approach led to an exploratory, multiple-case study approach (Yin, 2018) to facilitate an in-depth investigation into the complex, real-world context. It means examining the organisational modes and structures that are specifically developed to mediate and produce interdisciplinary work, asking how these structures are informed by, and respond to, wider economic and institutional pressures. By focusing on the intricacies of the creative process of conjunction, production studies allow the structural requirements and mediatory logics of interdisciplinary practice to come to the forefront. Using this methodology, the book structures its empirical investigation around five central analytical areas. These areas collectively map the lifecycle and context of interdisciplinary projects: (1) The cultural and political economy – examining the funding, finance, and resource allocation within the broader cultural and political economy that enables (or constrains) interdisciplinary production. This includes cultural policy, public and philanthropic investment. (2) The production process and relational work: considering how interdisciplinary cultural projects are made, from initial conception and ideation through to final realisation. This area interrogates who is involved, the various roles they play, and the mechanisms by which relationships, labour, and creative differences are convened, negotiated, and managed. (3) Contextual parameters and materiality: analysing the social, cultural, spatial, and temporal parameters in which the projects take place. This includes the subtle influences of disciplinary relationships (i.e., between art form categories), the specific sites of production, and the materiality involved, from the creative materials and technologies utilised to the physical objects and organisational documentation produced. (4) The organisational modes and structures – the structures specifically developed to mediate and produce interdisciplinary work, asking how these structures are informed by, and respond to, wider economic and institutional pressures or objectives. (5) Distribution, publics, and audiences – investigating the strategies for disseminating the work, the relationship with critics and publics, and the role of the organisations as mediators between the artists, the funding bodies, and the participants or audiences.

The core of the research employs a qualitative methodological framework incorporating several data-gathering techniques. The primary data source consists of a series of 19 anonymous and non-anonymous semi-structured, in-depth narrative interviews. These interviews were conducted with key producers, managers, curators, and artistic directors, all centrally involved in the commissioning, development, and realisation of interdisciplinary projects across a range of different organisations. Participants were selected using a purposive sampling strategy to ensure the inclusion of individuals with specific, deep knowledge and experience. This allowed for the collection of rich, contextualised data and personal accounts of the production process. In addition, the methodological framework incorporated analysis of archival and contextual sources, grey literature, which included organisational documents, marketing, internal reports, and social media communications. This was supplemented by a policy analysis of relevant policy and strategy documents, research reports, and funding applications. To understand the reception and public positioning of the work, the research involved a systematic analysis of media coverage and critical reviews. Additional contextual data was gathered through interviews with artists and cultural producers associated with the case studies, as well as the analysis of video and audio documentation of public events such as talks, discussions, and symposia. The book's key case studies were selected because of their distinctive and expressed commitment to interdisciplinarity as a core mode of production. The focus is primarily on non-profit, small-to-medium-scale arts organisations operating outside of traditional academic contexts. The common thread is the particular form of interdisciplinarity expressed within their working processes and organisational structures, in a way that does not restrict them to a single art form. This strategic selection allows for the derivation of broader, more transferable insights about interdisciplinary cultural production. Focusing the analysis at the organisational level is intentional, as it allows for an examination of institutional obligations to funders and to publics, as well as a detailed study of their production and mediatory roles. With such a broad frame, there is no sense that the book is attempting to be comprehensive; many significant projects, organisations, and approaches have not been covered due to pragmatic constraints associated with geography, time, access, and language. However, the book is intentionally international in its outlook and case study selection. This decision is motivated by a critical desire to move beyond the traditional dominance of European and US-centric histories of interdisciplinary arts. While this international perspective is necessarily qualified by the accessibility of English-language materials and interview access, the book aims to begin the process of providing a more geographically and culturally diverse perspective on interdisciplinary cultural production.

To a certain extent the trajectory of the book aims to follow the production lifecycle and context of interdisciplinary projects. The next chapter begins by setting the foundation through considering the interdisciplinary impulse in contemporary arts commissioning from the perspective of cultural production and arts management. We move beyond an oversimplified notion of novelty and innovation, arguing that a productive approach must first acknowledge and actively engage with the inherent tensions of disciplinarity. Disciplines are not fixed silos, but dynamic assemblages; therefore, meaningful boundary transgression requires practitioners to possess both a strong disciplinary grounding and the critical openness to challenge those conventions. The chapter identifies the complex, often entangled motivations for pursuing interdisciplinary cultural production – the desire for radical transformation, the pressure for utility (instrumentalisation to meet external demands), and the pursuit of innovation often linked to resources and audiences. This chapter provides the practical and operational insights to aid cultural managers navigate the dilemmas of instrumentalisation and seek rigor in practice.

From this broad opening perspective, in Chapter 3 the book then turns to look at the macro-level, through a specific national case study – the complex and often fragile funding ecosystem supporting interdisciplinary cultural production in the UK since 2010. While the rhetoric of interdisciplinarity, often tied to innovation, technology adoption, and commercialisation, has successfully advocated for new investment, cultural managers and producers face uncertainty navigating funding schemes that remain primarily focused on disciplinary objectives. The post-2010 austerity-led funding cuts reduced the appetite for artistic risk-taking and experimentation, but despite this, promoting interdisciplinary collaboration, especially with technologists, has been a central, if loosely positioned, policy priority for UK arts councils. The chapter examines the organisational forms of interdisciplinary cultural production, from it being a central curatorial concern, to it being strategically developed as an 'adjunct practice' that allow organisations to pursue innovation, diversify funding, and manage reputational risks without compromising their core artistic focus.

Chapter 4 articulates a framework defining the central parameters of interdisciplinary cultural production across different institutional contexts, with a specific focus on spatiality and temporality. The analysis is structured around key thematic areas: effective project structure and design, strategic functions, the consideration of time, place, and process, and the underpinning institutional logics. These themes are examined through a comprehensive series of organisational and project case studies. The discussion begins with the short, intensive artist-technologist collaborations staged by the New York-based net art organisation, Rhizome, in their *Seven on Seven* programme, and subsequently addresses the long-term, situated projects of Arts Catalyst in regional England. Further sections consider the public art collaborations of artist Katie Paterson and architects Zeller & Moye in the UK and US and explore the studio as a responsive site of collaboration through the creative methodologies of The Centre for the Less Good Idea in Johannesburg. The analysis then examines how AfroAsia in South Korea mediates the postcolonial present within its local neighbourhood. Finally, the focus turns to the festival as a cultural form and a key site and instigator of interdisciplinary cultural production. This phenomenon is examined through three distinct case studies: Pan-African cultural festivals in the 1960s and 1970s, the founding programme of the Manchester International Festival in 2007 and the Shanghai Project in 2016. The final chapter addresses a core tension inherent in interdisciplinary cultural production: the potential for audience discomfort and alienation caused by challenging established conventions, which must be balanced against an organisation's institutional need to justify and value public engagement. The analysis proceeds from the premise that interdisciplinary work is inherently risky for cultural organisations, as audiences may be alienated by perceived complexity, feel patronised by superficial execution, or perceive the work as reduced to mere spectacle. But the chapter also more generally seeks to account for how the audience is conceived in relation to interdisciplinary cultural projects – which is often through an objective of 'eliminating,' 'educating,' or 'developing' the audience. This can create a challenging dynamic for publicly funded organisations, which must balance the mandate for broad public relevance with the reality that the actual audience for highly innovative work is often a narrow, adventurous, elite group that embraces ambiguity. Therefore, to successfully manage these inherent risks and fulfil the promises of this kind of cultural production, the chapter considers the strategic approaches producers must adopt toward the audience.

In its totality, this book seeks to serve as an intervention into a field often obscured by superficial jargon and unexamined rhetoric. It critically interrogates the difficult dualities inherent in this work: the organisational need for stability versus the creative impulse for innovation, and the mandate for broad public engagement versus the reality of niche, risk-taking activities. By grounding the analysis in detailed case studies and the production studies framework, it provides a critical map for cultural managers, producers, and scholars to better understand interdisciplinary cultural production in practice. Consequently, the study asserts the necessary basis for rigorous practice.

Bibliography

Arts at CERN. (2024) '#CollideCopenhagen [Instagram post]', 26 April. Available at: www.instagram.com/p/C6Oa4vWIS-I (Accessed: 26 April 2024).

Augsburg, T. (2017) 'Interdisciplinary arts', in Frodeman, R. (ed.) *The Oxford Handbook of Interdisciplinarity*. 2nd edn. Oxford: Oxford University Press, pp. 131–143.

Barry, A. and Born, G. (eds.) (2013) *Interdisciplinarity: Reconfigurations of the Social and Natural Sciences*. Abingdon: Routledge.

Becker, H. S. (1982) *Art Worlds*. Berkeley, CA: University of California Press.

Bishop, C. (2012) *Artificial Hells: Participatory Art and the Politics of Spectatorship*. London: Verso.

Cecchetto, D., Cuthbert, N., Lassonde, J. and Robinson, D. (eds.) (2008) *Collision: Interarts Practice and Research*. Newcastle: Cambridge Scholars Publishing.

Cultural Relations Platform. (2023) *Apply for the Global Cultural Relations Programme 2023*. [Online]. Available at: www.cultureinexternalrelations.eu/2023/04/26/apply-for-the-global-cultural-relations-programme-2023 (Accessed: 1 November 2025).

Cultural Relations Platform. (2025) *Cultural Relations Platform*. [Online]. Available at: www.cultureinexternalrelations.eu (Accessed: 1 November 2025).

Hughes, L. and Lafortune, M.-J. (eds.) (2001) *Penser L'indiscipline: Recherches interdisciplinaires en art contemporain = Creative Con/Fusions: Interdisciplinary Practices in Contemporary Art*. Montreal, QC: Optica.

Kester, G. H. (2004) *Conversation Pieces: Community and Communication in Modern Art*. Berkeley, CA: University of California Press.

Klein, J. T. (1990) *Interdisciplinarity: History, Theory, and Practice*. Detroit, MI: Wayne State University Press.

Klein, J. T. and Philipp, T. (2023) 'Interdisciplinarity', in Philipp, T. and Schmohl, T. (eds.) *Handbook Transdisciplinary Learning*. Bielefeld: transcript Verlag.

Lehmann, H.-T. (2006) *Postdramatic Theatre*. Translated by K. Jürs-Munby. London: Routledge.

Mayer, V., Banks, M. J. and Caldwell, J. T. (eds.) (2009) *Production Studies: Cultural Studies of Media Industries*. New York: Routledge.

Moran, J. (2010) *Interdisciplinarity*. London: Routledge.

Morrison, K. (2022) *Making Socio-Ecological Art and Science Collaboration Work: A Guide*. [Online]. Available at: https://eprints.glos.ac.uk/11325/8/11325-Urquhart-(2022)-Making-Socio-Ecological-Art-and-Science-Collaboration-Work_%20A_Guide.pdf (Accessed: 14 August 2025).

Packer, R. and Jordan, K. (eds.) (2001) *Multimedia: From Wagner to Virtual Reality*. New York: Norton.

Rogers, H. S., Halpern, M. K. and de Ridder-Vignone, K. (eds.) (2021) *Routledge Handbook of Art, Science, and Technology Studies*. Abingdon: Routledge.

Shaw-Miller, S. (2004) *Visible Deeds of Music: Art and Music from Wagner to Cage*. New Haven: Yale University Press.

Triscott, N. (2017) *Art and Intervention in the Stewardship of the Planetary Commons: Towards a Curatorial Model of Co-inquiry*. PhD thesis. University of Westminster.

Triscott, N. and Santomauro, A. (2021) 'Transdisciplinary co-inquiry as curatorial methodology: From the Canadian Arctic to the Calder Valley, Yorkshire', in Rogers, H. S., Halpern, M. K. and de Ridder-Vignone, K. (eds.) *Routledge Handbook of Art, Science, and Technology Studies*. Abingdon: Routledge.

Yin, R. K. (2018) *Case Study Research and Applications: Design and Methods*. 6th edn. Thousand Oaks, CA: Sage.

2

THE INTERDISCIPLINARY IMPULSE IN CONTEMPORARY ARTS COMMISSIONING

2.1 Introduction – a warning

I want to start with a warning: 'interdisciplinary work is fraught with dangers' (Foster, 2003). Leaving behind your comfortable, known world and travelling to encounter something new is not without risks. It is common to view the processes of interdisciplinary cultural production as positioned against the ways art forms and mediums have been historically divided (Augsburg, 2017). And it is certainly the case that one impulse behind the creation of interdisciplinary cultural projects is a sense of frustration or irrelevance with how particular artistic disciplines, or their current practitioners and institutions, might be operating. As much as these projects are now often situated in relation to global challenges, they are also positioned against notions of medium specificity and autonomy in modernist aesthetics. They unfold out of the 'post-medium' practices of conceptual art from the 1960s, a period when the field of art expanded through such practices. Conceptualism, in effect, led to a pluralisation of art ontologies (Barry et al, 2008). This is where at least one of the dangers is lurking. As Foster (2015) notes, this freedom of association between art and almost everything else can come 'at the cost of disciplinary rigour, and the expansion of art has also meant an extension of its administration.'

It is therefore perhaps not surprising that one of the consistent criticisms levied against cultural projects that seek to integrate different forms of knowledge is that they appear to critics and audiences to be less than the sum of their parts – a convergence of disparate interests that lacks coherent expression. They are often criticised as clunky, awkward, compromised, instrumentalised, decorative, superficial, or simply bad art. Or, as Ede

DOI: 10.4324/9781003514947-2

(2005: 3) put it more bluntly in relation to collaboration between artists and scientists: 'Artists don't do prettification, product or propaganda for the public understanding of science. But they can engage with it and create images which suggest alternative ways of seeing.'

All of this points to the idea that interdisciplinary production in cultural contexts might be challenging for a myriad of reasons. Yet, this was not always how the process was necessarily conceived or presented by the practitioners interviewed for this research. In some cases, the difficulty was only truly understood after projects had been delivered. Essentially, achieving sound outcomes was harder than first perceived upon embarking on an interdisciplinary project, and the excitement, potential, or perceived benefits and promises of working with others from different disciplines was often considered a valuable end in itself. Consequently, on occasion little critical consideration was initially given by the practitioners to how the project might operate in practice.

The realisation of interdisciplinary cultural projects is frequently impeded by factors ranging from ill-defined intentions and divisive relationships between collaborators to significant power imbalances and the constraints of time, funding, or resources. Those in precarious financial circumstances, such as artists, can also feel pressured to contort their practice towards the specific requirements of a commission or residency, especially those from a prestige organisation, or to fit the parameters of a non-arts partner's project to access funding. This pressure is usually to the detriment of the final outcome.

The purpose of this chapter is to set out a series of six key considerations that may inform thinking around the production and management of interdisciplinary cultural projects. Distinguishing these points does not aim to provide an exhaustive list. There are undoubtedly multiple more factors that govern the production process of interdisciplinary cultural projects but highlighting these particular considerations aims to be generative, rather than restrictive. Such that these considerations can operate as starting points or provocations for cultural managers, producers and curators, acting as an aid to think through the possibilities and challenges of the process of creating interdisciplinary cultural projects.

2.2 Acknowledge disciplinarity

It can be tempting to launch into an interdisciplinary cultural commission or project without worrying too much about disciplinarity, assuming that interdisciplinarity is inherently progressive and will automatically generate value for funders, partners, or the public. However, simply combining things does not guarantee novelty, and juxtaposition alone should never validate the result. It is not a given that outcomes will be innovative, original, or even valuable; the underlying orientations, rationales, and working processes matter deeply. Failing to acknowledge this can generate or reinforce a view of disciplinarity as contrived and dull, contrasted with the supposedly exciting, new frontiers of interdisciplinarity.

It is therefore valuable to be aware of the consequences of properly acknowledging disciplinarity. Essentially, one must understand the internal dynamics of disciplines and their interactions within the process of interdisciplinary cultural production. This may seem obvious, but that is because interdisciplinary cultural projects are contingent upon disciplinary perspectives, people, fields, and discourses coming together. The space between disciplines is defined by how those disciplines are constituted, by their perceived stability, their territorialised boundaries, and the specific skills or knowledge they express.

As established, interdisciplinarity is not opposed to, but is instead fundamentally dependent upon, an awareness and knowledge of established disciplinary rules and practices. Therefore, the most productive starting point is to view disciplinarity and interdisciplinarity not as opposites, but as two concepts existing in a necessary tension (Osborne, 2013).

A conversation between Jon Wozencroft (co-founder of record label and multimedia project producer Touch) and sound recordist Chris Watson clearly exemplifies this tension (Blamey, 2016). They orient their discussion toward the consequences of digital production, which they believe has led to a downgrading of specialisation, where self-expression is prioritised over the specific knowledge of craft. In this context, 'knowing how' has been either downgraded or outsourced to digital technology, leading artists to identify with a wider range of creative practices than was historically common. As Wozencroft puts it: 'I think this relationship between specialism and interdisciplinarity is a crucial one, because it asks deep questions about our critical function as humans: is it an evolutionary step, or the opposite?' This follows the arguments of art historian Rosalind Krauss (2011), that a careless pursuit conceptual amalgamation can dissolve the critical rigor and technical support afforded by medium-specific constraints.

Central forms of disciplinary knowledge, practice, and experience are the foundational reality for most cultural producers, artistic directors and managers. Even those with decades of experience producing interdisciplinary projects generally began their careers within the terrain of a specific art form before expanding their work to other forms. The same can be for artists, as dancer and choreographer Merce Cunningham (1971) sets out in conversation with composer and artist John Cage noting the contingency of the disciplinary limits, while 'nothing is sacred to me in the terms of what one might think of as... possible in a dance,' on the 'opposite end, it's how the dancer, the individual dancer trains himself to be able to do that so that he can say repeat it without fear... of injury.' This perspective emphasises that the open willingness to challenge established conventions must be built on rigorous foundations and discipline in execution. Training and mastery of craft enable any art form to advance beyond its conventions. Thus, discipline itself should not be thought to hinder freedom in experimentation. Rather, it requires, as Cunningham describes the need to 'accept the mess' of putting oneself in an 'impossible' situation, only to discover through effort that it is now possible. Cage extended this idea with an analogy: 'think of the difference between an organized, cultivated garden and... a virgin forest. Entering the forest one is aware of what Thoreau called "wildness," and he said in this wildness, or we could say in the language we've been using, in this mess, is our salvation.' To borrow this thinking, acknowledging disciplinarity means embarking on an interdisciplinary cultural project by entering this wilderness with a set of disciplinary tools, skills, and knowledge that will facilitate the exploration, but being open to not using them and discovering new ones in the process.

Specialisation is also important simply because many complex cultural projects cannot be accomplished alone. If we view interdisciplinary cultural production as a relational process, the bonds between collaborators are frequently defined as relations between existing specialists. Therefore, at the outset of such projects, it is vital to acknowledge that the value particular artists, practitioners, or representatives from different fields bring is often based on their disciplinary specialism, expressed as knowledge, skills, training, or previous work, or conversely, their openness to applying that knowledge in new contexts and having those foundations challenged. While the overall project is interdisciplinary, the individual's contribution is valued precisely because it is rooted in disciplinary expertise.

Working through interdisciplinary collaboration can also heighten a practitioner's sense of disciplinarity through relationality. By forcing practitioners to consciously articulate, defend, and recognise the specific boundaries, methods, or value systems of their own field, collaboration acts as a mirror. This process requires practitioners to express their tacit disciplinary knowledge – their 'knowing how' (embodied skill, movement, and craft) – by explicitly articulating their methods and conceptual frameworks as 'knowing that' (conceptual knowledge). While these knowledge forms may be separable in theory, making this distinction helps in assessing skill, rigour, expertise, and specialisation in the interdisciplinary context (Ryle 2000 [1949]; Gobet, 2016; Bammer et al, 2020).

This friction arising from the coming together of disciplinary forms can sharpen an artist's understanding of what their discipline values most. This does not dissolve the discipline; rather, it allows practitioners to see existing boundaries more clearly, often leading them to reaffirm or selectively deterritorialise those boundaries. Disciplinary identity (e.g., as a musician, engineer, or choreographer) can be amplified and reinforced through their relational role in the collaboration.

For interdisciplinary cultural production to yield effective boundary transgression, however, the relations must go beyond mere identity affirmation.

As Barry and Born (2013: 1) state in their definition of interdisciplinarity, 'the disciplinary and disciplining rules, training and subjectivities given by existing knowledge corpuses are put aside.' There needs to be a willingness to set aside such components, though not necessarily to dissolve them entirely. If practitioners are too set in their ways, the potential transgressive value of the collaboration may be hard to realise. This points to an important lesson for cultural managers, who may need to facilitate such collaborations by carefully selecting participants and assessing their openness to setting aside fixed ideas.

This discussion connects to a wider question of hierarchies: should the traditional emphasis on mastering a specialised body of knowledge take priority before interdisciplinary work is introduced, or is developing cross-contextual skills more important for understanding the contemporary world (Klein and Philipp, 2023)? There is an enduring risk, as Foster argues (1998: 162 in Moran, 2010), that 'many young people now come to interdisciplinary work before they come to disciplinary work. As a result, they often fall into an eclecticism that does little work on any one discipline; it is more entropic than transgressive.' This perspective reinforces the need for an acknowledgement of disciplinarity. In Foster's words: 'to be interdisciplinary you need to be disciplinary first—to be grounded in one discipline, preferably two, to know the historicity of these discourses before you test them against each other.' The risk is that entering the 'wilderness' (to use the earlier metaphor) without the depth of rigour and training required to repeat new practices could lead to a lack of quality, or, as Cunningham (1971) put it, an 'injury'.

Given we are emphasising the importance of considering interdisciplinarity as something that should be imagined and practised as a response to the concept of disciplinarity (Augsburg, 2017). We should therefore not attempt to understand interdisciplinarity without first understanding disciplines (Moran, 2010). The word 'discipline' is associated with a specific body of knowledge, but also with modes of control and rigorous practice, whether through institutional forms (like the conservatoire) or through internalised dedication. In the arts, a high degree of skill and craft is acquired through extensive training and rigorous practice. Discipline is therefore more than just 'knowing that' (conceptual knowledge); it is also fundamentally about 'knowing how' (embodied knowledge).

As Cunningham (1971) expressed, discipline is not just a set of rules; it is 'something private' – a 'devotion' internalised by the dancer that allows them to perform. Disciplines and art forms can be conceptualised as self-perpetuating discourses or 'tribes', identifiable by their unique language, training, and culture. A primary critique concerns the power dynamics inherent in their use of inclusion and exclusion to control knowledge and authority. As Moran (2010: 17–18) puts it, they are 'a mode of thought, cultural practice or institutional framework that makes sense of and structures the world, often from the partial perspective of a particular interest group.' This historical formation shapes how we categorise art forms, leading to distinct training, critical vocabularies, and institutional structures.

When considering interdisciplinary cultural projects, we are not simply bringing together neutral entities, but art forms that carry a weight of historical tradition, established practices, and deeply ingrained notions of their inherent value. Interdisciplinary cultural production questions the modernist ideal of medium-specificity and seeks to explore the spaces between established categories, often echoing historical transgressions from Wagner's Gesamtkunstwerk to twentieth-century avant-garde movements (Augsburg, 2017).

For our purposes, it is useful to think of disciplines not as fixed entities but as assemblages (DeLanda, 2006). These constructs are stabilised through institutionalisation, which provides coherence and defines boundaries. This stability sets the scope of resources and power by monopolising 'knowing how' and 'knowing that,' which in turn shapes practices of cultural production, education, and research (Klein and Philipp, 2023). Disciplinary assemblages are made up of overlapping components: concepts, methods, techniques, tools, institutions, practitioners, funders, and social practices. These elements are not static; they evolve through a constant process of territorialisation, where boundaries are defended, and deterritorialisation, where core assumptions are challenged. This leads to the emergent properties of a discipline: its unique ways of knowing, its forms of expertise, and its distinctive culture.

If disciplines define what methods and concepts are rigorously applied, they are also about keeping out those that are undisciplined (Barry and Born, 2013). Fundamentally, acknowledging disciplinarity, means that arts organisations involved in producing interdisciplinary cultural projects understand they are implicated in disciplinary processes that manage inclusion and exclusion. Defining a process of inclusion is always, conversely, a process (even if unacknowledged) of also defining an exclusion. It is also worth remembering that disciplines themselves are fraught with internal differences and anxieties regarding status, purpose, and stability (Salter, 2021).

2.3 Understand the promise

The question of why cultural producers, curators, and artistic directors engage with interdisciplinary methods provoked a range of responses in the interviews. These ranged from a sense of it being 'important,' 'necessary,' or even 'urgent,' through to it simply being an 'exciting' way to work, a response to deep personal 'curiosity,' or an activity compelled by external factors such as funding requirements. However, there was also a pervasive sense of a common gap between the promise and the accomplishment of interdisciplinary cultural production in practice. That promise often takes on a mythic form, something actively sought by cultural policy makers and funders, but more elusive for arts and cultural organisations to realise successfully. This mythic element is referenced by the invocation of historical precedents (such as Black Mountain College or E.A.T.) as templates or justifications for new projects. Borrowing from the Barry et al (2008) analysis of academic interdisciplinary research, we can structure the rationales, or (somewhat mythic) promises, of interdisciplinary cultural commissioning around three distinct logics: ontology, accountability, and innovation. These logics can be entangled or sequentially at play within the same project. It is crucial for cultural managers and producers to reflect on these distinctions, noting how they create both dilemmas and opportunities for arts and cultural organisations.

The most radical and wide-ranging promise of interdisciplinary practices is that they will fundamentally transform or reorder art forms and disciplinary knowledge through the creation of new assemblages, objects, and practices that are irreducible to their original components. Barry and Born (2013) term this the 'logic of ontology' in academic research, a shift that transforms the objects and relations of study. These emergent hybrid objects cannot be reduced back into their original disciplinary components (whether social, technical, or natural), often necessitating new language for their description. It is perhaps in practices seeking such fundamental transformations that the most unease, friction, and disobedience are found. This is the realm of what Barry et al (2008: 38) call 'mutual interferences.' This tension is evident in the long-standing attempts to shift the ontological grounds of art in relation to emergent fields like the sciences, new technology, and social and political action (Barry et al, 2008).

These practices share a lineage with the post-medium condition and the pluralisation of art ontologies that occurred as a counter to formal modernism, a loss of the specific conventions that once defined a medium. This trajectory runs through postmodern and conceptual art, where the latter challenged modern art's material, visual, and economic forms by privileging non-object-based media and new temporalities, such as performance, participation, networked media, and installation (Barry et al, 2008). Such practices asserted an end to the philosophical conception of art as autonomous, where value is bound to aesthetics and formal properties alone, rather than to social, moral, political, or economic ends. This commitment to continuing to pluralise art's ontologies, or disobedience to form, is a central promise underpinning the interdisciplinary impulse in many contemporary commissioning contexts. While alluring for artists seeking to challenge the meaning and substance of art, this captivating idea also drives the impulse of cultural managers and producers. The inheritance of continually seeking to challenge what art should be becomes a motivating factor, yet it creates the challenge of mediating perceptions to retain critical distance and integrity while engaging meaningfully with other knowledge fields.

Beyond fundamental ontological shifts, a second promise of interdisciplinary cultural production is the more direct sense of utility. Here, accountability is the promise of utility, defined by how different art forms are made useful, politically, socially, and economically. This logic addresses how a discipline can appeal to or meet the external demands, needs, or requirements of another, making itself more accountable, relevant, or accessible to the public. Simply put, this is the strategic use of interdisciplinary cultural production to meet the specific objectives of one of the collaborators, thereby granting it greater public and political legitimacy. This is particularly relevant when arts organisations or other institutions (including scientific bodies) become more responsive and accountable to societal needs as opposed to being solely guided by artistic or market concerns. The promise here is twofold: firstly, in terms of problem solving – projects seek to address complex 'wicked problems' like related climate change, public health, and inequality. Secondly, this is in terms of audience engagement – projects aim to engage publics and stakeholders beyond the scope of traditional arts audiences, appealing to governments, funders, or specific communities.

Barry and Born (2013) notably map this logic of accountability onto the instrumentalisation of the art-science field, particularly through the work of funders like the UK's Wellcome Trust. The demand for scientific institutions to be more accountable and accessible to the public has led to interdisciplinary projects promising to make scientific research more readily communicable and understood by wider publics. This strategic relationship is a two-way process. Just as scientific bodies can seek to co-opt cultural production to promote science, arts organisations can co-opt scientific or social institutions to develop their work and enhance its utility, accountability, and legitimacy within the field of art, with funders, and with the public. As such, arts organisations and cultural producers strategically partner with laboratories, researchers, charities, or technical experts to gain credibility for their work through this association.

Thinking about the promise of accountability and utility requires understanding what perceived failure or deficit may exist for collaborating partners. Art is sometimes framed as a solution or panacea for social failures; for example, in the art-science field, this often relates to the deficit or failure of science communication (Sleigh and Craske, 2017). The key dilemma for cultural managers in this context is the degree to which they are comfortable working in such potentially highly instrumentalised practices and the risk that this may undermine or erode the integrity of an art form. The dynamics at play are complex, particularly when asymmetric power relations exist concerning funding sources or the attribution of legitimacy. These challenges are generally more likely to be overcome in projects designed with a more equal sense of authorship, involving co-design, co-inquiry, and co-production. In interviews, there was a strong awareness, and accompanying hesitancy, among interviewees regarding the risks of being co-opted or instrumentalised. A further challenge arises in complex, large-scale areas where individual funding is scarce – cultural producers must design projects that appeal to divergent agendas to secure financing from multiple sources. This highlights a collateral promise of interdisciplinary cultural production: resources. In situations of economic precarity, collaboration and the sharing of resources become a logic of resilience and financial survival (explored further in Chapter 3).

Innovation is the third major promise associated with interdisciplinary cultural production – the creation and subsequent visibility of new possibilities (Barry and Born, 2013). Innovation is framed as the emergent property, the outcome that is greater than the sum of its parts. However, like interdisciplinarity generally, it arguably suffers from being over-hyped, especially when tied to commercialisation (Klein and Philipp, 2023), and may be more difficult to realise than anticipated (Edmondson and Harvey, 2018; Triscott and Santomauro, 2021). This promise of innovation has a clear overlap with utility, based on the assumption that artists and practitioners offer unique 'ways of thinking' (sometimes framed as a monopoly on creativity) valuable for generating innovation when mixed into technological, scientific, or social contexts. Similarly, the problem-responsive orientation of interdisciplinary cultural production seeking utility often entails a parallel promise of innovation as solutions are sought through collaborative practice.

In theory, innovation emerges from an artist's ability to be provocative, to enrich discussions by bringing new perspectives, asking unexpected questions, and providing new ways of seeing, thereby generating novelty. Artists and cultural producers can also be co-opted to offer thier work as 'content' for testing or prototyping new technological tools (Barry and Born, 2013). Conversely, artists can also be subversive, playful, or critical in ways that may compromise the intended promise of innovation, which in itself can risk the arts not being taken seriously as potential collaborators. Triscott offers the interesting example of Arts Catalyst's projects placing artists in micro-gravity situations with partners like the European Space Agency (Triscott and Santomauro, 2021).

Nonetheless, innovation concerning media, technology, and social practice has been championed in the arts, with interdisciplinary work offered as the route to this outcome. This rhetoric has been common in the programming approaches of new arts organisations seeking to establish themselves, as examined in the case of The Public and Manchester International Festival (see Chapter 3). For other arts organisations, like The Foundation for Art and Creative Technology (FACT) in Liverpool, the search for innovation becomes a central ethos, with the organisation describing itself as a 'hub of innovation, a pioneer of interdisciplinary international partnerships, and a centre of excellence developing new models of local connectivity and collaboration' (Stubbs and Newman, 2009: 11). This question of 'connectivity' also entwines the promise of innovation and interdisciplinarity, as one key innovation sought is the ability to grow or change an arts organisation's audience demographics (examined further in Chapter 5). This appeal to innovation also fits into wider corporate and business practices, such as the concept of 'open innovation' (Chesbrough and Bogers, 2014), which encourages businesses to create more open boundaries for seeking new ideas (Salter, 2021). This also appeals to the neoliberal notion of competitive advantage through creativity and its entwinement with entrepreneurship, and the continual pressure for arts organisations to 'innovate' to remain relevant (accountable) to funders, publics, and wider society.

However, other models promise innovation more carefully, without resorting to bombastic rhetoric. In interviews, some cultural producers and managers discussed interdisciplinary innovation as a process of 'holding space' or 'creating space' through practices of 'incubation'. In this model, the practical process of supporting interdisciplinary cultural production purposefully keeps instrumental elements away from practitioners, freeing them from external demands. Collaboration is emphasised as a 'privilege' rather than a weary necessity, requiring a high degree of support, rigour, and sensitivity.

The specific role of the arts organisation here is to establish an ethos of mutual, supportive, and open collaboration, unburdened by any conceit to instrumentalism, accountability, or utility. Such experimentation and dialogue can happen within a designated 'safe' environment long before requirements for audience appeal or income generation are placed upon it. However, such situations are often privileged and hard to achieve, frequently dependent on specific cultural economies, such as that provided by The Centre for the Less Good Idea in Johannesburg (discussed in Chapter 4). In contrast, in the cultural economy of the UK (Chapter 3), the promise of innovation, particularly regarding new technologies, is typically tightly bound to accountability, as public funding bodies encourage dynamic partnerships to generate new income streams and audiences, thereby making the arts accountable to publics and politicians.

2.4 Consider scale and vocabulary

A common framing used by those interviewed in thier role as producers of interdisciplinary cultural projects to conceptualise the interrelationship between disciplines was the notion of 'distance'. In one instance, a discussion, when starting a new project, centred on whether to collaborate with those perceived to be at the greatest 'distance' from the project's own discipline. The argument was that working with those at the greatest 'distance' might potentially yield the most radical results, offer the most intrinsic value, or provoke the most profound reflexive introspection. Beyond the risk of simply creating the spectacle of juxtaposition, how should we conceive of such distance in practice? This is where the concept of scale becomes central, allowing for a clearer understanding of both difference and commonality in interdisciplinary cultural production.

Considering scale is crucial to how interdisciplinary cultural production is conceived, particularly in relation to ideas of difference and commonality. This pertains to three specific areas: acknowledging that entering the metaphorical wilderness requires breaking the 'myth of unity' that surrounds disciplines (Salter, 2021); clearly defining the level of engagement the project seeks to operate at; and examining the power dynamics that play out at those levels.

Many art forms – from film to dance, music, and theatre – are inherently hybrid and collaborative in some form. Each art form already implies others but establishes itself as a discrete convention by privileging core elements (such as movement, performance, sound, image, or text) and hierarchically ordering all other components to produce meaning. Interdisciplinary cultural production can thus mean recognising and challenging these internal hierarchies. As Evans (2008) notes, the slipperiness of the term 'interdisciplinary arts' is partly due to the way it captures activities playing out across different scales. This ranges from those easily defined as working across distant disciplines, such as painting and molecular biology, to those operating within sub-disciplines, like the relationship between painting and printmaking within the visual arts. What matters, however, is not the perceived distance, but the expected outcome of the collaboration and the degree to which that outcome entails reflexive criticality that genuinely challenges disciplinary practices. The arts are messy and divergent, not a singular entity, they are changing and competing just as science is. Therefore, defining them against each other as singular, monolithic entities is unhelpful.

As many scholars have argued (Moran, 2010; Barry and Born, 2013; Salter, 2021), assuming a starting point with a simple dichotomy between two entirely homogeneous, closed-off disciplines or art forms would be a mistake. Art forms and disciplines are inherently porous, often possessing overlapping components. Salter (2021: 16) builds on this in relation to the 'perpetual argument' between art and science: 'the arts are not unified – there is as much a distinction among the training, methods, and practices of dancers and visual artists as there is between molecular biologists and particle physicists.' Such simple binaries are generally highly problematic in interdisciplinary cultural production. Salter argues for 'actions that go beyond worn-out clichés, binary oppositions, and mistaken assumptions on both sides of the still problematic "two cultures" that C. P. Snow wrote about some fifty years ago.'

The largest scale at which this plays out in interdisciplinary cultural projects is what Salter (2021) calls 'the art-science complex.' More essentially, this is the persistent, perceived superiority of the sciences over the arts and humanities. Moran (2010: 12) traces a history of academic disciplinarity in Western thought, noting that from the very beginning, the term discipline was caught up in the relationship between knowledge and power. Academic disciplines did not emerge as an 'organic consequence of advances in knowledge, but were also the product of institutional and societal factors,' particularly the demand for specialists in a complex and technologically sophisticated society. It is valuable to note this history because the key features of discipline become the very substance of negotiation in interdisciplinary cultural production. Running through this history is the perceived superiority of the sciences, as it traditionally offered more effective examples of 'useful knowledge' (Moran, 2010). Ultimately, this points to one of the greatest challenges for cultural managers and producers: seeking parity and symmetrical power relations between diverse disciplines within a project, regardless of external hierarchies.

The next consideration is the abundant way metaphors are used to imagine processes of interdisciplinary cultural production. As we have seen, 'distance' is used as a geographical imaginary to conceive of difference, alongside dualities such as 'mess and order' or 'the garden and the wilderness.' Examining what metaphors are frequently used offers a deeper sense of the approach and process of interdisciplinary cultural commissioning that is worth examining in depth.

As Klein (1990) shows in her work on the rhetoric of interdisciplinarity, the working process is often conceived through a metaphorical lens. While these metaphors can be beneficial, they are also potentially problematic. Looking at metaphorical frames provides a wider sense of how cultural producers conceive of interdisciplinary projects. These metaphors act to rhetorically simplify the complexity of such projects, offering a way to find a shared vocabulary between collaborators and potential audiences, thereby making complex projects more broadly accessible.

However, over-reliance on metaphors can simultaneously obscure, territorialise, oversimplify, or sensationalise such projects. It can lead to an overly simplistic view of the collaborative process, potentially overlooking crucial aspects like conflict, transformation, or the ways projects may transcend the initial disciplines involved. Considering the metaphors used may reveal underlying assumptions about conceptions of disciplinarity and the modes and logics that define a project, potentially highlighting pitfalls in the working process. I will briefly set out a series of forms of metaphor encountered in this research: spatial and territorial, infrastructural, violent, emotional, and biological. What is appealing about Roland Barthes' definition of interdisciplinarity, and perhaps why it is so often cited, is that in a single paragraph he evokes at least three of these different metaphorical frames. For Barthes:

> Interdisciplinarity is not the calm of an easy security; it begins effectively (as opposed to the mere expression of a pious wish) when the solidarity of the old disciplines breaks down … in the interests of a new object and a new language neither of which has a place in the field of the sciences that were to be brought peacefully together, this unease in classification being precisely the point from which it is possible to diagnose a certain mutation.
>
> *(1977: 155)*

The first set involves the search for 'common ground' or the discovery of 'new territory.' In a two-dimensional sense, disciplines might be imagined as 'territories' on a map, 'isolated' or 'cut off' from others by a 'border' or 'edge'. This implies peripherality and a void that must be crossed, reinforcing a sense of distinct boundaries and making the action about the process of movement across that boundary. Similarly, there are three-dimensional forms used to describe isolation: 'echo chambers,' 'silos,' or 'bubbles.' To connect these distant territories' interdisciplinary cultural projects are presented as the 'bridge,' 'intersection,' or 'junction.' Here, interdisciplinary collaboration is imagined as a form of infrastructure that facilitates exchange and the creation of new territory. The notion of bridging however, may downplay the possibility of deep integration. These metaphors emphasise specific points of contact and the potential for both exchange and divergence, where a junction suggests shared outcomes and the branching off of new explorations. We can also point to shared processes that involve vertical movement either up or down such as collective 'excavating,' 'unearthing,' or 'bringing things to the surface,' or 'building' and 'constructing,' where collaborators contribute different skills, materials and perspectives to a shared outcome.

Then there are the violent metaphors – 'Crash!' 'Collision!' As a sudden transfer of energy, the crash turns kinetic energy into something else – heat, light, sound – it is highly productive in that sense – creative destruction. But just as friction creates a spark and starts a fire, while destructive, it can create a path for new growth. This perspective sees discipline or art form as a form of protection that needs to be smashed or broken down by outsiders. Sometimes these are playfully conceived as double entendre – as in the title of the book 'Collision: Stories from the Science of CERN' (Appleby and Potter, 2023). Here a group of contemporary fiction writers were paired with scientists and engineers connected to the particle physics laboratory Genève, known for Large Hadron Collider and asked to respond to each other's work in prose. This was similarly deployed in the founding artist' residency programme, at CERN, known as 'Collide@CERN' (Koek, 2013).

There is a propensity here for such language to play out as spectacle, novelty, or sensationalisation of the perceived friction or conflict between participants, used to generate audience interest. This dramatises the entertainment value of situating countervailing views in juxtaposition. Conversely, in invoking 'collision' in their work on interarts practice, Cecchetto et al. (2008), while noting its problematic nature, advocate for using violent metaphor because it reveals the inherent limitations and uncertainties within established disciplines. The forcefulness of the term is valuable in advocating for a more critical and nuanced understanding of interdisciplinarity, one that is open to risk and challenging disciplinary knowledge. Yet, in a practical sense, cultural managers and producers must tread a careful path to enable projects. In the interviews, they generally saw themselves in softer terms as 'mediators' rather than forcing confrontation.

This leads us on to the next metaphorical frame, which is based in the emotional language of feeling and affect. Transgressing boundaries breaks the protection of disciplinary certainty, invoking what Barthes (1977: 155) called the breaking of the 'calm of an easy security'. This is important as it relates to the sense of unease or anxiety that comes from being out of one's 'comfort zone' that interdisciplinary cultural production can enable. This sense of unease may be felt by the producers, collaborators, participants, or by audiences encountering work that sits outside of their normative cultural expectations.

Finally, as Klein (1990) notes, biological metaphors are prevalent, where disciplines are thought of as interacting systems, such as ecosystems, gardens, and wildernesses. This emphasises interdependence, dynamic interactions, and the potential for competition, evolution, and emergence within an environment. Key terms repeat, from 'hybridity' to 'symbiosis' and particular forms of biological reproduction that induce change, such as 'cross-pollination' or 'cross-fertilisation.' While such terms might not fully capture the social or power dynamics at play, they do highlight the mutual benefit and the emergence of innovation. Just as cross-pollination leads to genetic diversity, the interaction of disciplines can foster richer and more innovative artistic outcomes. This emphasis on autopoiesis (self-creation) over purposeful development is often missed by the cultural economics of interdisciplinary production, which seeks to service specific agendas. Perhaps there is a balance here for the cultural manager or producer, again as a mediator, or back to Cage's notion, the gardener entering the wilderness, which emphasises the importance of stewardship: time, care, rigour, and working with constraints through nurturing, activating and propagation.

The value of considering such metaphors in the process of interdisciplinary cultural production is that it encourages critical thinking about the underlying assumptions and the logic driving such projects. The question is whether disciplines are viewed as fixed entities or more permeable, and whether the outcome will be synthesis, juxtaposition, or something else entirely. It also forces an acknowledgement that anxiety may be an inherent part of the process due to friction. While these metaphors are vital for imagining the possibilities of interdisciplinary cultural production, by their very nature they risk oversimplification and obscuring the complex practical realities and nuances of these collaborations. In each case, across spatial, territorial, violent, emotional and biological metaphors, they inherently emphasise certain components of interdisciplinary cultural production while downplaying others.

2.5 Understand the form

There are numerous forms that interdisciplinary cultural projects and commissions take, but the geometry of those forms falls into a common set of patterns. These forms define the nature of the relationships between the components of an interdisciplinary cultural commission or project. The duality or relationality of such projects can create different degrees of balance or friction between these components. These imbalances play out across a spectrum of power relations and the degree of disciplinary friction within a project. This ranges from smooth integration to antagonistic relations that open questions around foundational assumptions and practices within divergent disciplines in the process of them seeking to work together. These different forms can overlap and are shaped by the promise or logic driving such projects.

The design of interdisciplinary cultural projects necessitates a critical examination of the symmetry, hierarchies or equities of collaborative practices. Cultural producers can easily overlook underlying issues of hierarchy, authorship and relational symmetry. Unpacking these assumptions is essential for understanding the practical operational processes of interdisciplinary cultural production, specifically addressing divisions of labour, power dynamics, authorship and participant relationships. This provides valuable insight for arts and cultural managers navigating these contexts.

Barry and Born (2013) set out three distinct 'modes of interdisciplinarity' that can help us set out these forms of interdisciplinary cultural production. These modes are the 'integrative-synthesis mode', 'subordination-service mode' and the 'agonistic-antagonistic mode'. Integration and synthesis could be considered the primary mode of interdisciplinarity, where knowledge and practices from multiple art forms or disciplines are integrated together, with components being slotted together on more or less equal terms – to create hybrid work in ways that are not possible from a single approach. In these contexts, it is a relatively smooth process, where the basic assumptions and functions of either discipline are not challenged, and there is a clear sense of common purpose or common ground, a shared issue, belief or problem, through which collaborations are oriented towards, and provide the driving emphasis. By contrast the 'subordination-service mode', reflects situations where there is a clearer determinism or asymmetry to the power dynamics within the collaboration. This form of interdisciplinarity operates where a primary discipline is supported or has a subordinate relationship with one or more other disciplines that offer it some utility. The third 'agonistic-antagonistic' mode operates where friction may become a productive force, this reflects collaborative situations that move beyond the neutral realm of mutual collaboration to a position where the fundamental assumptions of disciplinary practices involved are challenged. These are disciplinary components that may be latent or taken for granted but in some way shape disciplinary assemblages – values, methods, processes. This is harder in practice because those participating must be open to challenging their own understanding of these fundamental components, to accept limitations or blind-spots, or problems – emerging from this mode may be challenges to disciplinary practice that are felt within those institutions that defend, legitimate or legislate disciplinary boundaries. This means critique within an interdisciplinary collaboration is welcomed, as well as a starting point that acknowledges the very disciplinary edges or constraints. As well as an openness to self-criticality in the process of collaboration, this might also include an 'intervention' where one is not necessarily invited.

The practical case studies (set out in Chapter 4) considered in developing this book, connect to all these modes to different degrees. All three modes can also take place within a single project at different times – as negotiations take place and friction occurs, different paths through a project are navigated. Take a common form of interdisciplinary culture production such as the 'artist residency' where an artist is embedded in a non-arts context for a period of time. Here through the guest-host dynamic that may play out, it is possible to imagine how different forms of integrative, subordinate and antagonistic encounters, discussions and practices may develop over a period as the artist and the host institution navigate and negotiate each other's work – testing the boundaries of what it is possible to achieve or gain within that collaboration in context.

The case studies I have developed for this book show that interdisciplinary cultural production is shaped by distinct authorship / production dynamics. These dynamics operate along two primary axes: the first is the form of authorship, concerning the degree to which ultimate credit and potentially intellectual property are concentrated in a single individual or shared broadly among participants. The second is the modality of production, which addresses the extent to which the work is developed through direct collaboration and co-production (as a shared process) or by synthesising discrete, singularly developed contributions into a unified final project.

The most common authorship / production dynamic I encountered was a *singular (or hierarchical) authorship / shared production* relationship. There are many cultural production contexts in which a multiplicity of contributions from different disciplines, specialists or defined practices work together on a production. But where a sense of authorship is defined and expressed. These might take the form of service, subordination or sub-contracting. But can also be more fundamental to the intrinsic emergent properties of a project or working process in more conceptual projects. Such as where artist and activist Gustav Metzger's *Auto-destructive Art Manifesto* (1961) calls for collaboration with scientists or engineers to provide a means for self-destruction in the creation of public art. Similarly, projects may be about interpretation, translation and multiplicity of responses, which creatively repurpose those voices. Such as French artist Sophie Calle's project *Take care of yourself* (2007), where she asked 107 women from different professions to read a break-up letter sent to her by her boyfriend and analyse the writing from their specialist background. Here actualisation of 'boundary objects' (see Star and Griesemer, 1989) become a way to invite a multiplicity of voices into dialogue. Where such objectives have emergent relations with many different worlds – they become a rich source of response and creative inspiration across fields. But ultimately the form of such projects is rooted in the invitation of an artist, for others to respond and place their work into an arts context. Writing on the work of British artist Jeremy Deller, critic Charlotte Higgins (2025) characterises this form of *singular authorship / shared production*:

> Deller seeks out collaborators, usually from fields far removed from the art world: synchronised swimmers, archaeologists, power lifters, brass-band players, army veterans or simply willing volunteers. This way of working relies on Deller's manner and character: his genuine curiosity about the skills of others. Still, for all his punctiliousness at acknowledging those who have helped him, there is never any doubt about who is the creator, the artist. It is Deller.

All of this raises an interesting question about who actually undertakes the labour involved in the interdisciplinary element of a cultural commission. In many cases it is the artists themselves, but it is also possible that the difficult work of confronting, negotiating, interpreting and responding to other forms of knowledge – may be outsourced to curators, cultural producers and technicians – who realise this work on their behalf.

In a much broader sense, art forms rooted in hybridity, such as film and the performing art for example, also operate in this form of *hierarchical authorship / shared production* and are co-dependent on many multidisciplinary practices and specialists in those practices coming together that are subservient to the overall art form. This form of interdisciplinary synthesis is essentially normative practice within such highly collaborative, and industrial produced, cultural forms. The group dynamics between defined specialists within the creative production processes become fundamental to the emergent development of new ideas, innovations, improvisations and creative responses to specific constraints (Sawyer, 2012). But in general, the process is directed towards creating a cohesive final form or product in line with established conventions, rather than as an experimental practice with unknown outcomes at the start. Although many of those conventions will have started out as experimental forms for integration and collaboration before being commodified and folded into market capitalism. Ultimately although the production process might be highly interdisciplinary – authorship generally resides through an established hierarchy. Think of the idea of auteur theory and film production for example, where the director's creative vision may supersede those of their production collaborators – each with their own distinct crafts – composers, writers, editors, set designers, actors etc.

We could also point to the myriad forms of visualisation, sonification and the aestheticisation of data and scientific materials that artists, composers and designers undertake (see for instance, Manovich, 2010; Hermann et al, 2011). While artists can draw upon scientific expertise and methods to create work that primarily serves artistic ends ('engaging' with science in material, practical, technical and epistemic ways, as Ede [2005: 3] notes), the dynamic also operates in reverse. Since science can also be inherently an image-making activity, those images possess disciplinary mobility (Galison and Jones, 1998). In this reciprocal direction, art functions as a tool for the natural sciences, aiding in the conception and visualisation of scientific phenomena in aesthetically compelling ways (Salter, 2021).

Then there are authorship / production dynamics, where there is a *singular authorship / singular production* relationship. Here these are generally set out as interdisciplinary cultural frameworks that synthesise discrete contributions. We can see this in the way curator Hans Ulrich Obrist (2015: 152) characterises relations in an early project he was involved in that sought to bring disciplines into together – 'my sense was that to force artists and scientists to collaborate felt wrong: that would be to dictate the production of new works in a rather authorial way. Instead, I thought it could be more interesting, and more unpredictable to produce a context for chance encounters.' This approach is mirrored in his subsequent curatorial frameworks, such as Marathons where diverse contributors present work in response to a thematic frame, relying on the emergent properties of proximity, or juxtaposition for resonance with an audience. We can extend this to how in multidisciplinary thematic presentations created by festivals, biennials, museums or other cultural institutions. Here both the curator and the audience are in a sense the interdisciplinary agents, but not necessarily the individual work shown. In such situations it is possible to argue that interdisciplinary work is delegated to the audience, who must seek to synthesise and integrate the multiple disciplinary practices or materials to construct a holistic sense of meaning from it all. Something similar could be said for projects such that take a 'call and response' approach, rather than aiming for co-production – for example the writing model for the book *Collision: Stories from the Science of CERN* (Appleby and Potter 2023). Where fiction authors and scientists responded in individual prose to each other's work.

While such examples of form imply a clear reciprocity, it is also possible to identify *singular authorship / singular production* dynamics, that are less mutually beneficial or, indeed, extractive. This is a phenomenon we could characterise as a form of 'disciplinary tourism' – a brief excursion by artists, curators, or cultural producers into a foreign discipline (or vice versa) to observe its working methods before returning to their primary field. More bluntly, such a process has been labelled a 'looting expedition' (Penny in Barry and Born, 2013: 12). During these extractions, elements, including concepts, methods, or materials, are borrowed or appropriated and repatriated to the home discipline. There, they are typically presented as evidence of novelty, innovation, or as souvenir, sometimes packaged through the spectacle of conjunction or juxtaposition.

While a defined sense of authorship is central to the practices discussed above, a key motivation for many practitioners and cultural organisations engaging in the interdisciplinary cultural production process is the dissolution of singular authority. This intention to work with others without reinforcing the notion of singular authorship leads to forms of practice with an emphasis on *co-authorship / co-production* dynamics. In this model, authorship is shared, diffuse, or negated, and collaborators from different backgrounds work together in an appeal to non-hierarchical structures. It is important to acknowledge, however, that these collaborative collectives may still operate through external service or subordinate relationships during the final realisation of their work.

This form is reflected in the many multidisciplinary collective practices that explicitly seek to flatten such hierarchies and create a symmetrical set of relations within a project, notably by not always explicitly imposing collaboration, but creating the condition in which it may occur productively. This dynamic also extends to large-scale creative research investigations such as Feral Atlas (Tsing et al, 2021) as well as the approach of the Indonesian collective ruangrupa, exemplified by their direction of documenta fifteen that took place in 2022. Furthermore, Chapter 4 will examine the 'incubator' approach of The Centre for the Less Good Idea in South Africa and the 'transdisciplinary co-inquiry model' developed by curator Nicola Triscott at Arts Catalyst (Triscott and Santomauro, 2021). This form of *co-authorship /co-production* dynamic also extends to structures which fit more closely in as structural or spectacle of conjunction or justifications. This might be the 'equal-billing' of artists in the large-scale collaborative partnership projects of Manchester International Festival (see Chapter 3 and 5) or Rhizome's *Seven on Seven* programme putting artists and technologists together to create new work in 24-hours (see Chapter 4). Overall, this form of practice, as described by RAQS Media Collective (in Cornell and Halter eds, 2015: 86), is characterised by: 'curatorial collaborations and artist-practitioner-technician-curator-theorist net-works that transcend borders and disciplinary boundaries, that give new twists to the 'publicness' of public art projects, and that raise vexed questions concerning the 'ownership' of the ephemeral and networked works and processes that they generate.' This also points to how the 'agonistic-antagonistic mode' (Barry and Born, 2013), offers productive conflict and disruption – that reshapes what art making might mean and therefore require new legal concepts of authority, as well as economies of usage and participation.

The three dynamics of form explored here, across singular and shared authorship and production map the core tensions that define interdisciplinary cultural production. The dissolution of singular authority is reflected in practices that flatten hierarchies and seek a symmetrical set of relations, but this can also create conditions where productive conflict and emergence can occur.

Within these dynamics, the location of interdisciplinary work – the burden of conflict, synthesis and negotiation – can shift between the artist, disciplinary collaborators, producers, technicians and the audience or participants.

2.6 Conclusion

This chapter has presented a set of key considerations that inform the interdisciplinary impulse in contemporary arts commissioning, from the perspective of cultural production and arts management. Firstly, by acknowledging disciplinarity and actively seeking to engage with the tensions between disciplinarity and interdisciplinarity, the production of interdisciplinary cultural projects can move beyond an oversimplified promise of interdisciplinarity in relation to novelty, innovation, futurity and progressive practice. Rather interdisciplinary cultural production should embrace disciplinary contingency and aim for a productive awareness of disciplinary practices, existing in tension, not opposition, with specialisation. Ultimately, disciplines are not fixed silos but dynamic assemblages of concepts, methods and institutions, defined by processes of inclusion and exclusion. For interdisciplinary cultural production to achieve meaningful boundary transgression, practitioners must bring their specialised tools into the collaborative wilderness, possessing both a strong disciplinary grounding and the openness to set aside and challenge those same conventions. This approach, which acknowledges disciplinarity, is valuable for cultural managers tasked with facilitating the promise of such work.

This promise is multifaceted. The motivation for undertaking interdisciplinary cultural production is complex, extending beyond mere curiosity to encompass a range of distinct, yet often entangled, promises. One defining promise is that of radical transformation – the logic of ontology (Barry and Born, 2013) – the creation of new artistic assemblages and practices that fundamentally reorder disciplinary knowledge and are irreducible to their original components. This impulse, often inherited from post-medium conceptualism, drives artists and cultural managers alike to continually desire to challenge the meaning and form of art. However, as Rosalind Krauss argues, a careless pursuit of this can dissolve the critical rigour afforded by medium-specific constraints. Therefore, the question of rigour in pursuit of interdisciplinary cultural production comes to the forefront. Secondly, is the promise of utility, often derived from a logic of accountability (Barry and Born, 2013). Where strategic use of the arts promises to meet external social, political, or economic demands, that might include, public engagement, 'problem-solving' or improving science communication. While this can secure resources for precarious organisations and practitioners, it creates a dilemma for cultural managers who must navigate the risk of instrumentalisation and erosion of artistic integrity, particularly under asymmetric power relations. Finally, the promise of innovation offers to yield new possibilities, often by applying the artist's seemingly unique way of 'seeing differently' to technological or social contexts. Such a promise is often overestimated, and innovation is frequently entwined with questions of accountability, as public funding pressures arts organisations to seek new income streams and audience growth or diversification.

In practice, such promises are also shaped by how interdisciplinary cultural projects are conceived in terms of scale, metaphor and form. Critically considering these frames aims to help producers assess and understand a project's underlying assumptions and desired outcome. Doing so can avoid an oversimplification of practical realities, creating or reinforcing oppositional binaries, or generating spectacle. Part of the challenge is recognising which fields are already fragmented. While metaphors are beneficial for creating a shared, accessible vocabulary for collaborators and audiences, over-reliance can obscure, oversimplify, or sensationalise the genuine complexity, conflict and promise of the work. The varied forms of interdisciplinary cultural production are shaped by balances of friction and power relations between their components. Understanding the modes of interdisciplinarity as integrative, subordinate and antagonistic, as well as the authorship / production dynamics at play within interdisciplinary cultural production enables a valuable set of insights into the practical and operational reality of such projects. This provides an awareness and acknowledgement of how inherent power dynamics and existing hierarchies operate within the collaboration.

Bibliography

Appleby, R. and Potter, C. (eds.) (2023) *Collision: Stories from the Science of CERN.* Manchester: Comma Press.

Augsburg, T. (2017) 'Interdisciplinary arts', in Frodeman, R. (ed.) *The Oxford Handbook of Interdisciplinarity.* 2nd edn. Oxford: Oxford University Press, pp. 131–143.

Bammer, G., O'Rourke, M., O'Connell, D. et al. (2020) 'Expertise in research integration and implementation for tackling complex problems: When is it needed, where can it be found and how can it be strengthened?' *Palgrave Communications*, 6(5). [Online]. Available at: https://www.nature.com/articles/s41599-019-0380-0

Barry, A. and Born, G. (eds.) (2013) *Interdisciplinarity: Reconfigurations of the Social and Natural Sciences.* Abingdon: Routledge.

Barry, A., Born, G. and Weszkalnys, G. (2008) 'Logics of interdisciplinarity', *Economy and Society*, 37(1), pp. 20–49.

Barthes, R. (1977) 'From work to text', in Heath, S. (ed. & trans.) *Image, Music, Text.* London: Fontana Press, pp. 155–165.

Blamey, D. (ed.) (2016) *Specialism.* London: Open Editions.

Calle, S. (2007) *Take Care of Yourself.* Translated by C. Renwarden. 2nd edn. Arles: Actes sud.

Cecchetto, D., Cuthbert, N., Lassonde, J. and Robinson, D. (eds.) (2008) *Collision: Interarts Practice and Research.* Cambridge: Cambridge Scholars Publishing.

Chesbrough, H. and Bogers, M. (2014) 'Explicating open innovation: Clarifying the construct and identifying for future research', *Journal of Product Innovation Management*, 32(1), pp. 15–28.

Cornell, L. and Halter, E. (2015) *Mass Effect: Art and the Internet in the Twenty-First Century*. Cambridge, Massachusetts: The MIT Press.

Cunningham, M. (1971) 'Merce Cunningham and John Cage in discussion with Studs Terkel'. The Chicago History Museum/WFMT [Online]. Available at: https://studsterkel.wfmt.com/programs/merce-cunningham-and-john-cage-discuss-music-and-dance (Accessed: 12 February 2025).

DeLanda, M. (2006) *A New Philosophy of Society: Assemblage Theory and Social Complexity*. London: Continuum.

Ede, S. (2005) *Art and Science*. London: I.B. Tauris.

Edmondson, A.C. and Harvey, J-F. (2018) 'Cross-boundary teaming for innovation: Integrating research on teams and knowledge in organizations', *Human Resource Management Review*, 28 (4) , pp. 347–360.

Evans, B.M. (2008) 'Five problems for interdisciplinary art', In Cecchetto, D.,

Cuthbert, N., Lassonde, J. and Robinson, D. (eds.) *Collision: Interarts Practice and Research*. Cambridge: Cambridge Scholars Publishing, pp. 19-34.

Foster, H. (1998) 'Trauma Studies and the Interdisciplinary: An Overview', in Coles, A and Defert, A (eds.), *The Anxiety of Interdisciplinarity*, London: BACKless Books and Black Dog Publishing. pp. 157–168.

Foster, H. (2003) 'Nutty Professors', *London Review of Books*, 25(9), 8 May 2003, [Online]. Available at: https://www.lrb.co.uk/the-paper/v25/n09/hal-foster/nutty-professors

Foster, H. (2015) 'Exhibitionists', *London Review of Books*, 37(11), 4 June 2015, [Online]. Available at:

Galison, P. and Jones, C.A. (eds.) (1998) *Picturing Science, Producing Art*. New York: Routledge.

Gobet, F. (2016) *Understanding Expertise: A Multi-disciplinary Approach*. London: Palgrave.

Hermann, T., Hunt, A. and Neuhoff, J.G. (eds.) (2011) *The Sonification Handbook*. Berlin: Logos Publishing House.

Higgins, C. (2025) 'From acid house to ancient rites: Jeremy Deller's enormous, collaborative, unsellable art', *The Guardian* [Online]. Available at: www.theguardian.com/news/2025/apr/01/acid-house-ancient-rites-jeremy-deller-collaborative-unsellable-art (Accessed: 02 April 2025).

Klein, J.T. (1990) *Interdisciplinarity: History, Theory, and Practice*. Detroit, MI: Wayne State University Press.

Klein, J.T. and Philipp, T. (2023) 'Interdisciplinarity', in Philipp, T. and Schmohl, T. (eds.) *Handbook Transdisciplinary Learning*. Bielefeld: transcript Verlag, pp. 195–204.

Koek, A. (2013) 'Creative collisions – Beyond paradigms', *NMC Media-N* [Online]. Available at: http://median.newmediacaucus.org/isea2012-machine-wilderness/creative-collisions-beyond-paradigms-2 (Accessed: 15 April 2025).

Krauss, R.E. (2011) *Under Blue Cup*. Cambridge, MA: The MIT Press.

Manovich, L. (2010) *What Is Visualization?* [Online]. Available at: https://manovich.net/content/04-projects/065-what-is-visualization/61_article_2010.pdf (Accessed: 18 April 2025).

Metzger, G. (1961) 'Auto-destructive art manifesto', Gustav Metzger Foundation [Online]. Available at: https://gustavmetzgerfoundation.org/texts (Accessed: 12 February 2025).

Moran, J. (2010) *Interdisciplinarity*. London: Routledge.
Nesta (2018) *Experimental Culture: A Horizon Scan Commissioned by Arts Council England*. [Online]. Available at: https://media.nesta.org.uk/documents/experimental_culture_report_2018.pdf (Accessed: 24 March 2025).
Obrist, H. U. (2015) *Ways of curating*. London: Penguin Books.
Osborne, T. (2013) 'Inter that discipline!', in Barry, A. and Born, G. (eds.) *Interdisciplinarity: Reconfigurations of the Social and Natural Sciences*. Abingdon: Routledge, pp. 82–98.
Ryle, G. (2000 [1949]) *The Concept of Mind*. Harmondsworth: Penguin.
Salter, C. (2021) 'The art–science complex', in Rogers, H., Halpern, M., Hannah, D. and De Ridder-Vignone, K. (eds.) *Routledge Handbook of Art, Science, and Technology Studies*. Abingdon: Routledge, pp. 105–123.
Sawyer, R.K. (2012) *Explaining Creativity: The Science of Human Innovation*. 2nd edn. New York: Oxford University Press.
Sleigh, C. and Craske, S. (2017) 'Art and science in the UK: A brief history and critical reflection', *Interdisciplinary Science Reviews*, 42(4), pp. 313–330.
Star, S.L. and Griesemer, J.R. (1989) 'Institutional ecology, 'translations' and boundary objects: Amateurs and professionals in Berkeley's Museum of Vertebrate Zoology, 1907-39', *Social Studies of Science*, 19(3), pp. 387–420.
Stubbs, M. and Newman, K. (2009) *We are the Real Time Experiment: 20 Years of FACT*. Liverpool: Liverpool University Press.
Triscott, N. and Santomauro, A. (2021) 'Transdisciplinary co-inquiry as curatorial methodology: From the Canadian Arctic to the Calder Valley, Yorkshire', in Rogers, H.S., Halpern, M.K. and de Ridder-Vignone, K. (eds.) *Routledge Handbook of Art, Science, and Technology Studies*. Abingdon: Routledge, pp. 536–561.
Tsing, A.L., Deger, J., Saxena, A.K. and Zhou, F. (eds.) (2021) *Feral Atlas: The More-Than-Human Anthropocene*. Redwood City, CA: Stanford University Press.

3

WORKING IN THE RUBBLE

Cultural economies of integration in the UK after 2010

3.1 Introduction – the cultural economy of UK interdisciplinary arts

If we take interdisciplinary cultural production to be a complex practical process, often highly risky, with uncertain outcomes. With that complexity and risk, most likely comes cost, and a high demand for financial or other resources (time, commitment, a willingness to collaborate and experiment etc). Given that, who is willing to invest and support such work outside of market-based logics and academic research contexts becomes a central question. As does seeking to understand the motivation or rationale for that investment or support – which are not always simply reducible to aesthetic or intellectual curiosity.

Take one recent large-scale interdisciplinary cultural project created in the United Kingdom (UK) in 2022 – *Dreamachine*. This project was conceived by producer Jennifer Crook, working with a broad interdisciplinary team (including art and architecture collective Assemble, the musician Jon Hopkins, neuroscientists David Schwartzman and Anil Seth, philosopher Fiona Macpherson, technologist Dev Joshi and sound designer Christopher Shutt). The project itself was an immersive experience inspired by the artist–inventor Brion Gysin's 1959 *Dreamachine* contraption that sought to create kaleidoscopic illusions, both hallucinatory and dreamlike. Crook's 2022 *Dreamachine* was commissioned as one of ten large-scale temporary projects. Each project cost between £7m and £10m. These commissions made up the programme of what became known as 'Unboxed', a nine-month 'festival' that took place in multiple locations across the UK through 2022 (NAO, 2022). The event was commissioned by the Conservative Prime Minister Theresa May in 2018 to celebrate British ingenuity, as a marker of national pride and

DOI: 10.4324/9781003514947-3

renewal following the UK's tumultuous departure from the EU. With a budget of £120m, funded directly by the government, it became known colloquially, and somewhat dismissively, as the 'Festival of Brexit' (Razzall, 2023).

While large-scale, one-off investments made for statement public cultural events are rare, when they do occur, it is often the case that interdisciplinarity as a mode of cultural production is present – with its associations of innovation, futurity, problem-solving and the spectacle of juxtaposition. In this sense *Dreamachine* and the Unboxed festival are a useful example of how a specific cultural economy can be seen to underpin interdisciplinarity in cultural production. Particularly, as with this case, where interdisciplinary cultural production is deployed, with an underpinning logic of invention and novelty, but is also ultimately, tied with nationalist political ends. Unlike other commissions within Unboxed, *Dreamachine* has gone on to have a life beyond the event and toured internationally to critical acclaim.

While this is perhaps a somewhat unusual example of how interdisciplinary cultural production can be caught up in the service of specific agendas, that may be political or otherwise. What it points to, is the importance of considering how interdisciplinary cultural production is enabled through specific cultural economies, driven by their own logics. This chapter therefore sets out to contextualise the cultural economy of interdisciplinary cultural production by considering the UK funding ecosystem and organisational forms that shape it. This includes considering business models, resources, funding, and cultural policy, to understand how such structural contexts enable and also limit the creative and organisational decisions of producers of interdisciplinary arts in the UK. Fundamental to this is understanding how, within these contexts, producers develop a rigorous practice and navigate the risks and challenges of interdisciplinary cultural production set out in the previous chapter.

To do this the chapter focuses on how the cultural economy of the UK, particularly since 2010, has enabled and hindered the production of interdisciplinary arts, while also setting out how interdisciplinarity manifests in different forms through the production processes of arts organisations. This begins by setting out the changing ecosystem of funders and supporters in the UK. First by looking at the strategic approach of the four national Arts Councils to interdisciplinary collaboration, where interdisciplinarity has become synonymous with the adoption of new technology, and a search for innovation in business models at a time of austerity and reducing budgets in the arts. Then by considering how key charitable trusts, that have been essential to establishing interdisciplinary arts practices in the UK, have shifted their funding models away from directly placing artists into interdisciplinary contexts. Following this, three key organisational modes of interdisciplinary cultural production are set out in relation to the way non-profit arts and cultural organisations in the UK relate to interdisciplinarity. These are where interdisciplinarity operates as a central programming or curatorial concern for a venue or festival, where interdisciplinarity operates as an 'adjunct' practice, and where organisations act as 'agency' or 'portfolio' interdisciplinary producers. Each of these organisational modes are shaped by particular cultural economies, but in examining them it is also possible to start drawing out what rigour means in the process of creating interdisciplinary cultural projects which is essential to our practical understanding.

The UK makes a valuable case study, even though it has not always been central to narratives of new interdisciplinary arts or foundational organisations, which have historically focused on the US and Western Europe throughout the twentieth century (see for instance, Augsburg, 2017). There is a long history of art and cultural practices that connect to and build on these movements and organisations and the UK, built through underground, counter-culture movements as well as commercial and public investment. From the Bloomsbury Group and Vorticism in the early twentieth century, through to significant post-war events such as the Independent Group's *This Is Tomorrow* exhibition at the Whitechapel Gallery in 1956, the *Destruction in Art Symposium* (DIAS) 1966 with artists like Gustav Metzger and John Latham in 1966 and *Cybernetic Serendipity: The Computer and the Arts* at the Institute of Contemporary Arts (ICA) in 1968. We could also point to the BBC's Radiophonic Workshop from 1958 with Daphne Oram and Delia Derbyshire or the work of the Artist Placement Group from 1966. As well as the experimental practice of COUM Transmissions (1969 to 1976), the Black Audio Film Collective (1982 to 1998), through to the critical media projects of Mongrel and YoHa or the social juxtapositions of artists like Jeremy Deller in the 1990 and 2000s. Such work, while certainly not always self-identified as interdisciplinary, nonetheless has some basis in modes of collaborative and collective enquiry or experimentation as methodology or approach rooted in a desire to collaborate with others from different disciplinary backgrounds or art forms. It is against this context that I want to explore the funding ecosystem for interdisciplinary cultural production in the UK after 2010 as contemporary interdisciplinary projects operate within a landscape already marked by these historical attempts at boundary crossing.

3.2 The funding ecosystem for interdisciplinary cultural production in the UK

Since 2010, funding for arts organisations in the UK, including those focused on interdisciplinary arts, has seen a profound shift and challenging environment. This era marks a decisive break from the preceding so-called 'golden age' of cultural investment. This earlier period began with the introduction of National Lottery funding in 1994 and was sustained by the subsequent New Labour government from 1997, which significantly increased public investment (Hewison, 2014). This policy instrumentalised cultural spending, emphasising the arts' contribution to social inclusion, regeneration, education and economic growth. This also led to the creation of the National Endowment for Science, Technology and the Arts (Nesta) in 1998 (funded by the National Lottery) to promote talent, creativity and innovation across disciplines and interconnected areas of the economy, particularly at the intersection of arts, science and technology. But as was noted by a Nesta report (2018: 4), the 'UK's high levels of economic inequality and low social mobility are reflected in the polarisation of audiences for art and culture in the UK – meaning that the most privileged are often (although not always) more likely to access the benefits of public spending on the arts.' This goes hand in hand with attempts to shift the focus of cultural policy and funding into a more accountable mode, from supply (art organisations, artists and artworks) to demand (communities, audiences and participants) (Jancovich, 2017). But alongside this, the financial crisis of 2008 and the subsequent politics of austerity led to substantial cuts to public funding post-2010, fundamentally re-shaping the cultural policy landscape and compelling arts organisations to re-evaluate business models. There has also been many shifting priorities over this period – the rising urgency of the climate emergency, the (somewhat failed) promise of digital technology and the internet to democratise the arts, the social turn in contemporary arts, and a wider crisis of accountability in the arts in the UK in terms of representation of those working within the arts, but also the social and geographic inequalities of investment and who engages with publicly funded culture. In addition, political shifts that then occurred such as Brexit, also closed transnational funding such as Creative Europe (see IETM, no date). Over this period (between 2010 and 2023) the Campaign for the Arts & University of Warwick (2024) found the UK now has one of the lowest levels of government spending on culture among European nations. This comes after core government funding for arts organisations decreased by 18% and local government revenue funding decreased by 29% in Scotland, 40% in Wales and 48% in England. With The Arts Councils' core Government funding decreased by 18% in England, 22% in Scotland, 25% in Wales and 66% in Northern Ireland. All of this has occurred while the 'Creative Industries' more generally has been expressed as an ever more important part of national economic strategy. And in purely economic terms, the 'creative industries outperformed the UK economy over the period between 2010 and 2023 in terms of growth in GVA [gross value added to the UK economy]' (Newson, 2025).

Given this shifting cultural economy, one response has been the promotion or encouragement of interdisciplinary working as a necessary strategy for survival, resilience, and to meet new funding priorities with specific and instrumentalised social, health or economic outcomes, rather than as artistic or intellectual endeavour. To develop more 'resilient' business models – i.e to be less reliant upon public funding, organisations have been encouraged to collaborate, build partnerships, share resources, create ‘cultural hubs’ and in some cases merge. Here arts administrators have turned to the logic of multi and interdisciplinary collaboration as a mode of cost cutting, aimed at allowing organisations to persist in their work through a shared mitigation of diminished resources. Through 2010 the rhetoric of resilience and the necessity of collaboration and partnership became commonplace in cultural policy (Arts Council England, 2013; DCMS, 2016; Woodley et al, 2018). Central to the appeal of the rhetoric of resilience, was that it gave arts organisations means to express and represent their ‘capacity to adapt to austerity’ through a performative exercise (Newsinger and Serafini, 2019). Beyond this, while interdisciplinary collaboration as resilience might offer a valuable logistical solution for managing and sharing resources, as a process such a logic seldom creates the necessary space, security, or freedom required for deep collaborations or new experimental work. Ultimately, such managerial pragmatism reduces the appetite for artistic risk-taking and can be counterproductive to essential experimentation, particularly when arts organisations are under existential financial threat.

Given this backdrop in 2018 Nesta published a report (commissioned by Arts Council England, to inform their future strategic development) titled *Experimental Culture*. They argued that to address the challenges the UK arts sector faced (‘a complex set of technological, demographic and socio-economic trends’) – greater experimentation was needed (2018: 9). The conclusion was that ‘cultivating a culture of experimentation within organisations – from opportunistic and small-scale testing to the larger and more structured experiments –should be a key priority’ (2018: 9). The report acknowledged that with declining public investment, many arts and cultural, and particularly smaller ones, needed to fundamentally change their business models. The report (2018: 8) pointed to how the: ‘significant technological developments in creative practice as interdisciplinary collaborations between musicians, artists, performers and technologists have generated artworks spanning multiple media and challenging conventional art form definitions.’ But it also noted that the predicted development of digital technologies had ‘not led to a seismic change in the relationship with audiences’ and many major institutions continued to operate with ‘a recognisable mix of activities’ (2018: 4). Nesta’s report argued that interdisciplinarity could be a route to innovation, but with a strong technologically oriented focus, as – ‘new technologies have increasingly been used in creative collaborations which blur art form boundaries’ (2018: 4). Here interdisciplinary collaboration between cultural organisations and practitioners with ‘technologists’ is placed centrally as a means to ‘advancing creative experimentation’. As they explained (2018: 40): ‘Interdisciplinary collaborations between musicians, artists, performers and technologists now regularly generate multimedia artworks mixing ‘high art’ with more popular forms and challenging conventional definitions.’ Essentially this promoted the view that the wider arts should adopt a multidisciplinary approach akin to the commercial industrial production of cultural products found in the film and games industries, where defined departments of specialists all contribute to the creation of a single product. An approach that would perhaps also already be very familiar to those working theatre and the performing arts for instance, where such collaboration is essential part of cultural production. This call for experimentation sharply contrasts with the economic instability and uncertainty facing arts organisations post-2010. So e now turn to examine how the UK's four national arts funding bodies have strategically positioned their response to this challenge.

3.3 The promise of tech and innovation: national arts funding strategies and interdisciplinary cultural production

Across the UK, public arts funding is primarily devolved and delivered at a national level by four distinct public bodies: Arts Council England, Arts Council of Northern Ireland, Creative Scotland and Arts Council of Wales. Each body operates with a specific remit for its nation, resulting in a differing strategic approach to investment, support, and development of arts and culture. Given the greater population in England, it is worth noting that Arts Council England has significantly greater financial resources than all the other nations combined. But nonetheless it is worth examining all four national approaches comparatively as there are nuances to their strategic engagement with notions of interdisciplinarity, particularly in relation to conceptions of innovation. The central aim here is to determine the discursive positioning of interdisciplinarity in cultural production within these national arts funding strategies. The analysis focuses on conceptual evocation in terms of if and how the concept of interdisciplinarity is explicitly invoked, defined, or articulated within the strategies. This includes considering how collaboration, partnership or working with other organisations beyond art forms or disciplines, both within the arts and with non-arts bodies, is encouraged, and what the logic underpinning this might be. With all of these bodies, staff are primarily, but not entirely organised, into disciplinary or art form specialisms within the organisation. So, it is also relevant to consider how different art forms are classified and categorised, and how these classifications either support or constrain the potential for interdisciplinary practice. Analysing the language and logic used to describe and promote interdisciplinary cultural production helps us understand what some of the underlying logics are of the strategic evocation of interdisciplinarity in the context of national arts funding. This allows us to better understand the promise of interdisciplinary cultural production at a national arts policy and strategic level.

While Arts Council England (2020) *Let's Create* strategy for 2020-30 makes no specific mention of interdisciplinarity or the interdisciplinary arts. It does set out the boundaries of the specific art forms it invests in as 'collections, combined arts, dance, libraries, literature, museums, music, theatre and the visual arts.' This was expanded at the start of 2026 to include a new art form discipline of 'digital art' (ACE, 2026). Although the strategy itself does not define 'combined arts', from other ACE literature shows it to be a category that operates as something of a catchall term. This points to a range of multidisciplinary activity and also incorporates those arts forms that may not have strongly sustained disciplinary structures, or historically have lacked status or legitimacy within the arts – 'festivals, carnivals, arts centres and presenting venues, rural touring networks and agencies' (ACE, 2025). An older definition of Combined Arts, relating to the 2018-2022 National Portfolio of organisations supported by ACE, does however make specific reference to interdisciplinarity, although it does not expand on the purpose of interdisciplinarity other than to 'create something new and exciting', in this definition 'interdisciplinary work' is set alongside outdoor arts, carnival, festivals, spectacle, live art and participatory and social art practice and as taking place in a range of settings from 'established theatres and galleries to communal settings, cross-artform venues and arts centres, pop-up spaces and outdoor sites.' (ACE, 2018). It appears this is very much focused on collaboration within the arts rather than expressly beyond the arts in any form.

Beyond art form classifications, a significant element noted in the 2020 *Let's Create* strategy (ACE, 2020: 9) was a retrenchment from 'innovation, risk-taking and sustained talent development' as a result of the more challenging cultural economy in the UK during the 2010s. Here the strategy acknowledges, 'funding pressures over the last decade have made it harder for many cultural organisations to experiment and undertake formal research and development' (ACE, 2020: 42). The answer to the retrenchment from innovation in the strategy is, somewhat circularly, to support 'innovation'. In this context innovation generally is set out in three specific modes – 'dynamic' ways of generating income, for instance reducing a dependence on public funding; seeking out audiences who are less likely to engage with the arts and seeking to 'adopt new technologies' (ACE, 2020: 41). The route to this innovation in the strategy, while not expressly related to interdisciplinarity – is situated in a collaborative mode of operation – where there is a strong emphasis on collaboration between organisations within the arts and externally to enable this innovation:

> We want them to become more collaborative: to learn from each other, share resources and jointly develop talent. We will assist them to forge new partnerships with further and higher education, the technology sector, the charitable and voluntary sectors and the commercial creative industries. We are confident that, in drawing on this wider pool of expertise, organisations will see new creative and business innovations emerge.
>
> *(ACE, 2020: 37)*

In the Arts Council of Northern Ireland's ten-year strategy published in 2024, interdisciplinarity is more explicitly invoked through a logic of innovation (ACNI, 2024: 28). In the strategy, innovation is the third most important outcome after financial sustainability and greater inclusion. Where 'experimentation' is set out as 'essential' for the growth of the arts sector – 'we aim to create an environment that supports artistic innovation, nurtures risktaking, and enables the sector to adapt and thrive in a rapidly changing world' (ACNI, 2024: 24). The Arts Council of Northern Ireland specifically define innovation to be the:

> Creation and exploration of new ideas and forms of artistic expression to bring fresh, exciting experiences for artists and audiences. This could mean the integration of technology, exploring interdisciplinary collaborations or introducing unconventional concepts or themes to inspire, provoke thought and contribute to evolving artistic practices. This could not only include a new product or output but also using new methodologies, techniques and processes to realise and bring ideas to life.

There is a greater emphasis here on artistic value and experience, rather than the instrumentalised economic innovation of the ACE approach. And a broader and more open focus on interdisciplinary collaboration for artistic development, that in scope goes beyond the arts, that is more than the promise of economic sustainability through shared resources.

ACNI (2024: 24) set out how they will specifically measure 'innovation and experimentation' in the work they support, through six areas: conceptualisation, originality, audience engagement, technological integration, impact/influence and 'collaboration/interdisciplinary – different art forms/sectors.' It is notable here that collaboration with other art forms or disciplines is a standalone category particularly in relation to technology. ACNI also has a less prescriptive art form categorisation, referring generally to the arts as a 'wide range of creative activities' encompassing many forms (2024: 29).

Creative Scotland, which also has a broader remit than other arts councils because it includes the screen sector which is not the case in England (where the BFI lead this) set out four strategic priorities as part of a 'refreshed' strategic framework in 2021 (Creative Scotland, 2024a). These are: equalities, diversity and inclusion; sustainability development – both in relation to 'helping tackle the climate emergency' and the operation of 'creative businesses'; fair work – promoting fair pay, conditions, and employment opportunities and finally developing and strengthening international collaboration, as well as artistic and cultural exchange. In relation to these areas, funding criteria for grants and support also take account of the quality and ambition of the work and engagement in relation to audiences. The strategy makes no specific mention of interdisciplinarity, but in the funding criteria set out in relation to Quality and Ambition, that consider the type of 'creative process' they want to encourage, there is a sense that challenge or transgressions disciplinary boundaries or practice is of central value:

> We want to create space for debate, critical thinking, risk and experimentation, encouraging connections across the arts screen and creative industries, and making the most of digital technologies, where appropriate. Research, development, critical thinking and self-reflection are all recognised as important to the work of the sectors we support.
>
> *(Creative Scotland, 2024b: 5)*

Again, 'innovation' is a central theme of the strategy – here it is primarily linked to development of 'new skills, networks and business models' but also in relation to 'experimentation' and 'risk'. But the strategy also sounds something of a cautionary note, that 'this will involve being adaptive to emerging models of practice or formats for the presentation of work, as well as protecting tried and tested models and building on them' (Creative Scotland, 2024b: 4). In terms of art form categorisation and definition, there is a broad acknowledgement of how cultural forms may shift and generate new modes of practice:

> We support individuals and organisations working across all areas of creative practice including craft, dance, design, Gaelic art, literature, music, screen, traditional arts, theatre, visual arts, and cross-disciplinary practice. We also recognise that artistic and creative forms are constantly evolving, and increasingly developing links and overlaps driven by new knowledge and collaborative approaches to creativity.
>
> *(Creative Scotland, 2024b: 5)*

This is important as elsewhere in analysis of their funding they have noted that the largest proportion of arts organisations they support (31%) are 'working on a multidisciplinary basis...[to] produce work that crosses art-form boundaries' (Creative Scotland, 2025). Creative Scotland has also operated with a specific subset art form categorisation, called, 'Interdisciplinary Performance' – that is a term used to describe funded to develop new projects related to live art and contemporary performance. For instance, a project by artist Craig McCorquodale, *In Search of Social Sculpture* at Tramway in Glasgow, a collaboration between the artist and a cinematographer, a composer and an architect exploring the intersection of performance and live cinema. Or a project by theatre practitioner Rachael Macintyre, titled *Where Oceans Meet* bringing together Gaelic and Sami culture in a new performance.

The Arts Council of Wales released a new ten-year strategy in 2024. It is perhaps the simplest and most open of the four national strategies. In relation to working across artsforms or with non-arts partners, the strategy makes no specific allusions to interdisciplinarity. But it does point openly to the value of 'networking', to 'create new relationships, including those outside of the sector, identifying local, national and global connectors and champions' (ACW, 2024: 15). This is also extended to a strong emphasis placed on the value 'collaboration' and 'partnership working' – pointing to the need to collaborate 'beyond the arts sector', with the aim of increasing 'reach and impact' (ACW, 2024: 13). Unlike the other national strategies there is limited focus on innovation, or its binding to the adoption of 'new technologies', in fact, the strategy makes no reference to technology at all. The single reference to innovation within the strategy, specifically relates to artistic practice – 'encouraging artistic innovation of the highest quality' (ACW, 2024: 15). This perhaps reflects the wider qualified sense of risk taking promoted within the strategy through an awareness or caution emerging from a sense of public accountability. As the strategy sets out, 'we will take risks, build resilience and be responsive to change, whilst remaining relevant to the people and communities of Wales' (ACW, 2024: 10). While the strategy itself sets out a very broad set of values and principles – that do not strongly connect, interdisciplinarity, new technology and innovation. This is clearly also something that has emerged in its implementation, as ACW has a specific 'Relationship Manager' role focused specifically on 'Innovation, Digital and Interdisciplinary Arts'. The role is focused on developing 'innovative practices across digital art, immersive media, AI creativity, XR' within Wales. (ACW, 2025)

Throughout all these strategies it is clear that there is a general positive emphasis placed upon collaboration within the arts, across art form and disciplinary boundaries – but also quite generally and loosely defined with a range of non-arts institutions, bodies and business. Generally, there appears to be a lack of strategic consideration of how this should be supported, enacted, or enabled in practice – especially given diminished resources. Where interdisciplinarity emerges as a mode of cultural management, it is generally underpinned by a broad innovation logic. This is primarily tied to how arts organisations should adopt or develop their work in response to new digital technologies. In some cases, interdisciplinarity is almost set out as synonymous with engagement with new technologies in the strategies. This overriding emphasis on logic of interdisciplinary cultural production as a route to innovation, based in engagement with new technologies follows the NESTA (2018) call for innovation, but overall, perhaps less rooted in enabling 'experimentation'. The strategic approach of the four national bodies, follows more generally another NESTA (Bakhshi et al, 2013) defined understanding of innovation within the arts and culture – that privileges digital technologies, but promises innovation in relation to four key areas of arts and cultural management and production: business model innovation and value creation, which can be both be generally read as new forms of commercialisation and audience 'reach' – engaging social groups not generally associated with specific art forms and art form development.

The risk with this kind of stipulation towards innovation through external collaboration – is that the answer to structural issues is that the arts seek collaboration to service the demands or requirements of other industries or areas of economic activity, whether market or socially driven – in a subordinate way, rather than focusing on artistic development or the more intrinsic cultural value of their activity.

There is also little sense or acknowledgement here of the challenges of successful complex collaboration – that require nuance, time, skill and resources to develop. Given the acknowledgement that risk taking has diminished in the arts through austerity, this raises the question of whether cultural organisations and their new partners have the capacity and skill-set to forge and sustain such complex, mutually beneficial partnerships effectively. This is especially the case for smaller arts organisations.

In a different sense, while the aspiration and ambition is clear, one of the other risks that is rarely acknowledged is that a consistent demand to collaborate with a 'wider pool of expertise' as set out in ACE's strategy, also has the potential to diminish art form specific knowledge, quality of delivery and expertise within organisations that specialise in specific art forms, particularly where areas like 'new technologies' are promoted as a panacea for requirements for 'innovation' as seems to be central in the strategic approach here. One of the risks or outcomes of this can be that when interdisciplinary collaboration is solely associated with a logic of innovation – and therefore promoted and encouraged by arts funding bodies – working within art form conventions and boundaries or not engaging with 'new technologies' is viewed as anachronistic or amateur.

3.4 The changing support of independent UK trusts towards interdisciplinary arts commissioning

National funding bodies must necessarily tread a tight path between demands on their focus and support for divergent art forms, as well as accountability in terms of allocation of resources to both the 'supply side' creation of public arts and culture and the 'demand side' consumption and participation of public culture at a universal level. However, in the UK the other significant form of funding comes from independent grant giving trusts and foundations. These private sector, grant-making charities play an important role in the cultural economy of the UK, particularly in relation to targeted investment that may encourage arts organisations to work beyond the boundaries of their particular root discipline. In some cases, this form of funding can offer a valuable opportunity for arts organisations to take risks, or seek to innovate their work through collaboration in a supported mode – where activities might fall outside of the conventional funding programmes of public bodies. This is particularly the case for piloting projects and the creation of new work that might be interdisciplinary in nature.

Since the early 1990s major trusts such as the Wellcome Trust and Leverhulme Trust have historically been significant supporters of interdisciplinary cultural production in the UK. However, more recent changes to their approaches to investment in the arts have shifted this. The Leverhulme Trust, one of the largest national grant-making Trusts in the UK, established in 1925, primarily funds research across academic disciplines. Up until 2017 Leverhulme supported an 'Artist in Residence Grant Scheme', that placed artists into a range of academic research institutions – to explore the collaborative potential of creating new work in such contexts. Described as 'one of the foremost mechanisms in the UK for interdisciplinary collaboration involving artists', the initiative had enabled artists to work with collaborators across the sciences and humanities (Fremantle, 2017). But the funding was ended in 2017 as pressure on the trust's funds meant it was no longer a priority. As those involved in the scheme described at the time, it had offered a uniquely open and supportive opportunity for academics to collaborate with artists through a rigorous and long-term collaboration (Fremantle, 2017).

While the Leverhulme Trust's focus in its Artist in Residence scheme was broadly open to a range of collaborative disciplines. Other trusts have a more narrow focus. The Wellcome Trust is a UK based global charitable foundation focused on health and biomedical science research. But alongside this Wellcome has had an evolving relationship with funding interdisciplinary cultural production, using interdisciplinary art commissioning in a range of modes to engage the public with bioscience related research and issues – through focus on health from social, cultural, and ethical perspectives.

Wellcome's first significant movement into commissioning interdisciplinary art focused on biomedical science was the 'Sciart' programme that ran between 1996 and 2006. The programme aimed to: 'stimulate interest and excitement in biomedical science...foster interdisciplinary and collaborative creative practice in the arts and science' and 'create a critical mass of artists looking at biomedical science and build capacity in this field' (Glinkowski and Bamford, 2009). Over the period 118 projects were supported with close to £3m of funding. The programme offered a route to interdisciplinary cultural production that was not available from other sources. As the evaluation report to the scheme acknowledged, the projects supported would have 'struggled to proceed' or 'been severely restricted' without the investment of the programme (Glinkowski and Bamford, 2009). According to the evaluation this led to 'considerable innovations, new explorative processes and methods of working, and interesting outcomes [that] attracted high levels of public and media interest' (Glinkowski and Bamford, 2009). But as Born and Barry (2010) and Sleigh and Craske (2017) note the emphasis of the programme was science communication and the public understanding of biomedical science in response to a perceived deficit of public understanding of science in the UK that was felt to be undermining the case for public investment in scientific research (Sleigh and Craske, 2017). This presented the sense that such interdisciplinary initiatives emerged with strong asymmetries of power, could be reduced to a 'science PR project' where 'art was subordinated to science in the pursuit of Communication' (Sleigh and Craske, 2017).

Subsequently Wellcome moved away from this mode of direct interdisciplinary art commissioning, alongside the opening of the Wellcome Collection as a public museum and visitor attraction in 2007, hosting temporary curated exhibitions, featuring artists work and new commissions that responded to the Wellcome collection itself and themes related to biomedical science in historical and contemporary context. Beyond this, Wellcome has continued to invest in arts research in a wider scope of global health challenges, climate and trust in science (see for example, Aggett, 2016). Where the emphasis is still very much on public engagement and the use of art as a tool for dialogue, understanding and change related to critical global health challenges, with a growing emphasis on collaborative, community-led and impactful initiatives. One project partially funded by the Wellcome Trust in this mode is *Wrecked on the Intertidal Zone* that is examined in Chapter 4.

Through the late 1990s and up to the mid 2010s funding from trusts such as Wellcome and Leverhulme made a significant contribution to the ability of individual artists and smaller, non-profit arts organisations to develop and commission interdisciplinary projects, working with respected non-arts partners. From this developed a much more nuanced understanding of the practical process of interdisciplinary cultural production – particularly in relation to service modes and allowed for a 'maturation' away from 'deficit models of science communication' (Sleigh and Craske, 2017). But in the UK context there has been little in the way of funding or support models that have emerged since that acknowledges or seeks to address the issues with such schemes. Leaving those artists or arts organisations wanting to explore interdisciplinary collaborations with limited direct routes to funding, or requiring more complex project funding arrangements with multi-funders for single projects each with their own requirements.

3.5 Organisational modes of interdisciplinary cultural production in the UK

In a broad sense, an interdisciplinary impulse is fairly strong across the UK's arts sector today. It is common for major cultural venues to proclaim interdisciplinarity in one form or another as a component, sometimes a central component, of their artistic or cultural ethos. As they align themselves with the legacies of the dematerialisation of the art object as well as emerging and developed artistic practices in relation to science, technology, new media, the social, feminism, postcolonialism and ecology. We can see this in practice if we look at how some of the leading contemporary arts venues and organisations describe themselves and their programming and commissioning online. The Institute of Contemporary Arts (ICA, 2025) in London describes its programme as 'genre-fluid' where they 'commission, produce and present new work in film, music, performance and the visual arts by today's most progressive artists...the cross-disciplinary programme encourages these art forms and others to pollinate in new combinations and collaborations'. Tramway in Glasgow describes itself as having an 'interdisciplinary spirit' – where 'dialogue' between disciplines is articulated as its central programming metaphor (Tramway, 2025). Manchester International Festival has placed interdisciplinary projects at the centre of elements of its programme ethos since its initiation in 2007. The importance placed on modes of conjunction in commissioning by the festival became manifest in a new building as it was architecturally designed as an open set of interconnected spaces where forms of performance, exhibition or other technologically mediated events can be staged or presented that, in theory, are not constrained by the architectural disciplinary limits of traditional spaces such as theatres and galleries.

Some of this may just be the slipperiness of defining interdisciplinarity in this context, and the stylised rhetoric of arts organisations explaining themselves to the public, their peers and seeking to excite funders. In practice, the programmes of these venues tend to vary, mostly they present multidisciplinary work marketed through specific art form strands in their programmes, with occasional commissions or projects that attend more rigorously with interdisciplinarity. Yet at different points in their histories, often correlated to artistic leadership, they may have had a more expressed relationship with bringing art form and disciplines together in the creation and presentation of new work. Institutions such as the ICA have an important history of interdisciplinary work, following its founding as a centre for the avant-garde in 1946 (see Massey and Muir, 2014) – but this is something that has ebbed and flowed from being more multidisciplinary to more interdisciplinary and back again through the history of the organisation. Primarily based on the changing leadership of the organisation and wider concerns of the time. When Director of the ICA, Phillip Dodd departed the role in 2004 he summed up the approach he had aspired to take (Higgins, 2004): 'What I have done is accept that the walls between art and science, culture and economics, art and politics have collapsed...I have tried to work in the rubble of those walls and accept that the distinctions between those things don't exist any more.'

Thus, it is possible to identify an embrace or acknowledgement of the value of working counter to rigid disciplinary structures by some key arts venues that present new work in the UK, but how they are deployed may be inconsistent even in the histories of individual organisations such as the ICA. Regardless, there is still a broad spectrum of arts organisations of different types that embrace interdisciplinarity and seek to work in the 'rubble'.

Looking beyond the practices of individual artists (and there is generally no shortage of those who define their work as inter or multidisciplinary) whose work is presented in such venues and festivals – it is worth setting out the different organisational forms through which interdisciplinary cultural production is funded and produced in practice in the UK today. There are four primary organisational forms of interdisciplinary cultural production that I want to introduce and discuss here that define different cultural economics of interdisciplinary cultural production (1) as organisational form and collective artistic practice; (2) as programming or curatorial concern; (3) as adjunct practice and (4) as 'agency' or 'portfolio' interdisciplinary producer.

Many collectives or artist-led organisations – groups of artists that work together with those from different backgrounds to create new cultural work – have emerged over the last few decades. These collectives are multidisciplinary in form – but do not run specific venues or cultural events – they are funded on a commission basis to create new work in a range of different contexts or develop new work through self-initiated projects with external and commercial partners. They also develop their cultural work through bringing together artistic practice and engagement with new technology, science, and social or political issues. Their creative process frequently integrates artistic practice and engagement with social or political issues. The resulting work, which spans multiple forms and media, is commonly presented in both traditional gallery or theatre contexts and non-arts contexts as well. Their collective practice means they generally move beyond a single medium, creating work that is often research-based and participatory, but they tend to have a 'base' discipline they are primarily associated with and then interconnect with other disciplines in service or synthesis mode in the creation of their work. Ultimately, authorship is shared. Here we could point to examples such as Assemble (founded in 2010), the collective that brings together architecture, art, material culture, urban design, and social practice. Assemble describe themselves as a 'multi-disciplinary collective working across architecture, design and art'. As well as groups like Forensic Architecture (founded in 2010), based at Goldsmiths, University of London, whose work interconnects architectural theory, digital modelling, forensic science and investigative journalism to probe state and corporate violence. The team of architects, software developers, filmmakers, journalists, scientists and lawyers create multi-media visual narratives and legal evidence, presented in both legal contexts and galleries and museums (Forensic Architecture, 2025). Blast Theory (founded in 1991) creates 'collaborative, interdisciplinary work' through a hybrid of performance, interactive media and social commentary. New technologies are foregrounded to create immersive experiences that put the audience at the centre of the work, exploring themes of surveillance, public space and media culture (Blast Theory, 2025). Semiconductor (founded in 1997), are an artist duo whose films and installations connect science, moving image and sound. They often use raw scientific data from sources like space observatories and geological surveys as their primary medium, transforming abstract scientific information into experiential artworks. Complicité (founded in 1983) works across art forms, primarily creating theatrical productions integrating physical theatre, visual art, sound design, and technology to explore complex themes and narratives. All of these collective organisations operate independently but rely on the support of public museums, galleries, theatres, festivals and in some cases commercial partners to develop their work. Generally, their work has been extensively written about elsewhere, so does not require further elaboration here. But their work often intersects with the next organisational mode of interdisciplinarity I want to discuss, organisations that privilege interdisciplinarity as a central programming or curatorial concern.

3.5.1 Interdisciplinarity as central programming or curatorial concern

This form applies to building based arts centres, festivals, or office-based arts organisations that place interdisciplinarity at the centre of their programmes in some form. As noted with the history of the ICA, at points, organisational programmes may have greater emphasis on integration between and beyond disciplines and art forms, and at other times they may present more mixed art form models (hosting conventional film, theatre, exhibition presentations etc in a delineated programme structure). Regardless, these organisations can regularly commission, present or support the creation of interdisciplinary work in their venues or programmes. These range from major centres for contemporary arts such as the ICA in London, Tramway and CCA: Centre for Contemporary Arts in Glasgow or Factory International in Manchester, to those with a more specific focus such as FACT in Liverpool, CAST in Cornwall or Delfina Foundation and Beaconsfield in London to major festivals such as Manchester International Festival or smaller events such as Abandon Normal Devices Festival across north west England, Sensoria in Sheffield or AV Festival that ran from 2003 to 2018 in north east England. These organisations commission new experimental work, supporting artists to work in innovative ways beyond disciplinary structures, sometimes developing education and public programmes alongside this work. They also work internationally, co-commissioning new projects with other venues, partners and festivals.

Preceding many of these organisations, there was also a host of forerunners in the field of interarts, media arts, transmedia, counter-cultural or avant garde organisations that supported the development of interdisciplinary work through the 1950, 1960 and 1970s (see for example, Walker, 2001). Spaces such as Arts Labs where artists from a range of disciplinary backgrounds would encounter each other's work and develop new collaborations (see Curtis, 2020). For example, the IRAT that opened in 1969 (Institute for Research in Art & Technology), to encourage 'cross-disciplinary work in cinema, video, print, theatre, music, photography and cybernetics' that included an eclectic mix of practices in its founding board including writer JG Ballard, architectural critic Reyner Banham, psychologist Dr Christopher Evans and artist Joe Tilson (see Ford, 2005). As Ballard later discussed with curator Hans Ulrich Obrist in 2003, the significance of such interdisciplinary spaces was that they focused on the exchange of ideas rather than the development and presentation of specific disciplinary practices:

> The ICA has always been enormously important as an ideas laboratory, not only in the days of the Independent Group in the 1950's but also in the late 1960s...the ICA was a hot-house where people with original ideas met to exchange ideas. In the last few years it's regained its old flavour. Part of the problem it faces is that the avant-garde is now the new establishment. The new is in danger of becoming the new old. But today's ICA seems to be successfully repositioning itself as a post-2000 ideas lab.
>
> *(Ballard, 2003)*

Ballard here also points to how within the history of such organisations there are internal tensions that play out in relation to how its artistic leadership has been structured between siloed disciplinary departments vs a more centralised form of artistic leadership (see for example, Higgins, 2010). At the point Ballard made this observation, under Philip Dodd's leadership, the ICA had writers and scientists in residence such as Zadie Smith and the Neuroscientist Daniel Glaser. In defining this approach to artistic programming, Dodd called it 'untidy in principle', an approach that as he put it, 'sits at odds with the disciplinary world of the UK' arts and culture establishment. But it was an approach that was also critiqued for its incoherence (Irving, 2004). What the tension evident in the history of programming at the ICA between disciplinary programmes and anything more inter or multidisciplinary seems to show is that the default programme structures of such organisations tend towards disciplinarity. Anything beyond that requires specific artistic leadership and a requirement a willingness to risk that form of untidiness we could interdisciplinarity or to break or challenge those disciplinary norms. Which may situate such organisations against existing funding structures, critics and publics that are comfortable with established disciplinary structures.

The ICA presents a particular mode of interdisciplinarity rooted in the legacies of the post-war avant garde – that seeks a more of integrative radicalism. There have also been attempts to root interdisciplinarity as central programming or curatorial concern in the context of community, grassroots arts and mass participation, although arguably less successful in the UK context at scale. Here we can draw precedent from theatre director Joan Littlewood and architect Cedric Price's design of the Fun Palace (see Bonet Miro, 2024). Created in 1961, the vision for a flexible, interactive, multidisciplinary space was never directly realised but inspired numerous projects in the UK and beyond (including the Centre Pompidou in Paris). The essence of the idea was to create a form of flexible architecture that would be reshaped and rearranged. With a central emphasis on mass participation (rather than spectatorship), through self-directed, pleasure-led cultural, artistic and educational activities from disciplines in a non-hierarchical structure. The emphasis was on the creation of space that would not constrain the uses of them or impose limits on what and how the public could engage and encounter within.

The influence of the Fun Place concept was felt strongly in a new arts institution, The Public, that was opened (partially) in West Bromwich in the West Midlands of England in 2008. The novel arts centre was created as a multi and interdisciplinary and interactive community arts centre, imagined by Jubilee Arts, a community arts organisation operating in post-industrial West Midlands from 1974. With the support of the local council and Arts Council England funding, the purpose-built venue was set to be a centre piece of a regional cultural regeneration programme, in an area with limited cultural provision. However, due to financial difficulties it closed in 2013. The Public's architect, Will Alsop, who had previously worked for Cedric Price, set out his vision for the building as fundamentally pushing against existing disciplinary structures:

> Arts facilities normally fall into a number of categories…you have things called 'theatres' and things called 'galleries' and so-called 'social centres', which are very well defined. If you try and mix all those things together without falling into archetypical responses to what they are, that's an extraordinary challenge. You couldn't define this project in terms of any other project. This is something new - and therefore we don't know what it is, quite'.
>
> *(Alsop in Rose, 2008)*

This insistence on moving beyond the well-defined architectural forms, was also taken up in the programme which sought to work outside expected categories. For Marlene Smith, the founding director of The Public, the most exciting and central aspect of the organisation's curatorial ethos was its commitment to crossing boundaries (Smith, 2008). With the initial programme featuring work by Blast Theory (an interactive, augmented reality installation called *Flypad*) amongst others working in interdisciplinary modes. While over the short time it operated, The Public did receive local support and increasing audiences.

The Arts Council withdrew funding in 2009 in relation to the failure of the central interactive gallery element, the local council then took control but subsequently withdrew funding in 2013 and the building was turned into a further and higher education college. The resulting inquiry showed significant financial and business planning failure in the project (costs rising from an initial estimate of £39m to over £60m) and Arts Council England being highlighted for their lack of oversight. Ultimately, it led to the project being described as 'a gross waste of public money' and a failure of leadership on the part of the Arts Council by a Parliamentary Committee (Culture, Media and Sport Committee, 2011). In the report commissioned by the Arts Council into the failures of the project, the author wrote 'The Arts Council became so persuaded by the transformative role of the project – for art, society and the built environment – that it was prepared to override due claims of prudence' (Blackstock in Dunton, 2014). One prevailing critique of the project set out in that report and by cultural historian Robert Hewison (2014) was an over-reach of New Labour's cultural policy into an explicit social and economic agenda – that stretched organisations like the Arts Council beyond their remit, as they sought to realise complex projects such as The Public. While the trials and tribulations of the creation of The Public in West Bromwich offers something of a cautionary tale in the large-scale investment in new cultural infrastructure and the yoking of cultural innovation to economic development agenda as François Matarasso (2016) notes, it was none the less a 'brave attempt' to realise Littlewood and Price's radical vision, 'in one of the poorest boroughs in Britain'. Ultimately in that sense the ambition was too great, and the project seemed to stretch the possibilities of how challenging it can be to achieve something outside of normative constraints of cultural economics concerned with disciplinary expectations and demanding economic abundance. As Matarasso (2016) put it:

> [I]t was on its way to working. Its closure was a sad moment for many people [and] seemed to underline how difficult it is to do something actually different. We're told nowadays to 'Think outside the box' – such a cliché – but try to think creatively, though, really leave existing assumptions, and you'll soon find the boundaries.

Ten years after the close of The Public another major cultural venue opened, funded under a similar economic rationale, that also sought to leave those assumptions behind and push disciplinary boundaries, defined in architectural terms. This is what has now become known as Aviva Studios in Manchester (previously, The Factory). The flagship £240m arts centre, opened in Manchester in 2023 to create 'meeting points' between different cultural practices and 'real and imagined lives, physical spaces and digital worlds' (Factory International, 2025). The OMA designed multi-use building was designed 'with flexibility in mind'. The promise of this 'flexibility' was that the building could adapt to a range of cultural presentation forms, beyond conventional disciplinary practices, as well as potentially accommodate those as yet undeveloped (Factory International, 2025).

The genesis of the new building and its form was rooted in the programme of the Manchester International Festival (MIF). Following a number of successful editions of MIF since it launched in 2007, Manchester City Council sought to create a permanent space for the festival that would be a site for presenting the kind of collective, multi- and inter disciplinary projects the festival had become known for. The venue's architects created two interconnected spaces 'The Warehouse' and 'The Hall', one a 'flexible container, left bare to be adapted by its users as they see fit' and the other 'a 1,603-seat auditorium with a flexible stage, able to accommodate opera, ballet, theater, music, and cross-art performances' (OMA, 2025). The idea of a major new cultural venue in Manchester was announced in December 2014 (BBC, 2014). Primarily it was financially backed by the UK government as part of the 'Northern Powerhouse' initiative, a programme introduced by the Conservative–Liberal Democrat coalition government aimed at generating economic growth in the north of England. Initially expected to cost £110m, with £78m coming from central government on the basis of the project's economic impact, it ended up costing over £240m by the time it opened. Manchester City Council was instrumental, acting as the lead developer of the venue. The project was championed as part of the city's regeneration, Sir Richard Leese (in Brown, 2015), the long serving council leader positioned it central to the future of the city:

> The importance of the Factory cannot be overstated. It will be of international significance, the cultural anchor for the next phase of economic and cultural regeneration in Manchester, Greater Manchester and beyond. It will help power Manchester and the wider region towards becoming a genuine cultural and economic counterbalance to London, as well as being a place where inspirational art is created.

Central to the vision of the venue, and how it was able to articulate a justification for such large scale public investment in the arts, at a time when the government was also engaged in a deep austerity programme (led by one of the key champions of the new venue Chancellor George Osborne) – was that it set itself out artistically with the promise of 'flexibility', the promise of interdisciplinarity – in a way for example that the other recently opened new arts centre in Manchester, HOME, that only just opened in 2015, with a delineated programme and spaces for theatre, cinema, exhibitions etc could not. The promise here that the new space would offer artists and their collaborators, 'unconstrained artistic and technical freedom' (Charcoalblue,

2023). With the creation of Aviva Studio, inward economic investment, large-scale urban regeneration, visions for the future of the city and the promise of interdisciplinary through creating flexibility in architectural space went hand in hand.

Since its founding in 2007, the MIF programme, under the direction of Alex Poots, focused specifically on commissioning and premiering entirely new work. One of the key routes to that novelty was through the creation of collaborative projects that specifically sought to defy traditional art form boundaries, combining music, dance, theatre, visual art and digital media, as well as cross-cultural interconnections. Projects such as *It Felt Like A Kiss* (2009), created by documentary filmmaker Adam Curtis and immersive theatre producers Punchdrunk, with music composed by Damon Albarn and performed by the Kronos Quartet and *Tree of Codes* (2015) – A collaboration between choreographer Wayne McGregor and artist Olafur Eliasson, musician Jamie xx. Such ambitious and complex staged events that brought together well-known artists within their fields to collaborate on new commissions became a signature for the festival. These events often took place in non-art venues, disused or in development spaces across the city, in most cases these are deployed as decontextualised, non-places, railway depots and car parks to churches and disused industrial buildings.

Such venues become an important site for the creation of interdisciplinary projects, exactly because they do not have specific components that align to art form conventions in form, or control. They offer a promise of openness and flexibility as spaces where 'anything could happen'. The practical and economic reality of working in such spaces is more challenging however and they are in themselves always nuanced, and site specific in the sense that whatever is created within them is necessarily shaped and constrained by their architecture, infrastructure, acoustics etc – that needs to be worked with or overcome at often great expense – especially for temporary and one-off projects.

The development of Aviva Studios was therefore conceived to provide a permanent space that could replicate the functional 'flexibility' and scale of a temporary warehouse while offering technical control and infrastructure. The risk of seeking 'flexibility' goes hand in hand with the wider risks identified around interdisciplinary cultural production, that of falling into a vague and ill-defined space, but with the added risk of an autonomy paradox, where anything goes, and nothing is tethered, and a lack of coherence emerges, for artists, collaborators, staff and audiences and funders.

But also, in this case the promise of interdisciplinary cultural production as artistic flexibility – became part of the economic and political argument for large-scale public investment in a new arts centre, alongside competitive urbanism, tourism, property-led urban regeneration, and a counter argument made by those also enacted deep cuts and austerity to the arts in general. With council estimates suggesting it will contribute up to £1.1bn to Manchester's economy in the 10 years after opening, it is the economic potential of the project was central to its realisation, but it wouldn't have been possible without the specific artistic vision for the promise of the space for flexibility under the logic of interdisciplinary cultural production rooted in Poots' original commissioning approach. For the city council the venue sits as 'an anchor to the development of the St John's area where it stands at the heart of Enterprise City, a major new mixed-use development of commercial, cultural, leisure, residential and cultural space' (Manchester City Council, 2023). But the city council also bore much of the additional costs of the project, where the buildings 'complexity and uniqueness' as a space that would operate between conventional disciplinary art form architecture was cited as more of the main reasons adding significant costs to the construction (Manchester City Council, 2023). The irony being that buildings supposedly designed for openness and flexibility in use, based on empty industrial warehouses, turned out to be more complex and costly to build than conventional arts venues.

With both the Public and Aviva Studios it is clear how the promise of interdisciplinary cultural production – in relation to wider artistic conceptions of flexibility, freedom, innovation, artistic progression and novelty – can be co-opted into cultural economies as part of wider arguments for cultural-led urban regeneration. But of course, at a very fundamental level, the changing programming ethos, vision and fate of all the organisations discussed here as examples of interdisciplinarity as central programming or curatorial concern, including the ICA, is that such curatorial endeavours, can either be supported, shaped or hindered by conventional architectural constraints related to art forms, but in practice – what matters perhaps more is artistic leadership. Which itself requires continual maintenance and reinvestment, and articulation of its importance for it to persist. The promise of interdisciplinary cultural production in relation to these venues, does not happen by default, – as default practice tends towards conventional art form presentation. Interdisciplinary cultural production is not something that can be in and of itself realised by their architectural form alone – but in relation to how those running such venues seek to use the spaces at their disposal.

3.5.2 Interdisciplinarity as adjunct practice

The default programming for most UK arts organisations is disciplinary specialisation; consequently, the most common way many organisations engage with interdisciplinary methods is through an adjunct practice. This manifests as time-limited, project-based experimentation, a kind of temporary flirtation with interdisciplinarity as method. These projects run as an additional area of activity alongside an organisation's core disciplinary work. Unlike organisations that centre interdisciplinarity, these institutions remain rooted in specific disciplinary practices, such as visual arts or theatre, but maintain an explicit interdisciplinary programme set aside as an adjunct to their primary presentations. Developing such an adjunct interdisciplinary programme is common for major public galleries and arts institutions.

For a time in the 2010s, Tate Modern supported this model through a dedicated curatorial role for 'Interdisciplinary Projects', focusing on live art, media, performance and film. This focus was directly connected to the creation of The Tanks space in 2012, which aimed to facilitate 'integrated and cross-disciplinary' work (Pringle in Tate, 2012). The stated aim of the programme was 'showing how contemporary art practice has evolved since the 1950s – particularly in areas such as performance, film and works that involve active social relations' (Noble in Tate, 2012).

In a different form, at the Serpentine Gallery in London, the curator Hans Ulrich Obrist has run several interdisciplinary projects alongside its core exhibition programme, focusing on specific themes such as ecology, law, or new technology. These programmes take many forms, from research projects and events to digital media presentations, engaging artists from a range of practices as well as academic and industry partners. Outputs are then presented via events, discussions, exhibitions and publications. Other major cultural institutions, such as the Royal Shakespeare Company, have also developed adjunct interdisciplinary programmes. For instance, their IF Interdisciplinary Fellowship is an annual, year-long programme centred on historically underrepresented voices for artists, researchers and cultural workers responding to the cultural change needs of the performing arts (IF/RSC, (2025).

For these large-scale institutions, this kind of adjunct interdisciplinary work offers an opportunity to explore, test and seek innovation, often connected to diverse artistic practices, or new technologies but also with a view to diversifying participation, or audiences, or to specifically speak to particular communities of practice, as well as meet various social objectives. Running adjunct programmes that move beyond the core discipline of such organisations also allow them to raise funds from non-traditional sources or sponsors. For example, the RSC's IF Interdisciplinary Fellowships are supported by the UK's primary arts and humanities academic research funder the Arts and Humanities Research Council (AHRC) as well as the Rothschild Foundation (IF/RSC, 2025). Such programmes, that are designed to be situated outside or alongside of the core activities of the organisation, could be seen as a 'safe' way to mitigate the potential risks of interdisciplinary cultural production identified in Chapter 2 and above. One of the key questions that emerges from this way of working is about the influence of adjunct interdisciplinary practice on the core disciplinary work. Although these temporary projects act as a periphery for experimentation and new institutional connections (with those from other disciplines, as well as funders and audiences) the extent to which they inform or shape an organisation's central disciplinary activities often remains an open question.

Adjunct interdisciplinary projects serve multiple strategic goals for large institutions. The 'distance' created between these projects and core activities is therefore determined by how project leaders perceive their roles, both in relation to their core discipline and to the wider landscape of knowledge sharing and dissemination. For Hans Ulrich Obrist (2015: 1), the curator's role is that of a mediator, 'simply about connecting cultures, bringing their elements into proximity with each other - the task of curating is to make junctions, to allow different elements to touch'. This idea of proximity (rather than integration or synthesis) is important, as it is specific to the adjunct model and offers insight into why this is a favoured method for interdisciplinary work among arts institutions. Obrist (2015: 152) also acknowledges the risks of interdisciplinary production, noting that 'reaching out to different worlds to connect them means going beyond the fear of pooling knowledge'.

Positioning interdisciplinary projects as adjunct or in proximity to core disciplinary activity potentially creates a less risky environment for experimentation, which serves various strategic goals, such as engaging diverse artistic practices, attracting new funding sources, and cultivating new partnerships and audiences. This distance also potentially insulates the core reputation, brand and status of the arts organisation from the uncertainties of convention-breaking cultural endeavours. Conversely, when such projects are deemed successful, the organisation can claim credit.

However, one of the greater, and often unacknowledged, risks of the adjunct model is that the institutional knowledge necessary to successfully design, lead, manage and produce these projects is frequently held by external freelance staff on project-specific contracts, rather than centrally within the organisation. This external reliance limits the institution's ability to develop rigorous internal working processes and knowledge, hindering the consistent realisation of high-quality interdisciplinary work.

3.5.3 The 'agency' or 'portfolio' interdisciplinary producer

The final mode of organisational interdisciplinary practice is something that has become more common over recent years in the UK. This is the 'agency' or 'portfolio' interdisciplinary producer. These are organisations that do not run venues or host festivals but are specialists in developing interdisciplinary projects working with both arts and non-arts partners. These types of organisations may take a curatorial role, inviting artists into specific contexts or they may collaboratively originate ideas with artists or those from other disciplines, but they then may operate as an expert producer, who facilitates or mediates the relationships between disciplinary partners within a wider interdisciplinary project. Often, they will have a thematic specialism as part of their identity, knowledge base or purpose, related to ecology or to technology for example. These organisations see themselves as mediators, able to 'talk to both sides' or act as experts in translating artistic objectives and ideas into languages and forms that may be understood and appealed to by others beyond the arts. In this sense they pride themselves on operating with a form of rigour or expertise in enabling interdisciplinarity, but that which might more commonly be associated with disciplinary rigour itself. These agencies work on all sorts of different projects across art forms, and geographies, and are generally not restricted to working in the UK, even if their base is there. However, place-based projects have become of greater significance to them in recent years as arts funding in the UK has developed a greater emphasis on place-responsive programming and investment. 'Agency' or 'portfolio' interdisciplinary producers are often sought out to create projects for major cultural events – e.g. European Capital of Culture, international festivals – and they necessarily move, and evolve in relation to funding opportunities such as these, both nationally and internationally. Part of their business model is that their expertise in developing interdisciplinary cultural projects is that they offer unique skills to organisations that lack that knowledge. So, they often work in response to external briefs from other cultural, research, university or public institutions that do not themselves have expertise in delivering complex interdisciplinary arts projects.

These organisations tend to be small, non-profits, with core funding from an Arts Council – and a small core staff team, but also a pool of freelancers that support each project. The core funding that might cover their basic overheads does not generally allow them to deliver much self-initiated programming – and therefore they are generally required to fundraise through grant funding, commissions, or competitive tender or similar sources to create work on a project-by-project basis. Some of these agency organisations have a more explicit artistic or curatorial vision, rooted in developing a particular kind of interdisciplinary arts practice. Some examples of such organisations include Invisible Dust (founded in 2009), based in Scarborough but working internationally, with a focus on art science collaborations connected to environmental issues. Arika, based in Edinburgh, who have worked through episodic programming and festivals across politics, experimental music, sound and moving image. FutureEverything (founded in 1995 with the original title FutureSonic), based in Manchester, formally a festival, but now operating on an agency model, with a focus on digital technology. Arts Catalyst (founded in 1994) based in Sheffield, previously in London, who have a long history of art science collaborations, but have more recently refocused on questions of co-inquiry, radical placemaking and ecology (their work is examined further in Chapter 4). Another similar agency is Mediale, based in Yorkshire. The organisation was launched as a university-backed interdisciplinary digital art festival in York in 2014 but also shifted to an agency model in 2021 to focus on producing a range of projects related to new digital technologies and talent development. This also allowed greater flexibility of operation and structurally provided a platform to manage the instability caused by short-term, variable funding commitments that have made staging large-scale events such as publicly funded festivals a challenge in the recent arts economy in the UK. As one creative producer working in this context set out to me, this brings both a sense of creative freedom but also challenges, as they explain this means they:

> could do any kind…of project, but also we have no anchor, no home turf… [so] we're only as good as our reputation… [we are] led by the artists and what artists are doing…which is a huge privilege and a huge opportunity, but also…incredibly fragile.

With this creative autonomy (from a specified format of presentation or building or venue) comes a particular sense of financial precarity as agency or portfolio interdisciplinary producers rely on project funding from a range of competitive arts and non-arts grant sources. Navigating which, in practice, requires time, expertise and constant partnership building. But as alluded to here, the success of these organisations also depends on their ability to successfully deliver the complex interdisciplinary projects that they have built their reputations upon. To achieve this, such organisations have developed their working practices and expertise in creating interdisciplinary cultural projects over many years and have staff that are highly experienced in the realisation of such projects. Central to the practical operations of these organisations then is how this expertise and experience offer a particular sense of rigour, thoroughness, precision and nuance in how they approach and manage interdisciplinary projects that becomes a key asset for them as an organisation in fundraising and developing partnerships and new projects.

It is this role as 'mediators' or 'brokers' or a 'middle entity' that those working in these organisations excel at and pride themselves on being good at. As a creative producer explained, this involved taking the 'seed of an idea' and realising it in practice by building relationships with partners, that might be universities, museums, galleries, festivals etc, that do not have the 'time or the energy or the remit to do that' to work in interdisciplinary ways, and perhaps in the process challenge their 'internal…preconceptions'. This expertise in mediating between disciplines to realise cultural projects – means having an expertise and understanding in how to realise interdisciplinary projects, from fundraising, working with artists, facilitating dialogue and development between different disciplinary partners, to creating multiple forms of presentation in a range of media, to communicating projects to audiences and participants. But also connecting their work to specific research, policy or advocacy agendas – which make a key part of their work understanding a specific 'context' – an issue, site, place, theme, concept, etc - and building relationships or getting 'buy-in' with creative practitioners and other partners around that context. Where they must 'articulate with confidence and with a dexterity what the value' these kinds of interdisciplinary arts projects are to different partners. In a practical sense, it means these organisations must be very linguistically adaptable, being able to 'speak different languages' or understand disciplinary knowledge forms to the extent that they can produce grant bids, and fundraising proposals to different funders, with different expectations and priorities. Being able to use 'entirely different language for the same idea without compromising it' becomes an essential skill of generating the financial resources for such a project – by funders with different goals (arts engagement, business innovation, scientific research etc) to invest in a project. Persuasion becomes an important skill for a mediator between disciplines and those seeking resources to realise such projects. When this mediation role works effectively, such organisations are able to achieve 'the transformational potential of well-crafted collaborations and rigorous context'.

The sense of rigour here is very important to the work of such organisations. This is particularly important to those who have professionally developed their work and organisations within a space that inhabits, embraces or is open to interdisciplinary ideas. As Jon Wozencroft (co-founder of record label and multimedia project producer Touch in McAuliffe, 2012), puts it:

> We are not proclaiming Touch as a model of inter-disciplinary work – I'm very critical of that, the way you get to do everything all at the same time and become a jack of all trades, master of none – but what we are trying to say is that there can be a rigour in working within this 'eclectic' context…It takes a lot of fine-tuning and fine-balancing to get this right.

One of the key elements of rigor in the development of new projects was being able to identify, champion, support and understand the needs and requirements of artists and those they work with within the creation of interdisciplinary cultural projects. This meant seeking out and working with those who shared a similar set of values and ideals around working beyond a central disciplinary practice and collaborating in various forms with others. For one artistic director I interviewed this was fundamentally about 'knowing the artist'. Part of the curatorial process of developing connections and relationships with artists was to find those artists that had a sensibility towards this form of practice. And part of this skill for producers was about not just identifying those who had already demonstrated an interest or created successful work in such a context, but also building relationships with those who showed potential or where it was evident their practice or research would benefit and flourish in such environments. Central to 'knowing the artist' was listening, and understanding their vision, through an empathy or attunement towards how artists work, think and collaborate. This was not about pushing their work in a particular direction, or finding situations it could be dropped into, but about being authentic to the ideas.

It also meant, in particular, understanding the degree to which artists have specific disciplinary specialisms that are at the centre of their work. And understanding what the boundaries of these might be, and therefore the kind of support they might need in realising an interdisciplinary collaboration. This ranges from an open to closed process – where the producer can either hand over all the elements of the production and collaboration to the artist, or can take on much of the complexity of realising a project with an artist focusing on a narrow area of their artistic creation. As a number of producers and curators noted in the interviews, this might be because the artist does not have the capacity, dialect or interest to deal with the often messy political reality of complex commissions with multiple partners, communities and financial backers. Or that the artist only wants, as one aristic director put it, a 'clean focus' on the 'purity of the idea'. But in other cases, and for other artists, it was noted that artists can seek to be involved in 'every detail…every single measurement, every single material.' For the producer then, part of the rigour of realising such projects is understanding these kinds of dynamics between the artists and partners involved and to mediate them, but also have a range of skills to be able to fill gaps where they occur. One of the factors that influences these dynamics within the practical production processes of interdisciplinary cultural projects in this context is how strongly artists view their identity and practice in relation to a specific discipline and their specialism within that discipline. In scenarios where artists strongly align their practice to art form conventions, open collaboration that may challenge those working processes can be hard to establish. As an artistic director noted, in some cases, particularly established or successful artists 'have their structures and their systems and their expectations…they have an industry built around them…so collaborating for them [is] quite a closed process, because their process is quite refined and quite expected…there's a tradition behind it'. In such situations, producers seeking to facilitate interdisciplinary work can feel they are themselves pushed to act 'outside of their expertise'. This is where the mediatory role can become challenging because the limitations of organisations and producers own own knowledge can be exposed and they may lack the discipline-specific authority required to influence established practices.

Part of the rigorous process of producing interdisciplinary cultural projects is also about understanding and working with different modes of interdisciplinarity, that might be multiple within a single project. Elements of collaboration might be rooted in a clear service-oriented relationship, where an artist's vision is realised or facilitated with knowledge, expertise or technical skills. Through situations that are more specifically focused on integration and synthesis in the process of developing a project – where managing an understanding of authorship in the creation of collaborative work can be complex. Through navigating the potential frictions in more antagonistic relationships in interdisciplinary projects, where collaboration may enable challenge to or critique of internal disciplinary assumptions and practices. This is perhaps the hardest element of the mediatory role of the interdisciplinary cultural producer – where projects can falter, break down or fail to progress but they are also potentially productive – where 'something exciting can happen'. As one creative producer explained, in such situations the producers role is to support those involved to be 'confident enough to be vulnerable' – to be open and curious about their own understanding and commitment to components of their own discipline that might, on inspection, be unsound. In developing rigorous production forms, producers must create the 'context for that comfort', space in which those involved can question their own practices to move beyond simply subordinate relationships or where disciplines are clumsily 'bolted onto the other.'

For one creative producer, the key component of rigour in interdisciplinary cultural production was a requirement for 'dexterity' in facilitating and mediating relationships within interdisciplinary collaborations. That meant, as a producer both, 'not being overly deferent' but also at the same time, not 'trying to dictate' or take a strong authorial position within a project. As other curators and creative producers described there needs to be a willingness to push back against artists at times – to challenge their thinking – both in a sense when it is too conservative, but also when it is potentially unethical – particularly where a proposed collaborative relationship might conceptually appear interesting, but is dominated by the spectacle of juxtaposition or might offer a problematic power imbalance between those involved, going beyond being merely subordinate into the exploitive.

This plays into a central notion that played out through conversations with 'agency' or 'portfolio' interdisciplinary producers – that they understood that rigor was a requirement of their work – but they were also aware that this rigour was heightened by the risks or pitfalls associated with interdisciplinary work more generally – from the 'jack of all trades' association, to the mantra of 'anything goes' – the risk being that interdisciplinary cultural production without rigour can lead to a loss of critical edge or meaning. In these contexts, rigour can still mean working against or within constraints, rather than simply discarding them entirely. The challenge that some of these producers therefore take in balancing freedom and fragility is to support the development of practices beyond mere spectacles or easily consumed commodities, to realise something that offers the potential of profound or significant aesthetic or intellectual inquiry.

Many of the producers I talked to were happy to admit that this did not always work. That the collaborations they facilitated or the projects they produced fell short. But there was a sense of an openness to failure was an important part of their work – they themselves needed to be confident in their own vulnerability towards art forms, disciplines and practices they were not expert in, nor had worked with before in order to embrace the promise of new interdisciplinary projects. Those working in such organisations also clearly embrace and enjoy the risk and uncertainty of these kinds of collaboration and are also driven by a form of curiosity into the new knowledge they can gather in the process.

3.6 Conclusion – working in the rubble

It is clear from tracking the changing cultural economy of support for interdisciplinary cultural production in the UK that working in the 'rubble' means navigating a fragmented and at times fragile funding ecosystem. Interdisciplinarity as a mode of practice moves in and out of fashion as attributes towards science, technology and ecology change. Shifting political, cultural, ecological and social priorities that operate beyond individual art forms, push and pull this ecosystem in different directions, often leaving cultural managers and producers in states of uncertainty and insecurity. Yet the rhetoric and deployment of interdisciplinarity under the logic of innovation and novelty in the arts has also served some well in contributing to advocacy for new investment at scale. This is all the more remarkable against a backdrop of declining resources.

Yet from the perspective of those seeking funding to support their interdisciplinary work, this often means, in Barry and Born's (2013: 256) conception, 'inhabiting a state of radical uncertainty'. This goes beyond the central uncertainties of interdisciplinarity more generally, of contested practices, definitions, and historical foundation, to how cultural managers and producers navigate funding schemes that support disciplinary objectives, often while nodding to the value of interdisciplinary collaboration. All the while placing themselves within or in relation to such 'unfurling lineages' (2013: 256).

As we have seen, one response to the post-2010 austerity-led funding cuts was a compulsion to the adoption of interdisciplinary collaboration as a managerial strategy for survival and resilience. This was aimed as much at cutting costs, sharing resources and securing new funding as it was delivering instrumentalised social, health or economic outcomes. But what characterised this period was ultimately a reduced appetite for artistic risk-taking and experimentation due to existential financial pressure. Despite the financial instability, cultivating cultures of experimentation (Nesta, 2018), especially through interdisciplinary collaboration with technologists has been promoted as a key priority within = UK arts council strategies, particularly in England. This was proposed as a route to innovation as well as in business models, mirroring the multidisciplinary production approach of commercial creative industries, in sharp contrast to the economic reality faced by some organisations.

In practice, interdisciplinarity has only been = loosely strategically positioned across all four UK arts funding bodies. Where it primarily emerges as a mode of collaboration that is underpinned by a logic of innovation tied to the adoption of new digital technologies and commercialisation. Despite a general positive emphasis on collaboration, there has been a lack of strategic consideration of how interdisciplinary collaboration should be supported, enabled, or resourced in practice, which risks making arts organisations subordinate to the demands of non-arts sectors and diminishing the value of artform-specific knowledge and expertise. Here interdisciplinarity needs to be treated as a complex and contested process, that requires rigorous engagement, rather than a quick fix. Otherwise it falls into something of a false economy, that leaves the arts enmeshed in serving other agendas, less inherently concerned with intrinsic cultural value. Ultimately, a balance needs to be struck. One additional risk is that the policy entanglement of interdisciplinarity and the imperative of technology-driven innovation, is the possible stigmatisation of those who nonetheless still seek innovation but not through the continual pursuit and integration of new technology.

Despite this there is a strong interdisciplinary impulse to be found in parts of the UK's arts ecology, as both a rhetorical and conceptual ideal. But such a commitment varies across time, fluctuating historically within individual institutions as they seek to embrace or shun radical uncertainty. In practice, the realisation and persistence of interdisciplinary programming is ultimately dependent on specific artistic leadership through a continual commitment to operate in that uncertain space, as the organisational default tends towards conventional, art-form-specific presentation. This is particularly the case where financial resources are limited or under pressure.

To mitigate the challenges, risks and inherent instability of interdisciplinary cultural production, but nonetheless acknowledge its value in multiple domains, many arts organisations in the UK have developed it as an 'adjunct practice'. Such an approach offers a 'firewalled' or distanced activity, and strategic way to pursue innovation, diversify funding and audiences, expand networks and manage the reputational risks associated with unconventional cultural production, as well as potentially reshape core art form presentations.

Whether deployed as a central curatorial concern, an adjunct practice or through an agency model – it is clear that the range of different forms of interdisciplinary cultural production in the UK have been both led by and developed by a set of cultural leaders, managers and producers who must operate as expert mediators. This is a role that perhaps goes under acknowledged. The value of the role of this facilitator, broker and sometimes arbitrator between disciplines is derived from their ability to translate and enable complex interdisciplinary projects between arts and non-arts partners through a rigorous approach.

This rigour is crucial for managing the inherent risks of interdisciplinary work. It involves nuanced relationship management, understanding different modes of collaboration, and actively pushing back against uncritical or exploitative collaborations while simultaneously holding space for new experimental ideas to emerge. We can also see how the development of this knowledge itself shapes interdisciplinary practice, how for example the art-science field has matured since the 1990s as critical engagement with its practices, funding schemes and agents have reflectively responded to critiques, particularly around the deficit model of science communication.

Increasingly, post-2010 as project funding reduced and became more competitive, such a role has also been about being able to communicate the value of projects to diverse funders and stakeholders with different priorities (e.g., arts, tech, research, business) through 'speaking different languages' without compromising the space required for experimentation. For those organisations with a focus on interdisciplinary production that has survived this period, many have had to change their business model, often through becoming radically introspective, challenged to think about who they are for, who they serve, how they operate and how they will survive with less. In some cases, this has led to a greater emphasis on localism rather than internationalism, with organisations becoming increasingly concerned with addressing questions of ecology and place in relation to conceptions of community and situated knowledge.

For the small 'agency' producer, that operates on a non-profit basis but may only have core funding (some wages and rent) from an Arts Council, financial precarity despite their expertise is the norm. As they rely on increasingly competitive project funding, commissions and potentially look to meet external briefs from ever more divergent fields. This organisational model, in some cases adopted to manage the instability of short-term funding and excessive demands of large-scale formats such as festivals, gives them creative autonomy but simultaneously makes them fragile, with their expertise and reputation they have developed at risk. As it was stated to me in multiple interviews, it is harder to make this kind of work today than in the last three decades in the UK. Yet many artists, curators, cultural producers, managers and leaders persist. Working in the rubble is a messy and uncertain process and that is also something those who choose to work in this way embrace, often regardless of the support they receive.

Bibliography

Aggett, S. (2016) *Art in Global Health: Insights and Considerations for Future Artist Residencies in Health Research Programmes.* Wellcome Trust. Available at: https://media.tghn.org/medialibrary/2016/08/ArtinGlobalHealth_ProjectReport.pdf [Accessed 25 March 2025].

Arts Council England. (2013) *Great Art and Culture for Everyone - 10-Year Strategic Frame, 2010–2020.* 2nd edn. Arts Council England. Available at: www.artscouncil.org.uk/sites/default/files/download-file/Great_art_and_culture_for_everyone.pdf [Accessed 24 March 2025].

Arts Council England. (2018) *Our National Portfolio, 2018–2022: Combined Arts Narrative*. Arts Council England. Available at: www.artscouncil.org.uk/sites/default/files/download-file/Combined%20arts.docx [Accessed 24 March 2025].

Arts Council England. (2020) *Let's Create*. Arts Council England. Available at: www.artscouncil.org.uk/our-strategy-2020-2030. [Accessed 24 March 2025].

Arts Council England. (2025) *Supporting Arts, Museums and Libraries*. [Online]. Arts Council England. Available at: www.artscouncil.org.uk/supporting-arts-museums-and-libraries. [Accessed 24 March 2025].

Arts Council England. (2026) *Digital Arts becomes Arts Council England's tenth supported artform*. [Online]. Arts Council England. Available at: https://www.artscouncil.org.uk/blog/digital-arts-becomes-arts-council-englands-tenth-supported-artform [Accessed 29 January 2026].

Arts Council of Northern Ireland. (2024) *Strategic Plan 2024–2034*. Arts Council of Northern Ireland. Available at: https://artscouncil-ni.s3-assets.com/acni-10-year-strategy-2024-34.pdf [Accessed 24 March 2025].

Arts Council of Wales. (2024) *Our Strategy 2024–2034*. Arts Council of Wales. Available at: https://arts.wales/sites/default/files/2025-02/ACWStrategy.pdf [Accessed 24 March 2025].

Arts Council of Wales. (2025) *Relationship Manager - Innovation, Digital & Interdisciplinary Arts*. [Online]. Arts Council of Wales. Available at: https://arts.wales/news-jobs-opportunities/relationship-manager-innovation-digital-interdisciplinary-arts [Accessed 22 August 2025].

Augsburg, T. (2017) 'Interdisciplinary arts', in Frodeman, R. (ed.) *The Oxford Handbook of Interdisciplinarity*. 2nd edn. Oxford: Oxford University Press. pp. 131–143.

Bakhshi, H., Hargreaves, I. and Mateos-Garcia, J. (2013) *A Manifesto for the Creative Economy*. NESTA. Available at: https://media.nesta.org.uk/documents/a-manifesto-for-the-creative-economy-april13.pdf

Ballard, J.G. (2003) 'Nothing is Real, Everything is Fake. Bizarrely, Most People Like It that Way.' J.G. Ballard interview by Hans Ulrich Obrist. [Online]. Available at: www.jgballard.ca/media/2003_catalogue_for_beck%27s_futures_art_exhibition.html. [Accessed 14 March 2025].

Barry, A. and Born, G. (eds.) (2013) *Interdisciplinarity: Reconfigurations of the Social and Natural Sciences*. London: Routledge.

BBC. (2014) 'Manchester to get new £78m theatre named the factory', *BBC News*. [Online]. Available at: www.bbc.co.uk/news/entertainment-arts-30314737. [Accessed 18 March 2025].

Blast Theory. (2025) *Who we are*. [Online]. Available at: www.blasttheory.co.uk/about-us/. [Accessed 12 March 2025].

Bonet Miro, A. (2024) *Architecture, Media, Archives: The Fun Palace of Joan Littlewood and Cedric Price as a Cultural Project*. London: Bloomsbury.

Born, G. and Barry, A. (2010) 'Art-Science: From public understanding to public experiment', *Journal of Cultural Economy*, 3(1), pp. 103–119. https://doi.org/10.1080/17530351003617610.

Brown, M. (2015) 'Rem Koolhaas wins factory design project as Manchester goes Dutch', *The Guardian*. 25 Nov 2015. [Online]. Available at: www.theguardian.com/uk-news/2015/nov/25/rem-koolhaas-wins-factory-design-project-as-manchester-goes-dutch [Accessed 18 March 2025].

Campaign for the Arts & University of Warwick. (2024) *The State of the Arts*. Campaign for the Arts & Centre for Cultural and Media Policy Studies, University of Warwick.

[Online]. Available at: www.campaignforthearts.org/reports/the-state-of-the-arts/ [No date accessed].
Charcoalblue. (2023) *Aviva Studios Opens in Manchester*. [Online]. Charcoalblue. Available at: www.charcoalblue.com/news/view/aviva-studios-opens-in-manchester. [Accessed 18 March 2025].
Creative Scotland. (2024a) *Creative Scotland: Strategic Framework*. Creative Scotland. Available at: www.creativescotland.com/binaries/content/assets/creative-scotland/resources-and-publications/applicant-and-recipient-materials/funding-criteria/cs-strategic-framework---may2024_final.pdf [Accessed 24 March 2025].
Creative Scotland. (2024b) *Creative Scotland Funding Criteria: 1. Quality and Ambition*. Creative Scotland. Available at: www.creativescotland.com/binaries/content/assets/creative-scotland/resources-and-publications/applicant-and-recipient-materials/funding-criteria/1-quality-and-ambition-fund-june-2024_final.pdf [Accessed 24 March 2025].
Creative Scotland. (2025) *Multi-Year Funding Outcome Announcement*. 30 January 2025. [Online]. Creative Scotland. Available at: www.creativescotland.com/news-stories/latest-news/archive/2025/01/multi-year-funding-outcome-announcement [Accessed 24 March 2025].
Culture, Media and Sport Committee. (2011) *Third Report Funding of the Arts and Heritage*. UK Parliament. [Online]. Available at: https://publications.parliament.uk/pa/cm201011/cmselect/cmcumeds/464/46405.htm#a7 [Accessed 15 March 2025].
Curtis, A. and Punchdrunk (2009) *It Felt Like a Kiss*. Music by D. Albarn, performed by Kronos Quartet. Manchester International Festival, Manchester.
Curtis, D. (2020) *London's Arts Labs and the 60s Avant-Garde*. London: John Libbey Publishing.
DCMS. (2016) *The Culture White Paper*. London: Department for Culture, Media & Sport. Available at: www.gov.uk/government/publications/culture-white-paper.
Dunton, J. (2014) 'Alsop hits out at 'decimation' of The Public arts centre', *Architects' Journal*. 7 November 2014. [Online]. Available at: www.architectsjournal.co.uk/news/alsop-hits-out-at-decimation-of-the-public-arts-centre. [Accessed 15 March 2025].
Factory International. (2025) *About*. [Online]. Available at: https://factoryinternational.org/about. [No date accessed].
Ford, S. (2005) *A Psychopathic Hymn: J.G. Ballard's 'Crashed Cars' Exhibition of 1970*. [Online]. Available at: www.slashseconds.org/issues/001/001/articles/13_sford/index.php [Accessed 14 March 2025].
Forensic Architecture. (2025) About. [Online]. Available at: https://forensic-architecture.org/about/agency [Accessed 12 March 2025].
Fremantle, C. (2017) 'Leverhulme Trust residencies: A plea for resuscitation of important interdisciplinary scheme', *a-n The Artists Information Company*. 30 June 2017. [Online]. Available at: www.a-n.co.uk/news/leverhulme-trust-residencies-plea-resuscitation-important-interdisciplinary-scheme/ [Accessed 24 March 2025].
Glinkowski, P. and Bamford, A. (2009) *Insight and Exchange: An Evaluation of the Wellcome Trust's Sciart Programme*. Wellcome Trust. Available at: https://cms.wellcome.org/sites/default/files/wtx057228_0.pdf [Accessed 25 March 2025].
Hewison, R. (2014) *Cultural Capital: The Rise and Fall of Creative Britain*. London: Verso.

Higgins, C. (2004) 'ICA director to leave', *The Guardian*. 20 July 2004. [Online]. Available at: www.theguardian.com/uk/2004/jul/20/arts.artsnews1 [Accessed 12 March 2025].

Higgins, C. (2010) 'ICA warns staff it could close by May', *The Guardian*. [Online]. Available at: www.theguardian.com/culture/2010/jan/23/ica-closure-threat [Accessed 14 March 2025].

ICA. (2025) *About*. [Online]. Available at: www.ica.art/about. [Accessed 12 March 2025].

IETM. (no date). *UK and Creative Europe: End of the Story?*. [Online]. IETM. Available at: www.ietm.org/en/news/uk-and-creative-europe-end-of-the-story [Accessed 24 March 2025].

IF/RSC. (2025) *About*. [Online]. Available at: https://if.rsc.org.uk/about/. [Accessed 12 March 2025].

Irving, M. (2004) 'Love to hate it - The historic ICA has lost its critical judgment', *The Times*. 15 December 2004. [Online]. Available at: www.thetimes.com/travel/destinations/uk-travel/england/london-travel/love-to-hate-it-0v8n60pswjr. [Accessed 14 March 2025].

Jancovich, L. (2017) 'The participation myth', *International Journal of Cultural Policy*, 23(1), pp. 107–121.

Manchester City Council. (2023) *Update as Aviva Studios Opens to Acclaim*. Manchester City Council. 18 July 2023. [Online]. Available at: www.manchester.gov.uk/news/article/9306/update_as_aviva_studios_opens_to_acclaim [Accessed 18 March 2025].

Massey, A. and Muir, G. (2014) *Institute of Contemporary Arts, London 1946-1968*. Amsterdam: Roma Publications.

Matarasso, F. (2016) *Fun Palaces Everyone an Artist: The Power of an Idea*. A Restless Art. [Online]. Available at: https://arestlessart.com/wp-content/uploads/2016/10/3-fun-palaces.pdf. [No date accessed].

McAuliffe, C. (2012) 'Interview: Touch', *The Quietus*. 19 November 2012. [Online]. Available at: https://thequietus.com/news/interview-touch-music-jon-wozencroft-mike-harding-john-kieffer/ [Accessed 22 March 2025].

McGregor, W., Eliasson, O. and Jamie xx (2015) *Tree of Codes*. Manchester International Festival, Manchester.

National Audit Office (NAO). (2022) *Investigation into the UNBOXED*. National Audit Office. Available at: www.nao.org.uk/reports/investigation-into-the-unboxed-festival/ [No date accessed].

Nesta. (2018) *Experimental Culture: A Horizon Scan Commissioned by Arts Council England*. Nesta / Arts Council England. [Online]. Available at: https://media.nesta.org.uk/documents/experimental_culture_report_2018.pdf [Accessed 24 March 2025].

Newsinger, J. and Serafini, P. (2019) 'Performative resilience: How the arts and culture support austerity in post-crisis capitalism', *European Journal of Cultural Studies*, 24(2), pp. 589–605. https://doi.org/10.1177/1367549419886038.

Newson, N. (2025) *Creative Industries: Growth, Jobs and Productivity*. House of Lords Library. 30 January, 2025. [Online]. Available at: https://lordslibrary.parliament.uk/creative-industries-growth-jobs-and-productivity/ [Accessed 24 March 2025].

Obrist, H.U. (2015) *Ways of Curating*. London: Penguin.

OMA. (2025) *Aviva Studios – Factory International.* [Online]. Available at: www.oma.com/projects/aviva-studios-factory-international [Accessed 15 March 2025].

Razzall, K. (2023) 'Unboxed: Under budget and on time, but was the cultural festival unloved?' *BBC News.* 30 March 2023. [Online]. Available at: www.bbc.co.uk/news/entertainment-arts-65107676 [Accessed 25 March 2025].

Rose, S. (2008) 'All aboard the fun palace', *The Guardian.* 19 Jun 2008. [Online]. Available at: www.theguardian.com/artanddesign/2008/jun/19/architecture [Accessed 16 March 2025].

Sleigh, C. and Craske, S. (2017) 'Art and science in the UK: A brief history and critical reflection', *Interdisciplinary Science Reviews*, 42(4), pp. 313–330. https://doi.org/10.1080/03080188.2017.1381223.

Smith, M. (2008) 'Opening the public to the public', *The Guardian.* 19 Jun 2008. [Online]. Available at: www.theguardian.com/artanddesign/artblog/2008/jun/19/openingthepublictothepubl [Accessed 16 March 2025].

Tate. (2012) 'Tate's curators reveal their vision for The Tanks' *Tate Etc.* Issue 25: Summer 2012. [Online]. Available at: www.tate.org.uk/tate-etc/issue-25-summer-2012/tates-curators-reveal-their-vision-tanks [No date accessed].

Tramway. (2025) *About Tramway.* [Online]. Available at: www.tramway.org/about-tramway. [Accessed 12 March 2025].

Walker, J. (2001) *Left Shift: Radical Art in 1970s Britain.* London: I.B.Tauri.

Woodley, S., Towell, P., Turpin, R., Thelwall, S. and Schneider, P. (2018) *What Is Resilience Anyway? A Review.* Golant Media Ventures, The Audience Agency, Arts Council England. Available at: www.artscouncil.org.uk/lets-create/strategy-2020-2030/investment-principles/investment-principles-resource-hub/what-resilience-anyway-review [Accessed 24 March 2025].

4

CASE STUDIES AND PARAMETERS

Time, place and festival

4.1 Introduction – holding space, holding time

In interviews, cultural producers, managers, and curators involved in numerous interdisciplinary projects identified many key parameters shaping collaboration, such as risk, depth, dialogue and discussion. However, two constraints consistently stood out: time and space.

Time, often conceived as a necessary temporality specific to interdisciplinary production, was viewed as a central requirement. It functions both as a resource to shape the project's form and as a necessity to overcome the inherent complexity of interdisciplinary collaboration itself. As one cultural producer put it: 'You definitely need more time when you are trying to work outside of your comfort zone, because people need more time to understand their limits...new challenges...new modes of thinking and new types of language that they're working with.' The working process essentially starts 'from scratch' meaning the time and resources required are 'greater than in other [conventional or disciplinary] ways of working.'

Space was also articulated as important: both as a relational and contested sense of place and in the abstract sense of creating or holding space for actions to happen. Cultural producers described this as 'holding' a project, often having to 'deal with [the] stakeholders without [the artists involved] a lot of the time' to remove limitations or protect artists from instrumentalised requirements or complex management issues. Creating this 'held' space and time is crucial for complex interdisciplinary 'conversations' to happen, fostering an openness towards possibility, where 'anything can happen.'

DOI: 10.4324/9781003514947-4

Producers noted an awareness of interdisciplinarity's risk of eclecticism, stressing that achieving rigour requires 'a long time and a lot of experience to manage artists and multidisciplinary projects...it is a skill,' underpinned by trust and empathy. The core role of the cultural producer, manager, or curator is thus explicitly about 'making that space and time for the participants,' because, as one producer stated, the 'complexity requires that.' It was clear these skills, responsiveness, empathy and rigour, must be learned, honed and developed by cultural managers over time. The need for this dedicated time to navigate and respond to complexity is even greater for 'those who are not so experienced... in that kind of thinking and that mode of sharing and like listening to others'. Ultimately, operating in this way fundamentally requires an openness to allow things to unfold, avoiding constrained or presumptive approaches.

This chapter uses these parameters as starting points to set out a series of case studies on the practices underpinning specific interdisciplinary cultural projects and the approaches of arts organisations, all defined by the range of promises and forms set out in Chapters 2 and 3. The chapter begins by looking at short but intensive durations of interdisciplinary cultural production in the form of Rhizome's *Seven on Seven* – where artists and technologists are paired together and asked to make something in only 24 hours. We then turn to an example of long-term unfolding collaborations in the work of Arts Catalyst, that take place over many years. Following this we turn to how an ongoing collaboration between the conceptual artist Katie Paterson and architectural practice Zeller & Moye – mediated particular spatial specifics in the creation of public art. We then consider how the incubator methodology and the site of the studio of The Centre for the Less Good Idea 'holds space' for new practices and relations to emerge. Before turning to how AfroAsia intervenes in their neighbourhood in bringing divergent communities, histories and artistic practices together. Following this we then turn to examine the festival as a mode of cultural organising that has acted as a prominent and privileged site of interdisciplinary cultural production. This brings the parameters of time and place close together as we can think of the cultural festival as a concentrated assesmblage of place and time. This is examined through three perspectives, the potential of festivals as a site of challenge and subversion of disciplinary conventions and practice by looking at the pan-African festivals of the 1960s and 1970s. As well as looking at the entwinement of cultural economics and interdisciplinary cultural production and the festival in the programming of Manchester International Festival in its early editions from 2007–2011. Finally, we will consider how interdisciplinary cultural production has been used as a means to push for novelty and innovation in the form of major cultural events such as contemporary art biennials, through a case study on the Shanghai Project.

4.2 In twenty-four hours: time constraints and the spectacle of interdisciplinary collaboration in Rhizome's *Seven on Seven*

One of the shortest forms of interdisciplinary collaboration that is facilitated by cultural organisations is that of a simple conversation. This dialogic form of interaction between two agents of particular disciplines, brought together to share and explore or seek to find shared affinity or play out some animosity, usually before an audience. While it is common for such public conversations to be presented as part of larger, or longer term interdisciplinary cultural projects, the conversation, or the short-term public encounter between disciplinary agents may be an event in itself. Here the form of the conversation within interdisciplinary cultural production has also been formalised into a mode of cultural production and presentation in its own right – both in a public sense, where this brief moment of interaction plays out before an audience. These types of short-term but often intense interdisciplinary presentation might borrow from the format of academic conferences – but where the role of the organiser, usually a cultural institution creates a short-term, intense format, that allows those working in different disciplines who have not encountered each other to interact, discuss, connect and share ideas – in a way that is contrary to the processes of dialogues that might be associated to their disciplinary norms.

A strong advocate of this conversational mode of interaction is the curator Hans Ulrich Obrist, who has created all sorts of contexts for 'chance encounters' or 'where unlikely things can happen,' as he puts it, where conjunction through conversation seeks to be productive 'in and of itself' (Obrist in Martin 2007). This element of surprise, mystery, and the unknown plays into the sometimes mythic promise of interdisciplinarity.

These forms become multidisciplinary and interdisciplinary 'un-conferences' or 'Marathons', where invited participants interact through a range of public and non-public events, discussions, and social events. Here Obrist sees the role of the curator, and by extension the organisations they represent, as mediators or facilitators of these interactions rather than authors, where 'space' is created for those participating to develop new relationships, without a specific requirement to produce anything. Obrist's Marathons are a 'twenty-four-hour polyphonic knowledge festival where all kinds of disciplines' meet (Foster, 2015). For instance, the Extinction Marathon in 2014 was curated around themes where numerous artists, writers, architects, scientists, etc., gave short presentations or showed new work (in Ellis-Petersen, 2014). Primarily, these are intense multidisciplinary events, staged with a multiplicity of voices, art forms, media, and ideas, where at least part of their allure is the sheer volume or concentration of participation in a very limited time period. They are staged in continual conversation in front of an audience over a single day. Representing the theatre of polyphony rather than deep interaction, the marathons generally operate with well-known speakers. However, the risk of such short, but intense, noise-creating events is perhaps that, as Foster (2015) notes, 'not enough attention is given to the quality of the discourse, or of the "community" effected'. As a short intense form of interaction, the conversation may be generative for those involved or the audience, and it may supplement understanding around interdisciplinary cultural projects. But where the conversation is treated as an end itself there is little else expected to emerge beyond that moment of interaction. So I want to focus in detail on an event that uses time as a specific constraint but also is orchestrated to allow the potential of novel ideas, artworks or projects to emerge from a short, intense burst of interaction between different disciplines. *Seven on Seven* has been produced since 2010 on a semi-regular basis by the internet art non-profit organisation Rhizome that is based at the New Museum in New York. *Seven on Seven* operates as a rapid collaborative event, where seven artists are paired with seven technologists and asked to make something new in 24 hours to present at a conference-style event. While *Seven on Seven* is primarily dialogical in form, it also works on the premise that through a short and intense interdisciplinary collaboration or 'rapid ideation' to use terminology from the tech world, something new or innovative might be created. As a process of cultural production and presentation it is rooted in the mythic promise and potential drama of interdisciplinary collaboration.

Rhizome began as an online email discussion list in 1996 in Berlin, founded by artist Mark Tribe. Through various guises, the online resource and archive evolved into a non-profit focused on preserving, commissioning, exhibiting and researching what it terms 'born-digital art' including practices such as net art and new media art. The organisation has explored the evolving interrelationship between contemporary art and the internet since artists began to engage with the internet as a means of making, sharing, presenting and discussing art in its early days. The organisation became an affiliate in residence at the New Museum of Contemporary Art in New York City in 2003. The first edition of *Seven on Seven* came in 2010, with the event then taking place annually at the New Museum, barring Covid-19 interruptions that saw the event run online in 2020 (when it was due to take place in Kunsthall Stavanger in Norway) and not return until 2024. There have also been editions held in Beijing in 2018 (as part of the Education, Arts, Science, and Technology festival (EAST) co-presented by Central Academy of Fine Arts at the Riverside Museum) and in London in 2013 (held in partnership with the Barbican).

Seven on Seven was conceived by the curator Lauren Cornell (and Rhizome's Executive Director between 2005 and 2012) in collaboration with three members of Rhizome's board, John Borthwick, Peter Rojas and Fred Benenson, who all came from tech backgrounds. Cornell defined the founding rationale for *Seven on Seven* as a response to two specific challenges Rhizome faced as an organisation in 2010. Firstly, 'connecting artists more with technologists' and secondly, how to situate Rhizome as an organisation in relation to the emerging growth in tech businesses in New York City, touted at the time as the 'new Silicon Valley' (Fino-Radin, 2022).

The format for the event is relatively straightforward but has a number of specific parameters that define how the working process of interdisciplinary collaboration is deployed, beyond the 24 hours time limit. This plays out as follows – the pairs are given a brief to create something new between themselves over 24-hours. There is no requirement from the curators as to what they produce (such as artwork, or some technical object, an application or website), how they do it or in what domain. Although in later editions the programme was structured in relation to specific themes for instance, Empathy & Disgust in 2015 or AI in 2024 and Law in 2025 and these shaped the selection of participants and their resulting work. While the pairs are not required to produce anything specific – each pair must present their collaboration at a conference style event to a live audience in a 20-minute talk, demonstration or performance, where they take questions and discuss their work over the preceding 24 hours. This is summed up in promotional material:

> This distinctive platform asks participants to make something - a prototype, an artwork, or whatever they imagine - and then present it at a major conference. Having catalyzed performance, apps, literature, and even a start-up, Seven on Seven challenges disciplinary boundaries and provokes sharp conversations about digital culture.
>
> *(e-flux, 2016a)*

Seven on Seven in form has a co-author – co-production dynamic, driven by the promise of innovation, but also entertainment. The artists and technologists involved in each edition are chosen by the programme curators. As participants, they generally represent themselves as individuals rather than as specific representatives of their tech companies, or wider artist collectives they might also be part of. There are no hierarchies expressed in the way the pairs are presented. Each artist and technologist involved has equal representation in the communications around the event and in the presentation of the collaborations, they sit side by side on the stage (usually behind an Apple MacBook) to present their resulting collaborative work. In the introduction and guiding principles set out by Rhizome it is always made clear that neither artists nor technologists are in a subordinate position. Although at the micro-level of the individual pairs it is clear in some cases subordinates may emerge as the collaborations play out over the 24-hour period.

The resulting work created by the pairs is presented in a conference style event that has mostly taken place at the New Museum and is promoted by both the New Museum and Rhizome to their audiences. However, especially in the early editions, the predominant sponsors of the events were tech companies or foundations affiliated to Silicon Valley. In 2011 sponsorship came from AOL, by HTC in 2012 and 2013, from the Sara and Evan Williams Foundation (Evan Williams being one of the co-founders of Twitter) and the Silicon Valley Community Foundation in 2016. In 2024 it was sponsored by the Hyundai Motor Group (their art sponsorship programme – Hyundai Artlab – has supported major events with museums such as Tate Modern in London and the Korean Pavilion at the Venice Biennale). As a non-profit that requires patronage to facilitate its wider work, the ability of Rhizome to build such sponsorship arrangements has strategic value. The interdisciplinary form of the event and Rhizome's work more generally obviously opens up the potential for sponsorship and patronage beyond those traditionally associated with the arts and museums. There is evident value to this for brands seeking to express a particular identity, or shift their identity through alignment with artistic practice, creativity and innovation through interdisciplinarity. As an AOL spokesperson (Sullivan, 2011) explained at the start of *Seven on Seven* in 2011:

> You all may be asking yourselves right now, what is my mother's internet company doing partnering with Rhizome for *Seven on Seven*? And the answer is quite simple. Rhizome's mission to simply support emerging artistic practices that engage with technology is a mission that we share at AOL…we've been focussed…on supporting and amplifying creativity as we reinvent our company and our brand.

Such alignments showcase the promise of strategic mutual utility that can exist in the cultural economies of interdisciplinary production. As was partly the intention, *Seven on Seven* has enabled new relationships to be forged between these arts organisations and corporate interests in the tech world for mutual benefit. *Seven on Seven* operates by raising the visibility of Rhizome as an organisation and non-profit, to build audiences, patrons, sponsors and relationships with artists and those working at the forefront of internet and digital development. The event is designed to present high-profile leaders in their fields of art and internet technology which feeds into this. Many of the artists and technologists that have participated in *Seven on Seven* are already well-known in their fields – as award winning artists or highly successful tech entrepreneurs. As there is no specific work to promote in advance, the draw for an audience, beyond the intrigue, mystery or interest in the spectacle of juxtaposition and conjunction that may play out – the draw is having the opportunity to hear and see the individual artist or technologist in person. All of this points to the way that the interdisciplinarity enacted through *Seven on Seven*, is a highly controlled, and defined format that is orchestrated by Rhizome and its organising partners. The process of interdisciplinarity that takes place in the project has in itself performativity or even theatricality.

Although as Cornell (2011) explained, their intention was not to create 'a "reality show" situation'. But that potential for friction and drama nonetheless has been essential to the event. As Rhizome's Executive Director Michael Connor (2015) sets out:

> the potential risk and reward involved in these encounters between leading figures in distinct but overlapping fields is what lends *Seven on Seven* its particular drama. Whatever the results, the conference is always a fascinating look at the process of collaboration and a snapshot of contemporary concerns in the discourse around art and technology.

But as one reviewer explained, it was also very much about the audience – 'in some ways, the relative ease of *Seven on Seven* (at times it felt almost like a series of pitch presentations, and not just because the audience, paying up to $350 per ticket, included more than a few venture capitalists) indicated how interdisciplinary we've all become' (Pasternack, 2010).

The format for *Seven on Seven* has been compared to '9 Evenings: Theatre and Engineering' in 1966, where ten artists and 30 engineers from Bell Laboratories created a blend of avant-garde theatre, dance and technology. Although the temporality was very different as the two groups worked together for 10 months to develop technical equipment and systems that were used as an integral part of the artists' performances. As Cornell (2011) explained: 'we see *Seven on Seven* as inspired by that, although it has a very different timeline, a day… we came up with the idea of a day… because that was really what we felt we could ask people to take out of their lives to participate in something like this and also created a kind of constraint of fairness'. This format is perhaps closer to the process in the tech and business worlds, where quickly generating many ideas and then rapidly filtering them to identify the most promising ones for further development through the mantras of 'rapid ideation' and 'failing fast'. The 24-hour time constraint emerged less from a specific methodological desire and more in relation to the pragmatic scheduling of the high-profile participants, with busy schedules and limited capacity to dedicate time to something entirely exploratory (Cornell, 2011). Perhaps connected to the wider demands of the always on, and attention demanding, digitally connected, 24/7 economy (Crary, 2013).

In the critical discourse around the event, there is a tension as to whether the dichotomy created by the organisers between 'artists' and 'technologists' is a false one, or valuable because of the distinctions between those groups. One theme that emerges is that artists and technologists – as they are conceived through the process of interdisciplinary conjunction that plays out in *Seven on Seven* already seemingly have a lot in common. With specific pre-existing overlaps in skills – it is not uncommon for artists to work with many new forms of technology, and artists have in many ways been at the forefront of exploring the social, ethical and cultural dimensions of emerging internet technologies – as Rhizome more generally as an organisation is testament to. But there was also potentially a sense that the event reinforced the distinctions between artists and technologists , where artists were positioned as holding the domain of 'ideas' while technologists provided 'solutions'. As one participant in the first edition in 2010 explained: 'A lot of artists now have all these ideas now, but they never learned how to articulate them and do them with the technology that exists, something like this bridges this so well' (Rhizome, 2010).

In a sense the distinction made by the organisers to situate artists and technologists as opposing fields is to a degree a false one. As one reviewer put it, 'this was a conversation in mid-stream, not a debate between beings from different planets' (Pasternack, 2010). This was also determined by the choice of participants, selected for their work and relative interest in the relationship between art and the internet. Something that is clearly carefully curated. In introducing the artist Frances Stark and software engineer David Kravitz at the 2014 edition, Rhizome's Executive Director Michael Connor (2014) defined a particular characterisation that the curators looked for in participants – 'when we are choosing people...one of the qualities we look for is a certain flexibility of approach, one that can maybe work in many different ways'.

Another element that emerges is the spectacle of collaboration, where there is drama to be found in these mostly unrehearsed improvised presentations – with pressure, awkwardness, politeness between the collaborators all mixed together. As a reviewer noted regarding the 2011 edition, 'the presentations gave more insight into collaboration than individual concepts' (Sneed, 2011). For the audience, then part of the interest and entertainment of the event is the experience of the dynamics between 'artist' and 'technologist' – the friction, productive or otherwise in the process of collaboration, played out on the stage and certainly amplified by the high-pressure 24-hour deadline.

Nonetheless the types of ideas and projects that have emerged, range from profound to the critical to the silly. From simple conversations, to complete technical objects and performances. Many projects have emerged as what has been called, 'unusual forms; they are cultural hybrids which may not fit easily into an art exhibition or the app store' (New Museum, 2018). Some projects have gone to much larger lives, for better or worse. The first non-fungible token (NFT) based artwork was created using blockchain at the event in 2014 by artist Kevin McCoy and tech entrepreneur Anil Dash. But as one reviewer put it, 'the projects themselves mostly boiled down to tweaking a tech phenomenon (image search, Bitcoin, video chat) along preset lines of what "art" is interested in - personalization, intimacy, privacy and the human - and it's within that range that they succeed or fail' (Cohan, 2014). Yet some projects have gone further, adopting a critical perspective on seemingly neutral or beneficial technologies, exposing how they may subtly produce detrimental effects.

In the 2012 edition the programmer and free and open internet activist Aaron Swartz worked with artist Taryn Simon to create a web-based artwork called 'Image Atlas'. A seemingly simple project, the web programme (preserved and active online via Rhizome's Net Art Anthology archive of net art), showed how image-based search engine results for keywords differed by the national location of where the search was conducted. The result neatly demonstrated the perceived neutrality of systems of information and language, highlighting cultural specificity very directly. The pressure caused by the time limitation was something acutely felt by Simon, as noted at the start of their talk – 'Aaron and I have been working together for the last twelve hours. I never imagined this pressure; my work usually takes years to complete so it's a little bit gut wrenching to go public with something after a 12-hour run'(Swartz and Simon, 2012). While technologists, especially those involved in programming may be familiar with 'hackathons' and short, intense bursts of productivity, it is perhaps something artists are unlikely to have experienced as Simon attests. But this collaborative experience nonetheless shaped Simon's later work (see Lau, 2013).

Rapid events such as *Seven on Seven* exemplify a model of interdisciplinary collaboration defined by intense time constraints and public presentation. In assessing how the participants discussed their collaborations, it was clear that the time pressure was a key structural element that amplified the psychological dynamics of interdisciplinary collaboration. Especially given that participants may have very different working styles. Such urgency led to challenges around establishing a shared language, navigating misunderstandings and left little time to revise or analyse early ideas. Yet the constraint was also a virtue in generating focus and decisiveness, establishing common ground quickly, pushing collaborators to immediate action.

Participants are challenged to quickly formulate and present an idea in a short, sharp way, suggesting a low commitment. Here the high-volume approach to idea generation mitigates risk. In a tacit and pragmatic sense, this acknowledges that deep collaboration is high-risk; these short-term, intense interactions allow practitioners to quickly test or build relationships. As the *Seven on Seven* collaborations are 'free from the usual pressures of success in software development, entrepreneurship, or artistic practice' (New Museum, 2018). Yet simultaneously, the public nature of the performance generates a high-risk atmosphere. As Cornell expressed, participants 'are really putting a lot on the line to sort of be vulnerable to each other, to try something out, to then have to present it in public. There is a lot of risk associated with that, but a lot of projects came out of it then the pairs or maybe an individual continued to work on' (Fino-Radin, 2022). Ultimately, this creates an unusual but generative dynamic in interdisciplinary cultural production, one that is high-risk, but low expectation. For the outcome is only ever expected to be the 'seeds of an idea' not a fully developed project (Chayka, 2011). While these brief encounters could be dismissed as 'fast-food creativity' (Cohan, 2014) they can also be set against Rhizome and the New Museum's other modes of long-term projects with deeper commitments. While the risk of sensationing interdisciplinary juxtaposition may be present in *Seven on Seven*. The events have enabled those involved to think more clearly and critically about what defines the contemporary fields of artistic practice and tech entrepreneurship. As Cornell explained, 'I think a lot of also like deeper questions came out of it about also why it's hard for these fields to work together.' This was summed up by one participant in terms of how the event had amplified a particular simplistic dichotomy between what artists and technologists may be seeking to achieve in their work – 'good technology is about solving problems while good art creates them' (Hill, 2011).

It is clear from examining *Seven on Seven* how the constraint and management of time can be a key parameter in interdisciplinary cultural production. Such formats are designed to facilitate brief but intense interdisciplinary interaction, where a high-pressure, high-risk public dynamic seeks to push collaborators toward action by exposing and challenging their disciplinary norms. Central here is the role of the cultural institution and curator as a mediator or facilitator who creates a space for interaction without a specific requirement to produce a finished work. But this can result in a high-risk/low-expectation dynamic, where the primary outcome is the spectacle of the collaboration itself. Likewise, the public nature also serves as a strategic tool for organisational visibility, audience building and attracting corporate sponsorship. The *Seven on Seven* format intentionally orchestrates a perceived dichotomy between two fields, often amplifying the notion that artists are critical and problem oriented, with unique creative insight, while technology is driven by utility and the provision of 'solutions'. While this distinction is often considered a false one given the participants' existing overlaps and interest in digital culture, the process of collaboration as it is played out on stage is inherently performative and theatrical. Something demonstrated to great effect in the collaboration between artist Miranda July and the technologist and writer Paul Ford in their 2016 collaboration that is discussed in Chapter 5. Ultimately, these events function as a snapshot of contemporary concerns cutting across art and technology and can yield innovative projects, while also providing a critical platform to challenge the perceived neutrality of technology.

4.3 Working to tides and seasons: Arts Catalyst

If short-term, rapid interdisciplinary cultural projects can be criticised for their inherent shallowness, then it would imply that long duration projects offer the inverse of achieving depth. Here we could define depth as the scale of transfer of disciplinary knowledge, methods and understanding between participants. It signifies a sustained and evolving dialogue that not only identifies shared interests but also confronts animosity or contention, either resolving these friction points or seeking a rigorous understanding of their origins. Over time, participants learn from and influence one another, acquiring new skills, grasping different methodologies, and internalising the specific language of other fields. Such projects inherently possess a pedagogical function, facilitating transfers of knowledge and skills. In talking to curators and cultural producers, it was clear that time in the context of interdisciplinary cultural production, was equated to thoroughness, robustness and rigour, in the working process. There was a sense that this generated greater capacity to ask more complex questions, embrace complexity and more specifically value the space and time created for failure and iterative development, leading to the possibility of more nuanced and multifaceted outcomes. With extended durations being credited with allowing new directions to emerge in the work and the ability to build on chance encounters and unexpected discoveries along the way.

For interdisciplinary projects led by non-profit arts organisations, longer-term approaches also offered the potential for resilience in funding generation, through building partnerships during the project lifecycle, not merely at the outset. If quick projects seek to capitalise on the tension of interdisciplinarity by creating a mythic, instantaneous 'spark' of connection, then long-term, slower interdisciplinary cultural projects are necessarily less spectacular. They rely less on the drama of interconnection and more on process, iteration, evolution, understanding and empathy. This slower pace permits failure and changes through cycles of testing, experimenting and listening. While all these activities can occur in a short, intense exchange, there was a strong sense from the case studies examined that time was both a necessity to achieve a rigorous process of interdisciplinary cultural production, but simultaneously it was always and often a scarce resource under pressure by budgets, delivery deadlines and impatient collaborators.

Sustained engagement is not without significant challenges. The essential resource underpinning time is money, and generating the requisite financial resources to maintain long-term efforts can be challenging. Long-term projects can be perceived as inefficient, demanding an exceptional openness from those involved to listen and learn, rather than simply performing or offering pre-determined services. Furthermore, external factors such as shifting funding priorities, political landscapes, or technological advancements can impactia project's relevance or feasibility. Sustaining relationships and motivation can also be a constant challenge; projects may close up rather than open out, or an open sense of possibility can lead to scope creep, diverting the overall focus. Finally, there is greater scope for antagonism between partners after the initial excitement and early goodwill fades.

This long term approach is evident in a range of practices and organisations. For example in the lineage of 'research-based art' as discussed by art historian Claire Bishop (2023), including organisations examined in this context such as the Center for Land Use Interpretation. Here we can see a form of long-term interdisciplinary cultural production as a specific mode of enquiry or research driven practice. Exploratory in nature, these projects typically coalesce around a specific object, subject, place, or system. While they may involve multiple public interactions, they are generally less directed toward specific outputs (e.g., a single text, exhibition, or event), although these may emerge as well. These projects become ongoing commitments, long-term interdisciplinary projects with undercurrents focused on social and political themes, such as climate change, ecological crisis and social justice. We could point to projects such as the Pan African Space Station (PASS), founded in 2008 by Chimurenga and composer Neo Muyanga, a platform for African writing, art and politics which operates periodically as an international pop-up live radio studio, archive and research platform. Or Council (2022), a 'international curatorial office', based in Paris that ran from 2013 to 2022, as a series of 'Inquiries' – that acted as 'long-term collaborative programs on societal issues by partnering with thinkers and makers from different fields of action and expertise'. These long-term engagements embrace ambiguity, positioning themselves to work without seeking immediate answers or resolutions, thereby creating space for new forms of knowledge to emerge through persistent, critical interaction.

To see how these principles of long-term, critical engagement are put into practice, next is a case study examining the work of the UK-based organisation Arts Catalyst, drawing on insights from CEO Claudia Lastra and Head of Programme Anna Santomauro. Founded in 1994 by curator Nicola Triscott (who led the organisation until 2019 when she became the Director/CEO of FACT in Liverpool) Arts Catalyst primarily operated as an office-based, nonprofit/charity art commissioning organisation, working project-to-project across diverse fields and numerous arts, academic, research and technology partners. Creating projects for artists in relation to science in many forms from airspace to bioscience to microgravity. In later years they have run exhibition and events spaces. Originally based in London, Arts Catalyst relocated to Sheffield in 2020. Since their first project key funders have been Arts Council England along with project support from the Wellcome Trust amongst many others. In the catalogue to an early project where Arts Catalyst facilitated a residency for artist, Helen Chadwick at King's College Assisted Conception Unit, to explore and make work around in vitro fertilisation (IVF), Triscott summed up the approach to expanding the disciplines and fields artists could work within and in. 'It is at the body that art, medicine, science and ethics collide. At this place of sensation and transformation, connections can be made which open up the potential to hear and see differently' (Triscott, 1996: 5). Finding and operating in such sites, moments or places where such disciplinary collisions can occur guide the practice of the organisation. This has allowed the organisation to outline one of the most well developed and coherently articulated methodologies of long term interdisciplinary cultural production. Developed over more than two decades of new artists' commissions and transdisciplinary projects, one-to-one artist–scientist collaborations and arranging artists' residencies in science labs to organising multidisciplinary research groups, field exchange trips and remote labs, Arts Catalyst have =articulated a specific methodology for producing research-driven interdisciplinary projects.

Drawing on their experience they have developed an advanced curatorial methodology based on processes of long-term 'co-inquiry' that focus on 'matters of concern' (Triscott and Santomauro, 2021). This has been situated against their early work, characterised as 'goal-oriented collaborative or residency programs' to what Triscott and Santomauro describe as 'spontaneous self-directed participation'. This practice of curating and producing aims to facilitate modes of interdisciplinarity that are more open and rooted in 'cooperation' between artists and other disciplinary agents rather than enforced output driven 'collaboration', with predetermined requirements from the outset of the project. Central to this methodology is their conception of 'co-inquiry'. A process of simultaneous or concurrent disciplinary and cooperative practice and research that seeks to expand knowledge and understanding around specific 'complex systems and issues' but without a defined set of methods, or relationships or social, artistic or other outputs given at the start. This shift was partly due to the limitations of traditional interdisciplinary cultural production models such as the artist residency, which can silo artists into limited contexts (Triscott and Santomauro, 2021). This change also reflects the broader 'social turn' in contemporary art, which favours engaging with site and community as dynamic social processes, around moments of social intervention and antagonism, rather than as fixed phenomena or spaces for purely phenomenological encounter (Kwon, 2002; Bishop, 2006).

As Triscott and Santomauro (2021) explain, the ambition is that 'co-inquiry groups work in a participatory and egalitarian way, using and valuing the knowledge of the whole group, particularly knowledge gained through experience. The participants in a co-inquiry group work together as both co-researchers and co-subjects'. This approach acknowledges disciplinary knowledge, skill and specialism, without requiring those involved to necessarily give this up, or operate in subordinate mode:

> Artists, anthropologists, scientists, activists, and other actors in the co-inquiry carve individual paths that may run parallel to each other, perhaps overlap, but only rarely fully coincide. Each practitioner brings their own languages, translations, and forms of expression: interviews, ethnographies, workshops, meals, field trips, and public programs become part of a multifaceted process that is both informative and transformative. Vitally, each practitioner never closes the doors to a transformative intention because of disciplinary boundaries.
>
> *(Triscott and Santomauro, 2021)*

Here the role of the organisation as curator is central, as the mediator, facilitator, manager, producer and often originator of such projects, drawing from the expanded role of the curator in the contemporary art field. This situates the organisation in an interstitial position – mediating as well as gathering of resources, funding, participants from different disciplines, publics, objects and ideas and connecting these with a politics of place and ecology – through projects that seek to intervene and potentially bring about notable change, rather than rooted in modes of representation, preservation and presentation (Triscott and Santomauro, 2021). The approach seeks a diffused agency and non-hierarchical approach to the production and gathering of different knowledge, through three phases – identifying matters of concerns, research and dialogue with and between artists, scientists and communities that ultimately enables the creation of an ecology of interconnected practices.

As well as the more open ended and non-hierarchical approach to project production, the other dimension that sets this methodology out most clearly from earlier Arts Catalyst work is the priority placed on incorporating 'situated knowledge' from specific communities that are external to the artistic and scientific communities involved. Triscott and Santomauro cite Donna Haraway's concept of situated knowledge, whereby knowledge is placed into a context, whether socioeconomic, anthropologic, intellectual, historic, or cultural (Haraway, 1988). One of the consequences of focusing on situated knowledge is a shift to open up their work to forms of knowledge that are not formalised into disciplinary structures or working with specific representative agents of disciplines. This approach shifts the role of the organisation from that of a finder of collaborators – matchmaking artists and scientists, then facilitating their projects – into an organisational working practice that requires long term relationship building and understanding the lived experience of people related to matters of concern rather than an infrastructure of specific disciplines (Lastra and Santomauro, 2025). Such an approach, by necessity, takes time. In ways that shape the 'cooperative process…shifting approaches, methods, and temporalities.' This allows for 'osmotic dynamics in the team' (Triscott and Santomauro, 2021).

Over a three-year period from 2014, Arts Catalyst produced a project called *Wrecked on the Intertidal Zone*. Developed through a cooperative series of investigations into the Thames Estuary, where the River Thames meets the North Sea, near Southend and Leigh-on-Sea in Essex, UK. The project was conceived by artist collectives YoHa (Graham Harwood and Matsuko Yokokoji) with Critical Art Ensemble (Steve Kurtz, Steve Barnes and Lucia Sommer) who worked with a wider group of researchers and technologists (Andy Freeman Fran Gallardo, Warren Harper, James Ravinet) to produce and document the project.

Focused on opening out and understanding of the complex changing ecological, social and industrial nature of the Thames estuary, the project sought to work with the systemic interconnections shaping the area without reducing it to scientific models or visualisations, while embracing the natural, non-human constraints of the environment. This meant working with what was already there – wilderness, weather, sea marshes, mudflats and the ebb and flow of tidal currents, migrating birds, as well as operating a spaces of leisure, tourism and fishing. This project was financed through a combination of grants from multiple sources, each representing a different characteristic of the project – arts funding from Arts Council England and the Wellcome Trust but also environmental and community funding from the Enovert Community Trust (previously known as the Cory Environmental Trust). The complexity of working on a constantly changing tidal plane required Arts Catalyst to develop relationships with multiple institutions that hold legal or other authority over the area, Leigh Town Council, Southend Borough Council, Focal Point Gallery, Natural England and Essex Wildlife Trust and local community groups such as the Belton Way Small Craft Club. While the project began with no specific outputs conceived, other than to explore the strange or eerie area of the estuary that Graham Harwood (of YoHa) lived, what emerged was a series of public artworks, participatory events and interactive citizen science workshops that were documented extensively online, through film and video production and written publications.

Beyond the methodology and production processes of *Wrecked on the Intertidal Zone*, Lastra and Santomauro (2025) cited Harwood's wider approach to art marking, cultural production and research more generally, as an influence in Arts Catalyst's process of long-term, situated mode of interdisciplinary cultural production. Harwood's work responds to a specific historical, institutional or geographic context which he and his collaborators are invited into, often creating technical objects that operate between ideas of sculpture, monument and technical contraption. Processes of co-inquiry, mediation and remediation rather than singular authorship are privileged – this operates as an assemblage of agencies, becoming a possible material to work and manipulate: 'I leave as much work undone as possible, so as it unfolds it can contest the space in which it is showing and the space/geography can contest the contraption[artwork]'(Fuller, 2010). As Harwood describes, 'the work doesn't make its argument through affirming a set of categories but by drawing out these formulae in uncannily clear ways through this process of conjunction' (Fuller, 2010). In *Wrecked on the Intertidal Zone* this process of mediation and conjunction emerged through a range of methods used to gather situated knowledge through informal processes of field research, observation and action, such as fishing, sailing, and bird watching. To facilitate this over the three years of the project Arts Catalyst organised a series of public events involving local food, sourcing, preparation and consumption – a 'recipe book' was published, called, *Talking Dirty: Tongue First!*' drawing on citizen science workshops, – 'we invite you to use the tongue as a tool with which to question the complex human and natural resources present with the estuary ecosystem' (Gallardo and Lastra, 2016: 5). The book was a manifestation of the situated knowledge of those living around the estuary, it contained instructions for cooking with estuary ingredients.

The most complex and time consuming public artwork to be created over the three-year project was called the *Graveyard of Lost Species.* This was an ephemeral and slowly decaying,public monument, established by remediating a local shipwreck, known as *Souvenir*, a 12-meter, 12-ton Bawley fishing boat, that lay deep in the estuary mud. Over many conversations with people living locally in Leigh-on-Sea and Southend the team gathered knowledge of 'lost species', this included 'wildlife, marine creatures, livelihoods, fishing methods, landmarks and local dialects that once flourished in the Estuary' but had disappeared locally, were slowly fading from the estuary, or were erasing from vernacular knowledge. The wreck was extracted from the mud, cleaned and strengthened to enable buoyancy, and the names of these 'lost species' were inscribed over its wooden surface. The boat was then sailed out into a new visible position in the marshes, sited back in the estuary landscape as a monument, to continue its slow decay into the earth. As Harwood (YoHa, 2015) writes on the working process of developing the register of 'lost species', the working process had an antagonistic relationship to formal research methodologies:

> We are not doing social science in any empirical sense, nor are we doing scientific ecological study. This is an exploration of the qualitative. We are working with personal and collective memory—in all its unreliability, misalignments, and fragmentations. So if someone were to say, "the eels of the estuary are gone," we accept that as told, regardless of whether an estuary biologist says, "There is still a population of eels in the southwestern section of the river bottom." The important bit in this example is that a relationship that was once productive and probably symbiotic is gone, and this absence has a place in this person's memory.

The process of developing situated knowledge and practical production of the *Souvenir*, from a wreck flooded with estuary mud, to a sited artwork was long and fraught. As Lastra and Santomauro (2025) set out 'it took about three years to be able to actually establish the artwork [the wreck 'Souvenir'] and sail it to a viable place where...people could actually see it...there was a lot of negotiation'. This negotiation required a triangulation with the agencies with that govern and have authority over the estuary space, the Environment Agency, a government body responsible for estuaries, Natural England an arms-length government body tasked with conserving and managing the natural environment and The Wildlife Trust, a non-profit/charity that protects and develop natural habitats such as those in the Thames estuary. Between these bodies, Arts Catalyst operated in a complex mediatory role 'we'd be working between agencies' but also in relation to the other knowledge domains of the project 'local people's ideas or aspirations' for the project and tasked with realising the artist's ideas, while balancing what was legally possible as an organisation in the estuary space (Lastra and Santomauro, 2025). While also ensuring the requirements of different funders were met. As an organisation arts Catalyst worked through this interplay of agencies carefully over time, creating environmental condition reports, and monitoring and ensuring safety around the waterways and positioning the boat such that it was visible to the public (Lastra and Santomauro, 2025).

In addition to these bureaucratic elements of the production process, the situated, spatial and temporal constraints of a project operating in an ever in-flux estuary were significant. The project was literally embedded in place, stuck in the mud. Here the process of creating the project was centrally about entering into the existing flows and dynamics of the estuary. As Lastra and Santomauro (2025) explained, to raise the wreck from the mud, not only were permissions required, but also a high tide that only came to the estuary three or four times a year. The production of the project necessitated a delegating or relinquishing of control to the temporalities of the tide.

Building on the approach undertaken in *Wrecked on the Intertidal Zone*, Arts Catalyst method of interdisciplinary cultural production through curatorial co-inquiry was then further developed in a long-term project in response to flooding, addressing the management of water through the Calder valley river catchment in West Yorkshire, UK. The four-year (2017-2021) project was called *Test Sites Calder*. The methodology of *Test Sites Calder* has been discussed in detail elsewhere by Triscott and Santomauro (2021) where they set out curatorial inquiry into the valley as 'a complex socio-environmental system'. So, I want to focus on the slow temporalities that were integral to the project here. As with *Wrecked on the Intertidal Zone*, the complexity and open nature of the proposed inquiry across questions of environmental stewardship, citizen monitoring, art making and participatory modelling required significant time to develop relationships and connections, both between the main interdisciplinary team and with the communities along the river. Arts Catalyst led the project and raised funding from a collection of different grant making bodies, including the Wellcome Trust and Arts Council England. Those invited to work on the project were artist Ruth Levene, artist group Invisible Flock, social anthropologist Megan Clinch and various social groups that interact with the river. It is important to consider the slow nature of the work here as Triscott and Santomauro (2021) place this at the centre of the interdisciplinary practice they enact – 'perhaps the long-term nature of the inquiry nurtures the potentiality of affective and osmotic dynamics in the team and puts an accent on the manifold micropolitics of the cooperative process that ends up shaping the inquiry'. This ultimately allowed Arts Catalyst to develop a nuanced and contextual understanding of the matters of concern of those people with relations connecting them to the river in a myriad of ways. This slowness, essentially related to the prioritising of discourse and relationship building within the project. The working process was slow because there was an open and tentative approach to relationship building through conversation anddiscussion that was rooted in Arts Catalyst's approach to developing an understanding of situated knowledge. The movement of the water through the valley set the pace here, as the tides had done in *Wrecked on the Intertidal Zone*.

Arts Catalyst led two narrowboat journeys along the Calder and Hebble Navigation in 2017 with anthropologists, scientists, artists and local people with connections to the waterway invited onto the boat to share food and discuss their different interpretations of the river. The journey on board allowed them to interact with these groups throughout the everyday temporalities of the waterway as they moved through it over a typical day, This included informal encounters with: anglers, boat owners, dog walkers, ecologists, local historians, town councillors, water engineers, and activists involved in natural flood prevention and citizen science river monitoring, in addition to more formal encounters such as interviews and group discussions. These journeys afforded those involved in the project a sense of close connection with the flows of deep ecological time.But this also allowed a shift in focus to urgent matters – which changed the perspective of the project as it became clear that a central local concern was the wider socio-political stewardship of the water system, not just flooding as an issue that had ignitedArts Catalyst's interest in the valley in the first instance. Flooding had been prevalent for 200 years and shaped the deep form of the valley, throughthe cyclical seasonal temporalities of high floods and low flow droughts, something exacerbated by climate change.

This gradual, evolving process allowed trust and knowledge to be built and shared by disciplinary perspectives (e.g. between Clinch as anthropologist and Levene as artist) that they could build on the situated knowledge of the locale. As Lastra and Santomauro (2025) articulated the group were able to begin to understand the complexity and inter-relationality of what they were addressing in the water system by simply spending time on it. Traveling along its course, 'grounding' themselves in its flows with the slow rhythms of the narrow boat navigation allowed them to observe as well as stop and have conversations with people – foregrounding the lived experiences of those for whom the river meant something in their everyday lives.

Without this deliberate and graduate process of gathering on route details would have been passed by through quick interventions, which would have hindered their appreciation of the valley and river in its relational form. The way the 'valley connects many different places' may be obvious on a map, but travelling slowly though them and meeting those connected to each point showed those involved how each place was also 'incredibly different from each other' (Lastra and Santomauro, 2025). Finally, acknowledging the historic and contemporary forms, flows and social connections of the river, the project also offered a perspective to imagine beyond the present moment when they encountered the water, by looking to the future of its management in the context of a changing climate. *Towards a Common Waters Policy* (2021) was a book published by Arts Catalyst created and written by Levene and Clinch that responded to all they had learned and gathered through the slowly evolving project. As the culmination of the project, the book was 'an attempt to understand and honour the often-challenging work undertaken by the many stewards who care for the Calder Catchment' (Lastra, in Levene and Clinch, 2021: 8) and to influence how future discussions and plans might account for that to shape future water governance.

Expanding the determination of ecological temporalities in interdisciplinary cultural production, Arts Catalyst's *Mind Garden,* that began in 2021 (see Pittwood, 2023) has infused the organisation with a particular form of earthly seasonality. Building on previous projects, *Mind Garden* continues to address the relationality of place and time, not in an abstract or infrastructural form, but as a 'set of relationships'. Arts Catalyst have continued to shift their work from aligning those with formal knowledge together (eg. artists and scientists) to create something new, into starting a project by 'building relationships with people and [their]...situated knowledge' (Lastra and Santomauro, 2025).

This basis of situated knowledge has then become the foundation on which other more formally defined practitioners, be they artistic, scientific etc, are invited in to build relations in specific situations. The starting point for Lastra and Santomauro has been establishing relationships with organisations not associated with the arts but are rooted in different forms of situated knowledge, where elements of Arts Catalyst and other organisations' work 'could be enhanced or supported by...collaboration'. That might be organisations in the voluntary sector or 'grassroots' initiatives in their infancy that do not necessarily have a legal structure, but where a connection can be made to Arts Catalyst ethos as an organisation, related to shared 'values...ideas...ambitions [or] desires'. This has led to projects such as the Mind Garden, where Arts Catalyst saw the possibility to assist and develop work 'mutual exploration', and where there might be value for their partner organisation in Arts Catalyst leveraging their network, knowledge and fundraising potential to facilitate an artist into connection with organisations or 'situated within those relationships' (Lastra and Santomauro, 2025).

The *Mind Garden*, was developed with the Sheffield branch of the national mental health charity Mind. Arts Catalyst built a relationship with the charity in Sheffield and proposed a project using an external plot of land Mind were looking to develop something on. Arts Catalyst were able to raise a small amount of money (via Arts Council England and two local charity grant making trusts in Sheffield, The Freshgate Trust Foundation and the JG Graves Charitable Trust) to invite the artist Harun Morrison to think about the possibility of creating a garden in the space. As an ongoing, constantly being made and living project, rather than a visitor space. As Lastra and Santomauro (2025) described:

> it wasn't like an overhaul "let's do an artist garden…and it's going to look fantastic". It was instead like "let's work with what is already there…let's make sure that we provide the healthiest conditions for whatever species are going to thrive in this environment, including people.

As with *Wrecked* and *Test Site Calder* working with what was already there was a defining principle of *Mind Garden*. To work with a group connected to Mind and over a series of seasons slowly develop the garden, where what is grown and who is involved changes each season. This brought together new knowledge, related to wellbeing and mental health, combined with ecological thinking around permaculture, that shaped how the garden developed through a slow, iterative process, where changes were introduced one at a time and there was time introduced for observation after each change.

Central to this notion of incremental change, and adaptation rather than intervention – also played out at an organisational level between Arts Catalyst and Sheffield Mind. As Lastra and Santomauro (2025) explained through developing the garden they were also 'navigating the partnership with Mind… having to make sure that we are on the same page and that [they understood they] were not there to just create something quickly and beautiful that would make that space pretty…it was about establishing a process that would happen long-term, a transformation…it needs time and [plants] need seasons'. This has also shifted how Arts Catalyst works as an organisation – with the team actively participating in planting and tending the garden, working directly with the seasonality of its development over years with a different Mind group. Working seasonally, with moments of flourishing and moments of fallow, is something that the project has inspired the organisation to aim towards more generally. As Lastra and Santomauro (2025) noted, this might be 'challenging in terms of structuring and planning [work], we had to adapt [but] it's been interesting and beneficial' to the organisation.

If we take all these Arts Catalyst projects together, what do they point towards in terms of our understanding of how interdisciplinary cultural production might practically operate through slow and long-term temporalities? What are the benefits or constraints of working with and against high tides and the seasons? Lastra and Santomauro (2025) described their approach as 'holding space'. This has a specific set of sensibilities – working with what is already there, in unorthodox ways, which is also a position that seeks to work against excessive consumption and novelty, the urge or desire to constantly be seeking to create something new, for its own sake. Something that is rooted in wider ideals of stewardship and sustainability. This approach is enabled through a slow process of polyphonic listening, where the organisation and those it brings into its projects from different disciplines attend to multiple voices simultaneously. But such an approach that offers this rigour and depth of engagement with constituents, requires the funding to provide the 'luxury to do that' (Lastra and Santomauro, 2025). It is only through a sustained funding of particular arts funding bodies and trusts such as Wellcome or 'being resourceful' as Lastra and Santomauro (2025) put it, that this privileged approach to long term work can be financially sustained. But this time to listen is fundamental in an approach where they feel a 'substance of responsibility' to those connected to their work such that they can engage with complexity and nuance, 'rather than just reacting to a specific issue in an immediate way' (Lastra and Santomauro, 2025).

But in the UK context the funding climate for non-profit arts organisations that want to work in this way, across disciplinary boundaries and embedded in ecological and social contexts has become increasingly challenging since 2010, with arts funding stationary or decreasing and much greater levels of demand for other forms of charitable grant making (see Chapter 3). The operational costs of the organisation are covered by an annual grant on a three-year term from Arts Council England as part of their National Portfolio funding. This allows the organisation to 'establish…develop and experiment' but it does not provide money to develop programmes that must be fundraised for separately. 'The culture of funding has changed so much' and there is less money available for this kind of work that there was 15 years ago (Lastra and Santomauro, 2025). With Austertiy in the UK over this period, larger grant making funders such as Esmée Fairbairn Foundation and the Paul Hamlyn Foundation are increasingly in demand.

Other large funders such as Wellcome Trust, have moved somewhat away from explicitly funding arts and culture projects and as a result of Brexit, the opportunity to participate in Creative Europe projects that often had an interdisciplinary approach was withdrawn. This type of international collaboration project had been central to the earlier work of Arts Catalyst, and whether directly or indirectly these changes align with their greater focus on situated knowledge and place in England.

The nature of Arts Catalyst's, long term, process rather than outcome-based approach means there are not many funders that support such work. This has also shaped the organisational form of these projects and itself contributed to their longer-term dynamics. Organisations such as Arts Catalyst must connect small pots of funding from different sources to try to build projects of substance and duration, through various grant applications.

This means projects must be designed in a way to meet the objectives of multiple funders, often who have a divergent focus, in relation to the intended outcomes of the funding, be it research, arts, social or ecological outcomes. The implications of this jumble of piecemeal funding from a production perspective are that there the mediatory role of the organisation can be pulled in different directions. One of the ways that Arts Catalyst has sought to navigate this complex mediatory role between funders and different forms of disciplinary knowledge is by carefully selecting who they work with. As is clear from the examples set out here the artists and practitioners they have worked with through these projects, all in some way or another have a strong curiosity and openness to knowledge forms, methods and research beyond the purely artistic. As Lastra and Santomauro (2025) put it 'finding the right person to work with' to 'co-host' the working process is essential. The centre of this process is finding affinity and 'shared values' with those from fields such as ecology, architecture, or environmental sciences – where there are common interests in relation to social or climate justice for example.

This offers an approach to strengthen relationships and knowledge exchange between disciplines that have shared concerns, but embedded in different histories and skills, but that seeks to create positive interconnection rather than antagonistic challenge to those practices. As one of the most experienced UK organisations in facilitating interdisciplinary cultural projects, Arts Catalyst have clearly evolved and developed as an organisation. What brings their later projects into focus – in some way a giving up or relinquishing of agency over knowledge ownership and production in the process of creating an interdisciplinary cultural project – to open up the potential to listen and learn from those with other forms of expertise both formal and informal. But also, in terms of giving agency in the production process – not willing something into being – but going with the flows of time and nature.

4.4 Public art and the interdisciplinary production of space and experience: Katie Paterson and Zeller & Moye

While Rhizome's *Seven on Seven* uses the theatrical stage as a site to create a performative interdisciplinarity and Arts Catalyst projects such as *Wrecked on the Intertidal Zone* worked through the inter-relationality of ecological time but rooted in what is already present in knowledge and materiality. Next, I want to look at how interdisciplinary collaboration is itself enacted in the process of conceiving, shaping and mediating the spatial, through the collaborative work of artist Katie Paterson and architects Zeller & Moye.

Rather than the determination of single organisations, interdisciplinary artworks are sometimes commissioned and produced through a constellation of agents acting together. They are not necessarily driven by an organisation seeking to develop a specific form of interdisciplinary practice or research, but rather come to this kind of work through the alignment of different streams of legislative requirements rooted in civic notions of public art and a relationship between organisational identity and expression of that identity in art. This is the case for some new public artworks commissioned outside the programmes of arts venues, or events like festivals. Here occasionally interdisciplinary arts projects have also found a home, especially where an association with interdisciplinarity as a concept itself might offer a strong and relevant sense of symbolic value to a project. To examine this form of interdisciplinary art commissioning and how spatiality has been a mediating parameter, we will look at two projects that were created by the same interdisciplinary collaboration of artist and architect, Katie Paterson, and Zeller & Moye that were commissioned in the UK and US through similar civic mandates for investment in public art required by local authorities as part of the permission to construct new buildings. These buildings were a major new life sciences building at the University of Bristol, UK and the Apple Park, the corporate headquarters of Apple Inc., in Cupertino, US, considered to be one of the most advanced office buildings in the world. Beyond developing functional and effective working spaces, the creation of public sculpture alongside both these buildings was utilised symbolically to express something about the nature of the endeavour through which the new buildings were created. Commissioning open and accessible public artwork in the landscaping around these buildings acted as a means to celebrate, or symbolically situate that newness, the sense of potential and futurity that a new building holds. In both cases new artworks were commissioned because of a locally mandated public art commissioning scheme, associated with the concept of the 'Percent for Art' – where public art is a requirement of formal planning approval at a local level for large-scale capital investment. When the investment in new buildings is of a relatively substantial scale, as it was in the case of both these buildings, an ambitious artwork can be paid for in full by a single funder – where managed carefully this allows for something novel and complex to be developed.

In Bristol, the Percent for Art concept has been part of the city council's development strategy since 2003, aligned with national guidance that dates to the Arts Council of Great Britain Percent for Art Campaign in 1991 (see Arts Council of Great Britain, 1991). As the local policy sets out – 'Bristol City Council recognise the 'percent' as meaning 1% of the capital construction cost of developments. In line with the national guidelines the City Council expects that 1% of the total build cost is allocated to public art and culture to mitigate the impact of the development on people and place' (APRB, n.d.). Similarly, as part of Cupertino City Council's approval of the $5bn Apple Park project in 2013 a requirement was that the development must include public artwork following the Cupertino Municipal Code (see City of Cupertino, 2025). In both these cases the costs for design, development, fabrication and installation of new public artwork were met by the developers of the new buildings, the University of Bristol, and Apple, inc (although in Bristol, additional elements of the project were supported by Arts Council England). But in both cases, it was not the local council nor the developer that directly sourced the interdisciplinary collaborators involved and produced the work, rather this was subcontracted to expert external consultants. In Bristol, the University worked with the non-profit arts organisation and production company Situations to develop the artwork and in Cupertino, Apple employed commercial art consultants, Artsource Consulting to advise on and realise the commission.

The project in Bristol began when the University of Bristol's Faculty of Life Sciences approached Situations to create a new permanent public artwork to be located in Royal Fort Gardens close where the new £56.6m Life Sciences Building (designed by architects Sheppard Robson) would be completed in 2014. For the University this was a significant investment and acted as a signifier for their commitment to the future of biological sciences research and as such any artwork commissioned as part of the building process would have a relationship to this (Sheppard Robson, 2025). Situations was created by curator and writer Claire Doherty as a public art commissioning programme within University of the West of England in Bristol in 2002. It grew to become an independent arts organisation in 2012 that ran until 2018. Throughout that period, Situations produced numerous notable public art commissions in the UK and internationally that challenged conventional commissioning practices exploring the interrelationship between art and place.

In post-war Britain there is a history of civic investment in public art linked to major construction projects and new buildings (Petherbridge, 1987; Garlake, 1998; Rosenberg & Cork, 1992; Pollock, & Paddison, 2010). While predominantly this manifests as modern sculptures dropped into the landscape around new buildings, for visitors, residents or workers to admire or contemplate. There have been occasional projects that have taken on an interdisciplinary approach to considering the relationship between sculptural form, art and architecture in greater rigour and depth. Victor Pasmore's *Apollo Pavilion* (1969) at Peterlee in County Durham is a good example, where the artist was appointed as the Consulting Director of Architectural Design of the Peterlee development corporation and shaped the design for the new town around a central sculptural pavilion. While the new work commissioned in Bristol did not take such a central role in the architecture of the new Life Sciences Building itself, its creation did follow a similar interdisciplinary approach to the development of space through the conjunctive work of Katie Paterson and the Zeller & Moye. With the brief from the University to develop a public artwork to meet the requirements of the Bristol City Council's public art requirements – and for an artwork to reflect the work conducted in the new Life Sciences building, initially Situations invited Paterson to develop a proposal for the project. At the time, Paterson was already working with Situations on the project called Future Library in Norway, – as part of a series of public artworks curated by Doherty in Oslo.

In Bristol, Paterson proposed an artwork titled *Hollow*. It was simple in concept, highly complex in execution. Her idea was to 'create a kind of miniature forest of every forest on the planet... making a microcosm of trees and forest life in one place' (Situations, 2015). This attempt to collect 'a planet's worth of trees' (BBC, 2016) was emblematic of Paterson's wider approach to art making. The concept for *Hollow*, reflected her artistic sensibilities to play with and crush deep temporalities and scales into the everyday, such as her work engaged with cosmology, *Earth-Moon-Earth 4'33"* (2008). From Nagano-Ken, Japan, using Earth-Moon-Earth radio transmission, 4 minutes and 33 seconds of silence was transmitted from Earth to the Moon. After travelling approximately 500,000 miles, it returned 2.5 seconds later. Or *All the Dead Stars*, 2009 – a map documenting the locations of just under 27,000 dead stars – all that have been recorded and observed by humankind. Her ideas are stark, conceptually sleek and neat but their practical realisation and the journeys undertaken to bring them speak to a sense of wonder (Larsen, 2014).

As with her other projects a vastly complex gathering process was required to create *Hollow*. As Paterson explained – 'you can say it in a few words but actually making that happen is a few years of research and working with huge networks of people' (BBC, 2016). Collaborating with those from other disciplines has been essential to her work. She describes the origins of her approach, 'while at the Slade School of Fine Art at University College London, I wandered into the Rock & Ice Physics Laboratory next door. They let me play my glacial-ice records in their walk-in freezers. That was when I found out how easy it was to approach others in different fields. *All the Dead Stars* involved hundreds of researchers. Some shared data, others developed the artworks with me' (Ball, 2019). As well as approaching and working with research and scientists directly she has also been part of schemes such as the now retired Leverhulme Artist in Residence programme, where she was based in the Astrophysics Group at the University College London (2010-2011).

This interdisciplinary experience provided the clear curatorial rationale behind Paterson's selection as the artist to develop a new project to sit alongside the new Life Sciences building, as an artist, although early in her career, already developing a high profile for her work drawing on scientific knowledge and collaboration with other disciplines. In a public conversation to mark the opening of *Hollow* at the University, the art historian Prof Simon Shaw-Miller noted Paterson's 'dedication to interdisciplinary art practice' aligned with the foundational principles of the University, where 'interdisciplinary conversation' was recognised as important by many of the first generation of academics (University of Bristol, 2016). As Shaw-Miller went on, 'the university takes the commitment to public arts seriously...we wanted to commission something which represents the important work taking place there, where our researchers are studying many of the acute challenges which face humanity this century' (University of Bristol, 2016). So, it is clear the commissioning context for a new work of art funded by the creation of the new building was one that embraced and valued interdisciplinarity as a practice more generally. And that the commission was also an opportunity for the University to demonstrate that value, particularly the interrelationship between art and science more generally (University of Bristol, 2025) as Paterson proposed a project that in her words 'could grow and take shape with the scientists at the university' (University of Bristol, 2016).

However what Paterson proposed for Bristol, went beyond what she had developed in previous work in terms of the requirements for interdisciplinary collaboration, it was not an image, map, sculpture, or sound work based on data sourced from elsewhere and installed in a gallery but rather a physical space, a structure that could be occupied and inhabited in some way. While much of Paterson's work has relied on her ability to work with sciences from all over the world in service of developing artworks, *Hollow* was something different in terms of the nature of the interdisciplinary collaboration required to create this spatial form. As she explained:

> The thing that I like doing is having ideas…that's at the core of what I do. But what I'm not very good at is visualising these things as forms… sometimes, yes, it's just very obvious…the form of the artwork just takes exactly what the idea is, but in other cases, you know, there's so many ways that it could come to life…I'd had the idea…the microcosmos of trees and bringing together all the forests, but I really could not visualise what an earth that was.
>
> *(SAIC, 2021)*

It was at this point that Paterson connected with the architectural practice Zeller & Moye. The relatively new firm had offices in both Mexico City and Berlin and was founded by Christoph Zeller and Ingrid Moye in 2013 who had both previously worked at Herzog & de Meuron leading on arts related projects such as the 2012 Serpentine Pavilion designed by Herzog & de Meuron (Stevens, 2017). What is clear from Paterson's outline of her invitation to Zeller & Moye to collaborate on the *Hollow* project, is that from the start there were highly defined roles – even if the working process was open. Paterson's role as artist and originator for the concept of the work delineated clearly, and Zeller & Moye situated the project through this self-acknowledged deficit. This openness to share authorship through the collaboration is central here. But there was also a stong shared affinity between Paterson and Zeller & Moye right from their introduction. As Paterson described there was an immediate 'chemistry' between them where they 'clicked' both aesthetically, as Paterson noted, Zeller & Moye have a 'minimalistic approach' and a 'sensitivity to materials' (SAIC, 2021) and 'visual sensibilities' (University of Bristol, 2016), that aligned with her own practice, but also more deeply in terms of working methodology. As Christoph Zeller put it Paterson started with 'lots of [ideas]...this is in a way how we start [a project] always with a lot of options, variations, and then slowly narrowing it down to the right solution…so in that sense, we felt at home' (University of Bristol, 2016). Central to this was a unified sense of trust within the collaboration, that went beyond a formal functional service into something deeper related to both their respective creative practices as Paterson noted 'that's really important because with many of the projects where I collaborate with scientists and others, it's often kind of drawing their expertise in, but it's not really the aesthetic side of it. And so this is the first kind of collaboration where we've really worked from the ground upwards on the form, and the whole experience of the artwork' (SAIC, 2021). But what was the influence of this collaboration on the final outcome of the work? Zeller & Moye brought their specific architectural understanding of 'spatial experience' into the project, to work with Paterson's ideas and shape them into something habitable in some sense. They also worked through various possibilities of how the project might manifest spatially, from early ideas of developing a chronological wooden boardwalk through the park. As Zeller noted, 'there are other parameters…we as architects can then already foresee all these issues' related to the preservation of wood and how it reacts to exposure to the climate over the seasons, which allowed them to rule out particular forms and processes. In the process of discussion, these possibilities gave them parameters to shape the work, such as keeping the wood untreated, but out of direct sunlight to preserve the natural colours (University of Bristol, 2016), developing an intimate and contemplative experience for the visitor. Paterson's early ideas for the space were situated around 'organic [crystalline] cave-like shapes, the idea of actually entering a tree…an intimate space where you were enclosed with every tree on the planet' (Situations, 2015). This meant that there was the need to strike a balance between privileging the wood at the forefront of the concept behind the project but also creating something that could create an encounter with it in a spatial environment. As Zeller put it, 'it's a little bit both. It's a little bit architecture, housing the wood, and at the same time, of course, creating that experience for the visitor. This very intimate experience' (University of Bristol, 2016). As a result of the collaboration, *Hollow* became an 'immersive piece of architecture'. Scaled down from initial design to allow only one or two people to enter the space at a time to provide this sense of intimacy, and sensory experience – the tactile, smell and feel of the wood. Over three years, working primarily remotely, Ingrid Moye noted the iterative and incremental design process went 'back and forth, all these ideas and thoughts and kind of massaging this thing. It was, was really fluid, really easy, although it was a long process with small, but solid steps, I think, was very successful'. A process that Paterson described as 'learning…and finding our way through' (University of Bristol, 2016).

Utilising a wide network of arboretums, wood collectors, research institutes around the world and with the support of Situations and the School of Biological Sciences at the University of Bristol, small samples of over 10,000 unique tree species were gathered, indexed, catalogued, cut and assembled into form by professional art fabricators, millimetre, which was then installed in Royal Fort Gardens. Although the collection of samples did not match the scale of all specimens of tree – around 73,000 – this did not ultimately matter for Paterson as the poetic and linguistic scale of the project enabled the same imaginary work for those encountering it. It became 'representatives of every single tree' (University of Bristol, 2016). The symbolic choices around the ages of wood and the status was brought to the forefront in the design instead. Paterson: 'I think the number 10,000 was also quite important in that way that it just goes over that number of something that's imaginary...100 is quite touchable...10,000 is suddenly, like, what is that? How does that feel?' (University of Bristol, 2016). Petrified wood from the earliest forests that emerged over 390 million years ago was placed at the base of the structure and extinct trees, vulnerable and critically endangered species placed higher up. With small apertures high up, the design sought to imply the way sunlight travels through a forest canopy. It is clear the resulting work both manifests the collaborative relationship between artist and architect in a distinct way. Fundamental to this was moving away from a didactic museological display, with easily directed interpretation for the visitor of the origins of each piece of wood. Rather the conversations between the collaborators led them to focus on the 'sensory' and 'imaginary' experiences that the space might evoke in relation to the histories of each specimen (University of Bristol, 2016). This process emerged through the technical architectural process of drawing detailed 3D models incorporating each individual piece of wood. It was this type of integration of conceptual thinking, and technical knowledge and skills, from their respective disciplines over a sustained period of discussion and collaboration that the final form emerged, and therefore *Hollow* could not be reduced to either single practice.

Given the success of the *Hollow* collaboration, Paterson and Zeller & Moye came together again to work on another complex public art commission when their proposal was selected for a commission to accompany the creation of Apple's new headquarters. As with the University of Bristol, beyond the specifics of the proposed artwork, there was a clear curatorial rationale for the selection of Paterson and Zeller & Moye as the interdisciplinary team selected by Artsource Consulting, Apple and Cupertino's Arts and Culture Commission. Here Artsource Consulting played an important mediatory role, through interpreting a brief from the client (Apple) that would meet the requirements of Cupertino's Arts and Culture Commission that needed to provide approval for the artwork.

Any proposal was required to meet a fairly exhaustive list of Cupertino's (City of Cupertino, 2025) public art specifications such as being sited as 'an integral part of the landscaping', that is 'easily visible from the public street' and be 'in permanent view to motorists and pedestrians' as well as make a 'major statement' when located at the entrance to a development and be composed of 'permanent materials requiring a low level of maintenance'. But more than that the collaboration between Paterson and Zeller & Moye and their respective artistic and architectural practices aligned with Apple's product branding and corporate identity, at one level in terms of clear and minimalist design aesthetics. But also, more generally in terms of an appreciation for and promotion of interdisciplinarity and an important working methodology. So, there is a clear sense of the values aligned in this commission, just as Apple's new headquarters sought to represent the brand values and identity in form and style. In this sense the Paterson and Zeller & Moye commission achieved this as well. In many ways Apple could be said to be the corporate embodiment of an interdisciplinary approach to technological development that brought design aesthetics of form and functions into a coherent relationship with advanced computing. As Steve Jobs put it in an oft-cited statement (at a launch event for the iPad 2) in 2011: 'It's in Apple's DNA that technology alone is not enough. That it's technology married with liberal arts, married with the humanities, that yields us the result that makes our hearts sing'. Jobs sets out Apple's approach to interdisciplinary thinking as a central mode of competitive advantage, as he went on to discuss how Apple, by using this approach, developed the iPad vs traditional PC. He goes on: 'we think we have the right architecture, not just in silicon, but in the organisation to build these kinds of products. And so I think we stand a pretty good chance of being pretty competitive in this' (Jobs, 2011). This interdisciplinary approach in Apple goes back to earlier developments for the company, especially in the Apple Computer Interface Design Project, initiated by Joy Mountford in 1991, who was identified as a 'strong advocate of interdisciplinary' at the company (Winograd, 1996: 185). This particularly presented in her approach to hiring, as she sets out: 'we looked for interdisciplinary-trained people, including those who had musical training, as well as computer literate minded. They were not rigidly trained but were more creative. I guess partly they had a good feeling for others, were creative and insightful' (Mountford, 2021). If this kind of interdisciplinarity can comfortably be described to be in Apple's 'DNA' then, curatorially, the selection of Paterson and Zeller & Moye was a good fit in this context.

Artsource Consulting announced Paterson and Zeller & Moye's project had been selected for the commission in July 2021, with local press reporting it as 'a multimillion-dollar project involving a team of dozens of artists, architects, geologists and desert experts, all with the goal of creating an outdoor public space at the company's massive Cupertino headquarters' (Toledo, 2021). The final work titled *Mirage* opened two years later in June 2023. As with *Hollow*, the work was realised through a complicated process of gathering. In this case, sand from all the deserts across the Earth. This sand was then cast into tall glass cylinders that were then presented as a flowing form of 448 colour-gradated vertical semi-transparent columns, placed in a curated arrangement through olive grove landscaping. Complex technical expertise was required to realise the work and required to as Moye put it 'collectively work together' (Otieno, 2023). With the team working with the Delft University of Technology in the Netherlands to refine the manufacturing process; specialised glass fabricators in California casting the glass columns; and structural engineering undertaken by Eckersley O'Callaghan, who also worked on the complex glass engineering undertaken for the Apple Park building, where glass was a prominent feature. Beyond these intersecting areas of technical expertise, operating in a service mode to realise the project, as with *Hollow*, the creative roles between artist and architect were well defined and complimentary in relation to the spatial necessity of the brief. With Paterson working in 'ideas' and forming these 'intangible thoughts' as she put it, into 'real, embodied, physical experiences' through the architectural 'understanding of space, embodiment, scale, light and immersion' brought by Zeller & Moye (Otieno, 2023). Zeller explained more about how this operated in practice:

> Our different disciplines complement each other. We approach a project together as one team that oscillates between strategic and systematic thinking, experimental and at times intuitive making. We each work with our own means of expression such as words, drawings, collages, computer models, then at certain intervals come together to exchange and discuss our ideas and drafts before returning to our studios to develop those further.
>
> *(Otieno, 2023)*

While a shared aesthetic affinity in this commission undoubtedly aided the working process. What Zeller points to here is how Paterson and Zeller & Moye used these representational 'means of expression' such as technical drawing and computer models as interdisciplinary 'boundary objects' to navigate, connect as well as transgress their respective practices. This enabled them to overcome the inherent technical complexity of the project, which necessitated continuous collective input and agreement from both the artist and the architect to drive discussion and decision-making forward. But as Paterson noted this was also possible because of a shared set of values toward work embodied in rigorous attention to detail in their respective practices (Otieno, 2023). The project's long-term duration and robust financial resources were also undoubtedly instrumental in facilitating this attention to detail. But the collaboration was not just about refining the aesthetic design of the glass column structure, more fundamentally, it was also about the relationship to landscape, site and place and how an imagined visitor would encounter the work.

The approach of Paterson and Zeller & Moye to conceiving the work in relation to its location also became a meeting point for their particular disciplinary interconnection. Landscape was central to Job's vision for the redevelopment of the whole site when he proposed the new headquarters to Cupertino council, prominently claiming the area would be remediated from 20 to 80 percent landscaping overall (Jobs, 2011). This was acknowledged by the architect of the building, Norman Foster, whose design for the building sought to establish a 'strong connection with nature and the landscape surrounding the building' (Foster, 2017). The gigantic ring-shaped office building would be 'set gently into a lush green landscape' (Hawthorne, 2011). One of the emphases placed on the function of this landscape, was on 'retreat', rooted in naturalistic design element – a space for Apple employees (but not necessarily the wider public as access would be restricted) could walk, exercise and gather in aid to their wellbeing, and achieve a correlated efficient productivity. Therefore, the design of the landscaping that *Mirage* would occupy, was based on a 'representation' of therolling topography of the surrounding Santa Clara Valley and the foothills of the Santa Cruz Mountains (Rybczynski, 2018). This was something Laurie Olin, the landscape architect contracted by Jobs and Apple to develop the landscape set out by deploying apple orchards, wildflower meadows, a pond, and clustered woodland, all interconnected with walking and cycling paths. Olin (in Rybczynski, 2018) set to meet two principles that defined the landscape from Jobs' brief: 'Health, in terms of mental and physical stimuli and ecology, and the regional landscape of northern California, in terms of history, fact, and myth'. The result was a highly engineered but naturalistic style, with more than 8,000 new trees brought into the landscape (Rybczynski, 2018). In a sense, the landscaping of the site – a pastoral corporate aesthetic environment,verdant but isolating, and not accessible to the wider public – is characteristic of what Mozingo calls 'pastoral capitalism' (Mozingo in Hawthorne, 2011; Mozingo 2014). This sense of exquisite remoteness came into further criticism when the media picked up the fact that the new building did not include on-site childcare facilities (Schwedel, 2017; Tibken, 2017). But as the artwork was a requirement of the City of Cupertino, as denoted by Cupertino's Arts and Culture Commission it had to be accessible to the public, not simply restricted to Apple employees. So, the commission was positioned as something of a civic counter to the wider isolated pastoralism of the landscaping.

It was into this context that Paterson and Zeller & Moye developed *Mirage*, as something subtle and interwoven into the landscape – enabled by the translucency and colours of the glass. As with *Hollow*, it sought to create an 'intimate interior offering space for contemplation and focus' (Otieno, 2023). This responded to the conceptual poetry of the work, set to evoke what Paterson described (in Otieno, 2023) as 'vastness' and 'mystery' of the desert. But also, in a practical and architectural sense this required evoking the simultaneity of place, embedded in the collection of desert sand turned into glass, to be distinct in each column and felt by the visitor. The balance played out between artist and architect is felt in the way the work was situated into the landscape, but also into how the visitors to the site would encounter it, conceptually and physically. Each glass column was chosen to be 2m high as Moye noted (in Otieno, 2023), this was determined by the 'scale of the visitor' – ensuring most could not see over them but rather would be drawn into looking through their hazy form. But from a distance they would not impose or obscure the wider landscape features, rather appearing as an 'apparition' within the landscape or passed by at speed on the road (Otieno, 2023). Ultimately this sought to immerse visitors simultaneously in the artwork and the landscape. Something aptly demonstrated during a 2023 Apple iPhone launch video, when Apple CEO Tim Cook introduced the new features of the device from the centre of the landscape created by *Mirage* (Apple, 2023).

Mirage and *Hollow* were not initiated by an aesthetic or research-driven impulse from the commissioning organisations, but rather by the logic of accountability through a legislative and civic requirement for public art. It is perhaps unusual that the civic mandate for public art generates such complex and ambitious interdisciplinary collaborations – as these tend towards the symbolic, ornamental or monumental. But in the case of both *Mirage* and *Hollow* this was enabled by how that appeal to interdisciplinarity also expressed the organisational identity of the commissioners by distinct spatial experiences. In both the UK and US examples, these public artworks were nonetheless symbolic of the new building's purpose, aligning the interdisciplinary nature of the artwork with the commissioning organisation's espoused identity and values. *Mirage* and *Hollow* are a direct product of an external legislative requirement driving an internal corporate/academic expressive need, which was then fulfilled by a highly synergistic and methodologically aligned interdisciplinary team. Paterson's artistic practice is inherently disciplinary, as she has noted, 'my work couldn't exist without a wide network of scientific expertise, yet it couldn't happily sit in a context other than art' (Quin, 2022). As this sets out her process synthesises and utilises the knowledge and expertise of others, often in a service mode, produced through a *singular author / co-production* dynamic. Yet the potential of the briefs in Bristol and Cupertino required a broadening of that interdisciplinary producing dynamic to a *co-authorship / co-production* relationship. The collaboration became important because Paterson's conceptually vast ideas lacked a predefined physical form, a deficit Zeller & Moye filled by providing architectural expertise in spatial experience, scale and light. The final forms in both cases emerged from a dialogue that balanced the artwork's conceptual resonance with the practicality of creating a contemplative, site-responsive and sensory environment. Through synthesis of their respective practice, neither *Mirage* nor *Hollow* are reducible to their antecedent disciplines.

From a cultural management perspective, what was also important was the involvement of the specialist external consultants, partners and producers

(Situations in Bristol, Artsource Consulting in Cupertino) who interpreted and responded to the original brief and the civic requirements, as well as facilitating the production of the projects. These organisations operated in a key mediatory role that was able to curatorially align the commissioning process with the identity and aesthetic values of organisations creating new buildings.

What is striking about the way both Paterson and Zeller & Moye discuss their collaboration is the strong sentiment and sense of privilege and gratification that is fostered around it (University of Bristol, 2016). As these examples show, the successful practical realisation of complex interdisciplinary projects can hinge upon the development of a key social dimension – a privileged sense of trust. As the curator Mary Jane Jacob (in Bewley and Tarbuck eds 2016: 13) noted writing on Paterson's wider collaborative practice, such trust can transcend more formal modes of service, contractual obligation or task delegation. This has the potential to 'open up an individual's disciplinary processes to thinking differently, using their knowledge differently, enacting who they are differently. Working on such projects unlocks for others their own questions, and in the process, their knowledge is validated and valued'. Such situations are rare and hard to cultivate in practice, but successful where the starting point is that interdisciplinary collaboration is a privilege, rather than something to be endured, from a position of disciplinary confidence rather than insecurity. The collaboration is positioned to facilitate a social and reciprocal foundation that creates a genuinely shared intellectual space, enabling integrative emergence that transcends the limitations of singular disciplinary practices.

4.5 The studio in response mode: The Centre for the Less Good Idea

Building on the sense of collaboration as privilege set out in the work of Paterson and Zeller & Moye, we turn to a small arts organisation in Johannesburg that places this social privilege at the centre of their work. Since The Centre for the Less Good Idea was founded in 2016 it has brought together hundreds of practitioners from different disciplines to create new work together. Key to the working process of The Centre, is a particular conception of 'the studio' as a critical site of creative interchange between disciplines. This case study examines this and the artistic leadership and economic foundation of The Centre to understand how it has developed this valuable mode of generative interdisciplinary cultural production. The Centre emerged from the artistic practice of William Kentridge, both in terms of its artistic ethos and operation but also its resources. Although deeply rooted in practices of drawing, his work has been celebrated for embracing a multiplicity of forms notably animation, performance and theatre. As art historian Rosalind Krauss sets out, this kind of practice does not follow the 'leeching of the aesthetic out into the social field' nor a 'retreat into etiolated forms of the traditional mediums - such as painting and sculpture' but rather embraces a 'differential specificity' – which seeks to reinvent mediums, sometimes through a conjunction or rigorous form of interdisciplinarity, rather than abandoning them (Krauss, 2000: 56). This is a practice that starts with the specificity of a medium, and expands through rearticulation – as Kentridge (2024) has put it, 'one doesn't have to a have brilliant idea for something to happen, one has to trust in the material in your hands and what you see emerging in front of you'. Kentridge's working methods and practice are well documented (e.g. Kentridge, 2014; Krauss (ed), 2017; Kentridge, 2024), but elements are worth briefly illustrating here. As he describes his practice, it is rooted in a resistance to narrow specialisation or the 'good advice' he received early in his career to focus on a single discipline (Kentridge, 2023):

> I was…making drawings in my studio, and eventually the drawings became animated films, and then a theatre company said…would I put my animated films behind them, and so the theatre came back in and the film came back in, and I discovered, against my will and against my better judgement, that I was, in fact, going exactly against that good advice and that I was doing all the different things together again. And it became clear at a certain point that the drawings were helped by what happened in the theatre, and the theatre gave rise to many new ideas for films and for animation…And this whole mixed cloud of activities was the only way for it.

Rather than focus on his practice directly, here I want to focus specifically on The Centre, as a wider manifestation of this 'mixed cloud of activities' and its approach to 'incubating' new interdisciplinary work beyond his own, drawing on insights from The Centre's co-founder and artistic director Bronwyn Lace. To understand how The Centre developed its unique approach to interdisciplinary cultural production, I want to explore the founding idea and principles behind The Centre, its location, economic model, curatorial approach and relationship to audiences.

The form of The Centre emerged after Kentridge approached Lace, herself a South African artist working across disciplines, with the idea of establishing an arts space in Johannesburg to 'extend' the elements of Kentridge's practice that were interdisciplinary and collaborative. By 2015 Kentridge had had two decades of major international success in the art world and art market and had the economic resources to fund the purchase of a building and support the running costs of a new organisation. What the organisation would be and how it would operate were determined by Lace and Kentridge, in a way that sought to build on Kentridge's approach to studio practice – where working 'response mode' rather than 'knowing mode' was primary (Lace, 2025).

As Kentridge acknowledged, 'the lot of 40 years of working in the studio has been trying to convince myself of the necessity for the less good idea, abandoning the good idea to only do one thing, and celebrating the possibility of the mess of many things coming together' (Kentridge, 2023). Kentridge describes The Centre, as the culmination of this idea. Taking its name from the Tswana proverb, 'If the good doctor can't cure you, find the less good doctor' – a call for seeking out new forms of knowledge, perhaps less conventional and obvious, than those that seem to offer initial apparent authority. Kentridge translates this as a fundamental artistic 'strategy for working in the studio'. Where the first impulse is to pursue the 'good idea', but in the process 'cracks' may appear in this 'perfect idea' – then new possibilities open – either an instance or enforced production of this good idea, or an embrace of what is happening 'at the margins' as he puts it perhaps 'a drawing that's not working, allow that, not working to happen and see in the mess of erasure what other things start to suggest...themselves'. This impulse is not focused on the 'category of knowing, but the category of recognition' – 'a capacity, even if we can't give a logical reason for something, to feel that something is either right or close to right or has an excitement, or provokes a series of associations in us that makes us want to follow an idea through.' (Kentridge, 2023). As Lace (2025) puts it succinctly, 'less good is not bad... it's unexpected...[it is an] incredibly rich and generative space'. The response mode is about focusing on what is emergent from a relationship of components and practices – it is not determined but about identifying and honing that emergent component.

It was important that The Centre was contextually specific to its location in Johannesburg. As Lace (2025) explained the city is 'always at the same time exquisitely beautiful and horrifically ugly...It's incredibly inspiring, and it feeds. It feeds you if you're an artist.' Rather than take on a dilapidated large and complex renovation project, where the building would be the focus, Kentridge and Lace, decided to start with a small unit, that was part of the Arts on Main complex in the Maboneng Precinct in downtown Johannesburg. Itself a contested and changing area of the city associated with debates about creative clusters, displacement and culture-led urban regeneration (eg. Gregory, 2015). The building was close to Kentridge's existing studio and where Lace had been a long-term resident. Both had seen the rapid urban changes in the area post-apartheid, with the growth of a 'thriving cultural community' in formal and informal ways and 'then a very quick shift from this rejuvenation into a sort of hard and fast collapse and gentrification happening simultaneously' (Lace, 2025). Over the first six months of 2016, as they toured many buildings to find a space, it became clear to Kentridge and Lace, that the structure itself was 'insignificant compared to the immaterial conversations that were going on around the philosophies that [they] were interested in' and their observations of the 'kind of challenges [there were for] artists in the city' (Lace, 2025). This placed the emphasis not on the building infrastructure itself, but rather how creating 'conversation and relationships' – could drive the definition of a new cultural organisation – its approach and methods of engaging creative practitioners from across the city would be prioritised. This approach stemmed from two particular directions – both Lace and Kentridge's sense of the limitations with the 'spaces and platforms built to hold us' as Lace put it. But also, the importance of creating a way that other artists could have the 'privilege' of collaborating with others from any background or discipline in a responsive mode. The sense that interdisciplinary collaboration could be a privilege, rather than something that is an economic necessity or requirement for relevance is valuable. Here the studio becomes an open space safe to explore, to challenge disciplinary practices through conscious dialogue and debate around the limits of established disciplines. Or to put it another way, what Kentridge calls a 'safe space for stupidity' – born out of a commitment to transcend or push against given disciplinary assumptions and practices – where what emerges from these processes, may be irreducible to the individual practitioners or their disciplinary backgrounds (Lace, 2025). This ultimately places an emphasis on process, rather than outcome. The necessity of such space was reinforced by Lace as she pointed out the increasing concern of the 'spaces built to hold' artists – whether universities, international festivals or theatres in major cultural capitals – was an imperative towards presenting a 'final product' – often driven by logic of economic return on that presentation. Given initial economic security provided by Kentridge's investment in the new organisation – one of the key ambitions was to be able to work in a way that without a requirement to such constraints could focus on process over outcome. But this also enabled in the early stage of developing the organisation, and in the 'responsive mode' of organisational development deployed by Kentridge and Lace, to free not to follow existing 'models' or 'best practice' or emulate the business models of existing arts organisations – but 'use what happens in the studio and what happens in a collective space as the…approach'. With an emphasis on 'the way in which people treat one another…[with] a deep…intimacy and empathy in the room…everybody making in the room together in a…a flat relationship with one another rather than a hierarchy' (Lace, 2025).

As artists, neither Kentridge nor Lace were 'cultural organisers or trained in…arts administration [or] leadership' – so they sought to approach building the organisation as they might a collaborative artwork or piece of theatre – 'bit by bit recognising that which seems to have legs and is compelling and giving that more energy, and letting that which didn't work go for a bit or even put it into a different space, and see if you can love it in a different way' (Lace, 2025). Here the lack of determined quantitative or qualitative evaluation frameworks of any particular ideas meant there was more space for surprise.

While they searched for a building, Lace also explored the breadth of the cultural landscape in Johannesburg by setting up new conversations across the city. These built into a series of weekly meals and discussions – asking those present from across the spectrum of the arts, education and civil society – what the cultural imperatives for Johannesburg were at that moment. One key thing that emerged from these early discussions was a sense of the 'deep network of relationships' that already existed across Johannesburg's cultural world and beyond (Lace, 2025). It was this sense of an entwined awareness of different practices that became a defining feature of how early programmes of The Centre were curated or rather unfolded and different practitioners invited into the space. An initial set of practitioners was asked to invite others who they had always wanted to work with, from any discipline or background, into the space. This approach consciously sought to build on the interconnected social networks in the city beyond disciplines. This approach was purposefully set against an 'open call' method of participant recruitment, where a jury would pass judgement on written proposals. Such processes are common when public money is involved, and a greater sense of accountability is required to be presented. But as Lace (2025) noted, such judgements by committee may privilege accountability over risk taking. As the project was a personal investment by Kentridge, it was an opportunity 'to push up against what is not working, and what is often quite brutal for artists' in such open call processes. Which can reward those good at writing, but perhaps not those who are: 'embodied in their practice, and who express and research through methods that do not translate into PDF documents' (Lace, 2025). This was fundamental to how Kentridge wanted to invest in the new space, as he expressed to her early on in the development of it, he was not interested in 'proposals' and 'even less interested in reports', the primary concern was towards 'what happens when we're in the room together…not having to come with their CVs and evidence, but just to come with themselves and for us to see how we can expand that' (Lace, 2025).

The first 'Season' of work created at The Centre was presented in March 2017. To develop the programme Kentridge and Lace invited an initial set of curators from a range of disciplines to start the process of developing new work that had been part of their earlier conversations. These curators were chosen because they had a unique network 'not only in their own industry or their own discipline, but also extending outside of that' (Lace, 2025). These were director and theatre maker Khayelihle Dominique Gumede, poet and performer Lebogang Mashile and dancer and choreographer Gregory Maqoma. The work developed out of two key questions Kentridge and Lace asked at the start of the first Season (and subsequently repeated over future seasons). Firstly, 'who is it that you have wanted to work with or been working with, that you desire to work further, or would want to bring into…the room'. This could be someone with a deep personal connection, a partner or best friend or someone they admired but had no personal connection to. Then secondly, 'what is that project that you've been wanting to do that you haven't been able to do…because it doesn't fit into the format of the spaces that have been holding you'. What became apparent from the discussion of these questions was that regardless of how successful an individual may have been within their specific disciplines, they also felt 'boxed[-in] by the spaces holding them' (Lace, 2025).

There was a clear sense that rigid disciplinary stereotyping of particular forms of practice, as they were seen to have a specific 'terrain' say spoken-word poetry, was limiting the possibility for those practitioners to work in other spaces and this was something The Centre's approach was well placed to challenge and overcome. But given the cultural economy of South Africa, where there are very limited resources for the arts, public or otherwise – being able to build a career can be predicated on the ability of practitioners to shift disciplines, or adopt a pragmatic versatility informed by economic necessity. In contrast to US or European contexts where it may be much easier to sustain a career within a single narrow disciplinary or institutional field of practice. The Centre sought to embrace this openness to disciplinary transgression, rather than 'punishing' those for wanting to step outside of the boxes they had been placed in or forcing them to 'disguise' themselves to fit into a pre-existing disciplinary frame. As Lace (2025) acknowledged, the 'complexity of a human is not encouraged in institutions. It's about saying…let's let the artists be in a state of not knowing'. The new work for the first season was devised by a large group of contributors, with the initial curators inviting more collaborators into the room – 'what was five became 15, became 30' (Lace, 2025). In total the first Season assembled over 60 different practitioners from a range of disciplines – acting, writing, dance, composition, visual art, filmmaking and boxing. This mesh of collaborators emerged through the initial group of curators inviting more into the room – 'artists choosing artists' – a process of branching progression or a kind of daisy chain curating.

The way the work for the programme was developed was through a devised approach – focused initially on an intensive five-day 'incubator workshop' (Mann, 2023), that became the recurrent method for developing new work in later seasons. The focus on this short but intense moment of improvised rather than planned collaboration, sharing, documenting and creating was about activating the studio space as incubator – as Lace (20250 put it 'we're interested in the room and what's happening [in the room]...the meaning and the sense and all of that comes later'. This sense of being in the room and feeling for the moment of connection as well as following tangential ideas down different paths was summed up by Kentridge and Lace in a performance they devised called *The Defence of the Less Good Idea*. The short performance starts with Kentridge giving a formal lecture but slowly being interrupted, drowned out by a swelling chorus of sounds and voices that builds to a joyous and cacophonous climax. What is central to this sense of being in the room in the studio is that it can be orchestrated to hold contradiction with both a rational clarity of intellectual articulation and feral, unrestrained energy – being welcomed and embraced. Such that is not a space that seeks to discipline what is emergent – but rather embrace those contradictions. This sense of space holding as being about to embrace both the formal minimalism of say a 'Danish architect, with her neatly ruled lines and her perfection which is needed [in that field]', where work and ideas are completed with 'finesse and nuance', using skills that have been finely honed and are deployed in a rigorous and disciplined manner. But simultaneously the same space holds a 'wildcat on amphetamines' with a fiery and unkempt creative energy – 'it's about the institution [as a] whole being enough…allowing for the collapse [and] the delight and… ravenous pursuit of something'. The power of bringing these forces together in the room is reward, in moments of recognitions, felt moments, when something unexpected happens – 'that oh, fuck! This is something that we didn't anticipate…that's been the privilege of being between those dynamics and recognising both' (Lace, 2025).

For some this working process has the potential to be 'deeply uncomfortable'. Some of that discomfort is being pushed to move outside of one's discipline or well-established ways of working but also in the physicality of the working methods used that encouraged embodiment and movement. Resistance to such practices generally came from those with a prescribed sense of disciplinary authority such as academics or those trained in singular disciplinary practices in the visual arts where the individuality of expression might be more prized. This was not an anti-intellectual stance, but rather about moving beyond merely talking – to 'being in room' where there could be an emphasis that what is emergent from interactions in a way that is not easily reducible to the individual, nor a singular sense of authorship. This was about understanding that there will people in the room that 'can do things that you can't do and that therefore you can do things that they can't do' and acknowledging that itself is a 'deep kind of very beautiful exchange, as you create something that belongs to both of you, and neither of you' (Lace, 2025).

Capturing these emergent forms, incidental flourishes, revelations, feelings and actions has been central to how The Centre has operated from the very beginning. Documentation in film, sound and writing of both the working process in the room and the resulting new work has been an important part of the methodology. But also building a high-quality archive of work, available online, was an imperative for Lace. This responded to the rich live but ephemeral performance culture in South Africa of the previous decades where much was lost in a sense because it had not been retained or documented in digital or other formats as might be the case in Europe or the US. Beyond this, documentation across media was also a strategy to allow the moments of discovery that took place in the room to be 'held and reflected back to' participants when they happened, to continually inform the process (Lace in Mann, 2023). The first people Kentridge and Lace hired to work with them on The Centre was a cinematographer, a sound recordist, a writer and a stills and a stills photographer – these 'mirrors in the room' acted to enable the practitioners to 'step outside of the moment of making' such that the work being created in the room could be reflected back and 'introduce itself' – literally through a different lens or a medium, such as writing. This ability to reflect the working process and creations of the centre was also about making this available to the wider world, beyond the 'magic that was happening in the room' (Lace, 2025).

Emerging from the workshops, the resulting work created for the first Season was expansive. There were performances featuring dance, poetry and music; four short Samuel Beckett plays; a boxing ring was created in the space and became a central site for performance developed in collaboration with the local Hillbrow Boxing Club; 12 short films were produced; a musical procession travelled streets of Maboneng; and Kentridge presented *The Defence of the Less Good Idea* with the Blind Mass Orchestra. All this work overflowed in abundance from the unfolding invitations and subsequent intensive workshops. Working with Hillbrow Boxing Club went beyond simply using the boxing ring as a stage in the round, a theatrical set for performances. Boxing was introduced as a provocation to the participants in the workshops. The club was founded by boxer George Khosi who works with local communities including supporting street children in an open-air ring set up in a former petrol station (Dougan, 2014). Boxing, with its restless movement, visceral physicality and drama, became a device or catalyst for the practitioners in the workshops to develop collaborations between disciplines. Khosi, led warmups in the workshops and intervened into the work being created. As a result, Lebogang Mashile developed play within the space of the ring, *Venus Hottentot vs. Modernity* for the first season based on the story of Saartjie Baartman. 'The boxing ring as the physical container for the story made sense, because every aspect of Baartman's life was contentious. Her entire world was a warzone' (Mashile, 2019). Mashile described the incubation of the work in the studio through the initial workshops – 'Beyond the individuals who were involved, being in an experimental multidisciplinary space allowed me to expand my own ideas of how and where the piece could live…it forced my ideas of what is possible' (Mashile, 2019). This experience is characteristic of the kind of expanded practice that Kentridge and Lace have sought to develop through the intense workshops where emergent ideas flow from the margins to the forefront.

Following the first Season of work in 2017 annual or biannual Seasons were produced at The Centre following a similar methodology and the work of The Centre has grown considerably. When Kentridge came up with the idea of dedicating financial resources to such a project in late 2015, the ambition was to try something out, for a short period of around two years. But the unique financial freedom has seen it grow, and Lace put it this 'is why The Centre is what it is'.

Kentridge remained the sole funder of The Centre's work over its first few years, supporting Lace to develop and run it without rigid or demanding financial reporting requirements, trusting her to work within specific limits each year. This sense of trust and openness to operative in a 'responsive mode' was extended to those invited to create work together in the space, without specific reporting requirements or output demands placed upon their participation. An openness to create something new without the required sense of 'officialness' or 'bureaucracy' that may come with a reliance or dependence on external funders and a freedom to approach running the organisation in a different way. But this also allowed them to operate practically in ways that other more formally constituted organisations might not have. Lace: 'I know my deep privilege of being able to drive an organisation without having all my attention and resources put to fundraising, and then also reporting and proving what you've done with your pennies'.

But other guiding principles or ethics related to resources have shaped the work, for example in relation to remunerating participants for their contributions: 'if you are at The Centre in any capacity, be it an intern, an artist, a production person, you are being paid for your time'. This extended in the first season where 60 artists were engaged in non-hierarchical approach to remunerating those involved, rather than basis this on their expected contribution or wider professional status or experience – all were offered the same amount – from which they could themselves derive how much they were able to contribute as individuals 'according to their careers, their expectations, their needs'. With the only 'compulsory time' dedicated to rehearsals and performing otherwise participants were asked to bring what they could to the space – with the understanding that what was being made intellectually and creatively belonged to them and would go with them out into the world after the season and not belong to The Centre.

As greater awareness was drawn to the work at The Centre, the space began to gather international recognition, which offered the possibility of new funding streams. New possibilities presented themselves beyond the original scope. An arm was established, The Centre Outside The Centre to focus on the international presentation of The Centre's work and methods and SO | The Academy was established as a learning programme for artists built within and around the other work being created at The Centre. As the ambitions of The Centre grew, particularly in relation to the Academy as it outstripped the potential of this funding – and where such external funding Lace was clear that is adopted the terms can't compromise the ethos and autonomy of The Centre. Additional funding became possible from different philanthropists and patrons that bought into the methods and ethos of The Centre. But this funding remains on specific terms dictated by The Centre. Having explored external international sources of funding during the pandemic to advance the work of The Academy, particularly through European cultural diplomacy institutes that have historically worked in South Africa (such as the British Council, Pro Helvetia, and the Goethe Institute) and invest in international cultural production. The Centre moved away from this approach because it challenged their ability to 'hold the artist' in the safe space they had created in the studio – as attention was shifted to reassuring and holding the funder instead, with time lost to admin and reporting, and the requirement of such funding to evidence social and cultural value. But as Lace acknowledged The Centre is in a unique position as a small organisation with an international reputation, that allows them to eschew entering financial relationships rooted in bureaucracy that collapses their approach to being progressive, prioritising artists and developing their work over anything else.

Part of the great value of imagining arts institutions as spaces built to 'hold' artists is that it creates space for imagining alternative forms of 'holding', as The Centre demonstrates. There is a forward-looking pragmatism to this, rooted in the founding ethos of The Centre, that keeps it in check with its time and place, rather than mythologising its own legacy. As Lace explained, The Centre may slip away when they recognise that is the right moment. 'It… just needs to be a project for as long as it's a project that works like this. And we're allowed to also say it did this for so many years. This is what we achieved… it's okay to stop it, too' (Lace, 2025).

What emerges from considering how The Centre has developed its unique approach to interdisciplinary cultural production is an important understanding of how the institutional context, or what is happening in the room – 'the frame' as Lace put it, is essential to shaping what emerges and defines the experience those involved have in the process. Where we encounter resistance to interdisciplinary cultural production, it may say more about the frame created to hold it than the individual participants. As Kentridge and Lace put so much thought and care into constructing this frame – to offer it as a safe space – a non-hierarchical space. Of course, Kentridge as an artist has also deeply benefited from this as a wider extension of his practice. As Lace explained, Kentridge is 'giving his resources and energy, and his mentorship to a space without… set parameters. So, where he's able to trust that space…William's practice is really interconnected right and circular. So many of the artists he meets through The Centre [he] gets to collaborate with. He makes work every season himself. He tests his own ideas in the space. He's often the kind of taking the biggest risk or being the biggest clown on that on day one which affords others the kind of allowance to be the same, and to let go of their sort of egos and anticipations. And that is, I think quite rare.' (Lace, 2025). This is the interdisciplinary studio as an open site of interchange, a space to respond openly and follow unpredictable paths. Not a site of knowing and articulation. Rather where connections can unfold and evolve, that push against disciplinary assumptions. Where recognition through reflection is privileged. Without the pressure of immediate perfection or external validation. To do this the imagined space must also have the capacity to 'hold contradiction' that allows such dynamic tensions to be sources of emergent creative power. This is the privilege of the particular form of interdisciplinary cultural production enabled at The Centre. For The Centre, the studio is much more than a building, it is a meticulously conceived and conceptually refined environment, that is importantly defined by artists, that actively facilitates, encourages and celebrates the fluid, unpredictable and collaborative nature of interdisciplinary creation.

4.6 Mediating the postcolonial present in the neighbourhood: AfroAsia

Dongducheon is a small city located north of the South Korean capital, Seoul and close to the Korean Demilitarized Zone. From 1952 until the early 2000s it was home to the largest concentration of US Army bases in Korea, that dominated nearly half the area of the city (Lee and Lee, 2025). The US Army's presence in the city has decreased from its peak though the remaining Camp Casey is still a significant element of the city. The location of the city within Korea means it is a geographic intersection of fraught geopolitics played at a local level. A city valued for its strategic infrastructure and proximity to the border. Dongducheon has also been at the nexus of South Korea-US relations, a site where the complex intersections of military expansion, economic globalisation, neocolonialism, immigration, and sex work converge. This is the city as 'contact zone' – a space where geopolitical power relations play out at a highly local level (Pratt, 1992; Kim, 2024).

Dongducheon is home to AfroAsia, a contemporary arts organisation built from the groud up in the Bosan-dong neighbourhood. In response to the city's unique historical and social context, AfroAsia uses a range of interdisciplinary cultural production practices to explore, understand and challenge the interrelationships between post-colonial African and East Asian experiences. This work brings together decolonial thought, historical research and community arts practice, with a primary focus on the experiences of recent migrants and long-term residents. Bosan-dong is often referred to as Africa Town; through its historical connections to the US military base, the area became one of the first and most significant African diaspora communities in Korea and is home to many Igbo Nigerian residents.

AfroAsia was co-founded through a collaboration between artist and curator, Che Onejoon and Sun A Moon who moved to Bosan-dong to establish the organisation. They now run two arts venues in the neighbourhood: Space AfroAsia (established 2021) and The AfroAsia Eco Museum (established 2022). AfroAsia has been funded through both personal investment and grants from arts bodies and local authorities. Their work includes community organising, historical research, educational programmes and creative training in various media, alongside creating a public programme of tours, talks, exhibitions and performances. Central to AfroAsia's practical approach is an interdisciplinary mode of cultural production that is rooted in their neighbourhood by integrating historical research and critical heritage with international contemporary arts production and community arts practice. Dongducheon, is a space where the daily lives of the South Korean population, migrants and the military exist as neighbours with complex, entwined spatial and economic relations. But while proximate, the everyday lives of these groups can often unfold in isolation.

This neighbourhood dynamic is central to AfroAsia's cultural work which has developed from the related artistic practice of Che and the curatorial work of Moon – both of which led them to Dongducheon in different ways. Che's starting point for AfroAsia emerged from his artistic practice of researching and documenting the historic relationship between Africa and East Asia, which led him initially to Dongducheon. Che's primary artistic practice is based in the medium of photography, where his early professional work was developed, but has expanded out to include film, installation and other forms. His primary interests have remained presenting and interpreting how the geo-politics of Korea's modern history is entwined with post-colonial Africa, often working with archive material. His work has been exhibited in international biennials and museums in Europe, Asia and the US.

Che's long term research project into North Korean-made monuments and statues in at least 20 African countries since the 1970s, was published as the book *International Friendship* (2022). The project began when Che was living in Paris in 2012 and was first able to find information about North Korea that had been suppressed in South Korea. Subsequently Che travelled through 12 African cities in nine different African countries over six years to document the monuments and statues. Most notably the 52m African Renaissance Monument in Dakar, Senegal. This work was partially supported by a Photography Award from the Musée du quai Branly – Jacques Chirac in Paris. Before 1990 such monuments had primarily been gifted to African countries as North Korean leader Kim Il Sung sought diplomatic influence with African nations to back North Korea's attempts at the UN to push the US out of South Korea. But the practice endured as North Korea sought foreign currency and was well known for its excellence in bronze casting (Kućma, 2022).

Che continued to develop this interest in the international relations of Africa and Korea in films such as *My Utopia* (2018) that was produced by Moon and explored the life of Monica Macias, daughter of the first President of Equatorial Guinea in Africa. From the age of seven, Macias spent 16 years in North Korea following a coup in Equatorial Guinea that deposed her father. Che was then invited to make work for the Lubumbashi Biennale in the DR Congo in 2019, where he created a new film *Ruashi's Boys*, about a Lubumbashi family, who were workers in a Chinese owned mine in the city. Following this, as the Covid pandemic emerged Che was curious about the experience of African migrants in Korea, so he began a documentary photography project to explore the everyday life of migrants in Dongducheon, where the largest population of African immigrants in Korea is located. Che soon began to build connections with the migrants in Dongducheon, who were predominantly part of an Igbo community from Nigeria, but also from Ghana. Through involvement in community churches and The Indigenous People of Biafra movement in the city, Che started to document family life in Dongducheon. At this stage it was not Che's intention to develop this work any further than as a documentary photography project, as he has done with previous research-based projects. But through discussions with Moon it became clear there was potential to develop a more long-term project in the local context of the city.

For Moon, as a curator and writer, with a background in art theory, her interest was focused on the interrelationship between contemporary visual arts and decolonisation. This was informed by her experience as a participant in the de Appel Curatorial Programme in Amsterdam in 2017–18. Where it was clear that the discourse around postcolonialism and decolonisation was a pressing focus in the contemporary visual arts discourse at the time, particularly around how European museums and arts institutions were seeking to address their colonial legacies. Although as she noted, such questions had been raised decades prior and its persistent return in the European context only confirmed that many of the underlying issues remained fundamentally unresolved.

In response to the ongoing European debates, Moon wanted to shift the focus and consider the Korean context, recognising its history of Japanese colonisation and Cold War interdependence with the US. This distinct background, further complicated by the rise of globalised capitalism, presented an interesting framework for a new Korean arts organisation. As Moon felt there was considerable work to do in the Korean context, particularly within the arts, to foster a better understanding of postcolonialism and decolonisation (Moon, 2025).

AfroAsia was built on these overlapping interests of Che and Moon – but central to the practical 'agenda for building the institution' was a core ethos towards exploring and deploying relationality as a mode of cultural production (Che, 2025). This saw the arts organisation as a mediator or intermediary between both different disciplines, art forms and social groups in the city – US army personnel, the local Korean population and African and Asian migrants. But also in terms of bringing together different forms of fields of knowledge to activate these relations, interconnected with creative practice, and forms of cultural display, performance and exhibition. Establishing AfroAsia in Dongducheon was born out of Che and Moon's ever deepening curiosity, initially with the story of African migrants in Korea, then understanding conceptions of decolonisation in the arts in Korea, but then into the city of Dongducheon itself and its people and neighbourhood dynamics. As Moon

(2025) noted, AfroAsia was built up from the ground in this sense but also built with those communities in the city involved, as it was important that knowledge through the project was co-created. What Moon (2025) called establishing a new 'co-founded discourse' in the process. There was initial hesitation about establishing an art space in Dongducheon. As a city dominated by the US military presence and situated near the North Korean border, its primary association in Korea was Cold War history, anti-US sentiment and sex work. This was connected to a history of exploitation and violence, including cases of sexual assault and murder perpetrated by US soldiers stationed there that perpetuated a particular form of historical sigma associated with the city (See Sang-Hun and Chung, 2023). Initially such dominant narratives cast a shadow of associations over the city seemingly leaving little space for the potential to open up new dialogue around postcolonialism. However, as they become more embedded in the neighbourhood, understanding and challenging this narrative became an imperative. As it became clear that postcolonialism was a fundamental shaping force in the history and contemporary life of the city but rarely acknowledged or discussed. As they explained, the town had attracted the attention of international scholars and researchers interested in the history of US military crime, feminism and movements for women. But as Che (2025) set out, 'that's the past… the African [diaspora and] life is the future in the town'.

Positioned at the centre of the Korean peninsula, Dongducheon's strategic geographic importance during the Cold War was not just due to its proximity to the front line. One of the reasons the US built their major military presence there was because of existing infrastructure such as railroads built by the Japanese during their colonisation of Korea between 1910 to 1945. These fraught, entangled and unresolved historical trajectories meant conversations in the city for artists and those living there were always embedded in complex questions of the 'present and the future, and also the past'. It was this sense of the need to engage with the postcolonial and Cold War history, to understand the present social and cultural relations that shaped the form of AfroAsia as an arts organisation. Che and Moon opened the first space in 2021 after 18 months of research in the city.

The initial venue was primarily self-funded, with the first exhibition receiving support from Arts Council Korea. While their early ambition was to establish the space for exhibitions, they also used it to support more discursive, research-based practice, concentrating on workshops and educational programming. However, after operating for a year, they realised the initial venue was too limited to fully accommodate such work effectively. To expand the organisation capacity, they received a grant from the provincial government's Gyeonggi Cultural Foundation, an organisation dedicated to promoting and preserving the cultural heritage and arts of Gyeonggi Province in South Korea. This funding was targeted to support new initiatives in geographic areas that were seen to be 'culturally undeveloped'. The funding borrowed its title from the concept of the *écomusée*, developed in France in the 1970s, shifting museum practice away from traditional museology towards community-focused, place-based institutions with deeper connection to the social, cultural environment. The funding denoted the name for the expanded space which became, The AfroAsia Eco Museum, but also gave them further impetus to think about their approach to 'activate the local people [towards] co-creation [within the] local community' – across the social groups in the city (Moon, 2025).

Central to the approach Che and Moon have taken with AfroAsia is to seek to generate 'solidarity' between these groups – using the integration of contemporary art and history as disciplines to generate new interactions. Their experience of working with the distinct communities in the city has been informed by their social isolation. As Moon (2025) noted, 'we wanted to build up...solidarity...because there is lots of misunderstanding between the communities'. This is compounded by language barriers that reinforce distinctions. An extended function of their work has been helping African immigrants with the everyday frictions – housing, bureaucracy, language, legal issues etc – that come with moving to a new country. As they put it 'we are now neighbour[s]'.

From 2020 they began a series of tours and workshops that sought to act as a 'bridge' between these groups. Che and Moon used the tours to begin to provide an alternative narrative about the city, one that was confronting history rather than seeking to sanitise it. This focused particularly on the presence of the US military in the town. As the local city government promoted the town to tourists for its mountainous landscape and good hiking opportunities without accounting for the fact that much of the land was controlled by the US military. The tours offered a multiplicity of voices, providing introductions and perspectives on the city's recent history, including sites of US military crime and monuments where land had been returned from US control. The tours were co-produced with Korean academic specialists in African Studies, activists involved in anti-US protests since the 1990s, and leaders from the Nigerian community, including from the Indigenous People of Biafra (IPOB) group in the city. The tours ended with performances by local musicians in the AfroAsia space.

While the tours were about reimagining sidelined historical narratives about the city. The workshops sought to think about the present of the city, and how it was seen by different groups – 'to record the Dongducheon now' – from their own perspective using different mediums (Che, 2025). The ambition was to bring all groups together but without directly forcing them to collaborate – as the language, communication and cultural barriers offered potential for misunderstanding. So they developed a more subtle approach to interconnecting the groups working with each group independently at first. Connecting with US soldiers was a particular challenge. There was a sense that the wider Korean population in the city, primarily saw the US soldiers stationed there as an economic resource, as customers to be engaged, so there were very limited educational or cultural ties being developed with them. To begin to counter this, Che asked a group of US military personnel to document their perspective of the city using photography. Given the military sensitivity of the area, civilian photography in many areas was illegal. Through a series of workshops Che was able to introduce the military personnel to the 'darker' history of the city that many US military personnel were unaware of. Similar workshops taught filmmaking skills to the Nigerian community, who valued the skills for potential employment upon returning to Nigeria.

In practical terms, the development of AfroAsia's projects has been fundamentally shaped by the nuances and challenges of communication between the city's three distinct communities, especially the need to overcome existing stereotypes held by each group. As Moon (2025) put it, Korea is relatively monocultural with low levels of immigration, and simply the geographic distance of Africa means there is an unfamiliarity with African culture. In addition, US soldiers were often reluctant to participate due to public relations concerns, fearing that interaction with local or immigrant populations might cause problems. Conversely, the local population has been hesitant to engage with the military outside of established commercial relationships, often concerned about generating social tension. This difficulty in generating interrelationships, combined with a growing awareness of differences in gender participation in their projects, led Che and Moon to adapt their approach to specifically work with women. One project used Macramé, an ancient North African weaving art form that is also popular in South Korea, to connect Korean, African and Filipino women through creative workshops.

However, the most persistent challenge has remained language. US soldiers speak English, but local Koreans often have only a functional 'commercial English'. First-generation Nigerian immigrants may speak Igbo or English, while second-generation immigrants primarily speak Korean (Che, 2025). This complex linguistic landscape made traditional, discursive programmes (such as tours, discussions and workshops) difficult to coordinate. Learning from these experiences, AfroAsia evolved the programme to include more non-discursive mediums, such as music – particularly performances by the African community. These became a way to effectively invite different groups into the space and connect. As a result, music production has become a crucial discipline that they have sought to integrate into the work of AfroAsia.

Outside of formal education, Che and Moon identified that there were limited opportunities for young African migrant children to meet or interact with Koreans of their age. As a response they set out to create a kind of creative 'playground' for these young people, where they could use cultural production to develop shared experience (Che, 2025). They did this through the creation of a K-Pop group made up of young women from Korean,

Ghanian and Nigerian backgrounds. The group went through a programme of dance and vocal training, and working with a professional song writer and choreographer they produced a music video. For Che (2025), K-Pop, as a transnational cultural form also symbolised a form of 'fluidity' – through which they could explore questions of nationality, ethnicity, and gender with young people. Such a 'versatile and diverse' process connected many of the elements of AfroAsia's wider work in the city – bringing together dance, music, performance, video to realise new co-produced creative work – that can be exhibited and distributed online (Che, 2025).

AfroAsia's practical approach is defined by a place-based interdisciplinary mode of cultural production that acts to mediate between social groups within the context of Dongducheon's complex geo-political history. This agenda seeks to build solidarity between the local Korean population, African and Asian migrants, and US Army personnel by intersecting historical research with contemporary arts production. AfroAsia's practical incremental approach has been characterised by constant adaptation in response to their developing understanding of the nuances of the communities they have sought to work with. This has allowed them to work through challenges, shifting toward non-discursive and co-creative mediums to overcome communication and cultural barriers present in the neighbourhood. This active confrontation of stigma and the reframing of Dongducheon's dominant historical narrative asserts the postcolonial condition, and shapes AfroAsia as an important force to influence the neighbourhood's future.

4.7 Festivals, biennials and the promise of interdisciplinary cultural production

Festivals, biennials, and other periodically recurrent, temporary cultural events can be important sites of interdisciplinary modes of cultural production. In some cases, this interdisciplinarity is their defining curatorial characteristic. Such events have a strong imperative to create, commission and present new work, this association with innovation and novelty responds to their spatial and temporal form – as place-specific, temporary and recurrent – festivals as a repeated, yet 'unrepeatable' moment of intensity. This temporary intensity is not only a conceptual trait but an essential component of their economic and social value. Such cultural events have become a central component of the economically important industry of cultural tourism (Hobsbawm, 2013). Their value here lies in their capacity to generate unique moments or offer a seemingly authentic sense of place, generating a symbolic capital associated with that novelty. The gathering process and publicness that underpins them – contrasts with the more closed spaces of interdisciplinary production, such as the 'lab' or 'studio'. This concentration generates an desire for co-presence – a specific, time-limited moment that creates a sense of the 'here and now' where presence in place is paramount. As Sassatelli (2011: 18) notes, these events seek to create the 'sense of unique, one-off experiences, for which it is important to say "I was there"'.

Major cultural festivals, from international festivals and contemporary art biennials to film festivals, have this association with what is new, now and what is here, but also with powerful notions of renewal, hope and change. Through their sense of recurrent temporality, they can function as signals of futurity, moments where narratives of novelty or innovation can be held up to showcase ideas and practices with future imperatives. However, such events can also act as legislative cultural organisations and as gatekeepers, with the ability to define, reinforce or subvert disciplinary art form boundaries. As Hobsbawm (2013: 36) notes 'the genealogy of today's festivals begins with the discovery of the stage as the cultural-political and social expression of a new elite'. Here the festival is an effective scenario that offers cultural expression and control for specific communities of interest, or groups who seek the advancement or preservation of its form. Performative desire borne of a need for the articulation of particular cultural sensibilities promotes the festival as a means of claiming 'territory' for social groups, to create a space for new relations through forms of expression. Festivals can therefore act as spaces of inclusion for art forms, practices, and communities while simultaneously excluding others. The social function and symbolic meaning of these events are closely related to the values that the organising community recognises as essential at that particular moment, ultimately celebrating the historical continuity and persistence of these associated art forms and social and cultural identities (Falassi, 1987). Given this, festivals can be an important mechanism for supporting the disciplinary foundations of new emergent practices, providing community, validation, status and legitimacy, as has been central to the development of strands of interdisciplinary arts practice, such as new media art (Palankasova and Cook, 2024). In these terms, a festival is a process of recognition, validation and affirmation; it is a claim to a set of values and beliefs. As Waterman (1998: 59) asserts 'the arts festival…is a 'cultural framework' reflecting the world view of a distinct socioeconomic section of modern society'. It is a process through which these values and beliefs are articulated outwards and defined internally.

Building from this I want to point to how interdisciplinary cultural production makes three interconnected promises in the context of festivals and similar temporary cultural events. Here the utility of interdisciplinary cultural production becomes entwined with the cultural form of these events. Firstly, interdisciplinary cultural production promises a route through which festivals seek to express a clear sense of their innovation, distinction, novelty and futurity. Secondly, festivals are often described in terms of their carnivalesque potential to 'challenge, re-order, subvert and disrupt' (Quinn, 2005: 934). Interdisciplinary cultural production in festival form offers a means to subvert disciplinary boundaries or established practices within a high-risk, low-stakes environment. This allows for the introduction of new interdisciplinary practices (high-risk) but in a framework where there might be many multiple new works showcased (low-stakes), and the high-risk is mitigated by the appeal to novelty and innovation that is held by the festival as institutional cultural form, rather than individual practitioners. Thirdly, in expressing innovation and novelty, interdisciplinary cultural production offers a route for festivals to develop a particular form of symbolic value or symbolic capital, deeply ingrained with imaginaries of place and economic relations, that has become central to the international neoliberal dynamics of intercity competitiveness over the last four decades. These three promises are all entwined and developed from one another and can be found to different degrees in individual events.

4.8 The Pan-African Cultural Festivals in the 1960s and 1970s

To begin to investigate the practical realisation and refinement of the three central promises interdisciplinary cultural production makes through the festival format, this analysis turns to three distinct large-scale events. The first case study examines the state-sponsored cultural festivals of post-independence Africa in the 1960s and 1970s, establishing how the confluence of artforms and historical lineages in a festival setting simultaneously facilitated cultural affirmation, political subversion and the negotiation of visions of futurity. Subsequently, the focus shifts to two contemporary urban settings to assess how these interdisciplinary promises manifest in relation to the cultural economies of interdisciplinary cultural production, specifically by looking at the creation of the Manchester International Festival (launched 2007) and the Shanghai Project (launched 2016).

The cultural festivals that took place in post-independence Africa in the 1960s and 1970s are an important example of the festival as a mode of cultural organising in decolonial contexts and as a site of disciplinary contestation, in terms of both affirmation and subversion, is This includes the Festival mondial des arts nègres (Fesman) in Dakar, Senegal in 1966; the Pan-African Festival (PANAF) in Algiers, Algeria in 1969; and the Second World Black and African Festival of Arts and Culture (Festac '77) in Lagos, Nigeria in 1977. Challenges to disciplinary boundaries were fundamental and strategic to these postcolonial Pan-African festivals. These events were strategically designed to challenge existing artistic, intellectual and political forms, instead orienting production toward African cultural renaissance and liberation.

The first festival, FESMAN, was conceived by Senegalese President and poet Léopold Senghor as an expression of his concept of Négritude, and became a platform for artistic, political and ideological contestation that extended beyond conventional cultural production and expression. Négritude interconnected black culture and identity, tracing its ideological lineage to the Harlem Renaissance. As Murphy, (2018) explains, 'Négritude was their response to this feeling of alienation, a return to their (imagined) roots that celebrated Africa, emotion, rhythm and spontaneity as the antithesis of a cold, European rationalism'.

The event gathered hundreds of artists, performers, musicians and writers from Africa and its diaspora, and juxtaposed and synthesised traditional African arts with the work of European modernists. This was the festival as a mode of expanding boundaries, rather than policing them (Apter, 2021). This integration fundamentally challenged the colonial-era disciplinary hierarchy, which typically separated Western fine arts (or 'high culture') from African forms often relegated to anthropology or craft (Morison and Rottenburg, 2024). The festivals sought to legitimise these practices as equal components of a global Black civilisation. The festivals aimed at 'building institutions for promoting postcolonial visions for the cultural, political and socioeconomic development of the Black world' (Morison and Rottenburg, 2024), a desire to forge a new 'transnational Black community' (Murphy, (2018)).

Yet, Senghor's racially defined Pan-Africanism contained inherent tensions, notably its narrowed cultural boundaries that initially excluded North African participants. The festival's official discourse was challenged by critics of Négritude, such as novelist and filmmaker Ousmane Sembène, who were nonetheless included. This demonstrates the festival's function as a site of contestation between the state-sponsored, top-down vision and counter-visions (Murphy, (2018)). FESMAN was also criticised for prioritising cultural affirmation over more direct political action (Apter, 2021). As a result, the later festival PANAF in Algiers (in 1969), broadened its scope to explicitly link pan-African culture with political liberation and invited representatives from liberation movements such as the ANC and PLO as well as radical artists and musician such as Nina Simone (Jacobs, 2024).

Through their structure, the festivals intentionally placed different fields into dialogue and presentation alongside each other. For example, the Algiers festival brought together American jazz musician Archie Shepp sharing the stage with Tuareg musicians from North Africa. The festival acted to showcased a confluence of many different performers, dancers and writers from across the globe (Jacobs, 2024). The act of bringing global Black and African arts together through the festival sought to legitimise all these forms equally, subverting hierarchies that privileged Western-defined arts and culture (Jacobs, 2024). Similarly, and at great scale, Festac '77 in Nigeria in 1977 gathered more than 17,000 people from 52 countries (Aterianus-Owanga, 2020). The 'heart' of the festival was a Colloquium gathering leading Black scholars for two weeks of intense debate around the cross-cutting themes of 'Arts and Pedagogy; Languages and Literature; Philosophy and Religion; Historical Awareness; and Science and Technology' (Southern, 1977: 104).

There is growing scholarship around these festivals (Murphy, 2021) and engagement with the archive (Chimurenga, 2019). The original festivals' success in fostering cultural intersections serves as a foundational reference point for contemporary organisations. This is particularly evident in the work of multi and interdisciplinary arts platforms in Africa, such as Chimurenga, a platform for African writing, art, and politics, which describes itself as an 'interscalar vehicles that mobilise knowledges outside of the academy along vectors unbound by disciplinary protocols' (Eshun et al, 2017). As Aterianus-Owanga (2020) notes, 'navigating between afro-futurism and Pan-Africanism, Chimurenga considers FESTAC as a haunting past that can provide powerful tools to reflect on the present and the future of Africa and the African diaspora'.

These Pan-African festivals were not defined by a single artform or discipline, but through a vast, directed synthesis of arts, science, literature and cultural tradition, that sought to confirm the scope of Black and African achievement, as well as to imagine and project possible futures. While sometimes failing in their utopian vision of political unity, they succeeded in fostering a complex, interconnected pan-Africanism by gathering Black artists and intellectuals together into dialogue and integration in unprecedented ways (Murphy, (2018)).

4.9 Risk and reward: The creation of Manchester International Festival in 2007

Since the 1980s there has been an acceleration of the growth of new festivals, biennials and large-scale temporary cultural events of an increasingly mobile and interconnected global industry of such events (Yeoman, 2004; Delanty, 2011). The development of arts festivals in the UK after the Second World War has been roughly delineated into three stages by Bianchini (1999) as the age of reconstruction from 1945 (e.g. The Festival of Britain of 1951 or Edinburgh Festival), the age of participation in the free festivals of 1970s and early 1980s (e.g. Glastonbury Festival) and the age of city marketing from the mid-1980s to present (e.g. City/Captital of Culture programmes). It is this last phase of new festivals where the promise of interdisciplinary cultural production has found a particular role. This phase is explained in relation to an economic restructuring of cities, inter-city competitiveness, and the drive to develop cities as large-scale platforms for the creation and consumption of cultural experiences. Waterman (1998: 60) asserts the significance of place here, 'arts festivals have as much to do with place as with art, and this concerns not just where they are held but why, and it refers to how they contribute to and assimilate from the characters of the places.'

The rationale for this festivalisation of urban space, can be considered in one sense as the result of neo-liberal economic policies, where policy interventions in urban culture have resulted in the creation of new spectacular events with the ambition to expand the tourist industry. To achieve this festivals must seek to generate a sense of distinction, authenticity and uniqueness and the promise of innovation and novelty derived from interdisciplinary cultural production can be one particular route to this. This brings together the instrumentalised and accountability logics of interdisciplinary cultural production and the instrumentalisation of the festival as a mode of cultural organising and purported engine of symbolic value for cities.

It is this sense of festivals as organisations searching for novelty in both their content and form that interdisciplinary cultural production sometimes becomes central to thier ambitions, where bringing together different disciplines in new configurations meets that search for distinction. It is also the case that urban cultural festivals are caught up with their own assertion of symbolic value that has been co-opted by various city officials, politicians, policy makers and cultural leaders all seeking a sense of distinction and cultural capital.

Since few urban arts festivals are privately funded, they inevitably depend on and must navigate the political and financial requirements of state subsidisers and corporate sponsors to survive. 'Selling the place to the wider world or selling the festival as an inseparable part of the place rapidly becomes a significant facet of most festivals' (Waterman, 1998: 61). Therefore, when contemporary cultural festivals adopt a programming strategy that is inherently interdisciplinary in its mode of production – we can see an entwining of the cultural form and place promotion. In the background a festival may be used as an economic policy instrument, a catalyst for urban regeneration and a device to change a city's image and attract capital and tourists (Moscardo, 2007). As Quinn (2005: 932) argues, 'many cities have seen in festivals a sort of "quick fix" solution to their image problems'. Cultural festivals in this context have been denounced as a 'carnival mask', hiding the problems of economic restructuring because of post-industrial decline, rather than directly addressing them (Harvey, 1988; Garcia, 2005).

Against this backdrop of policy-led urban festivalisation, this case study now explores the founding of Manchester International Festival (MIF) by looking at the interdisciplinary cultural production that defined its early approach to programming across its editions in 2007, 2009 and 2011. MIF was conceived by the Manchester City Council as part of a strategic effort to elevate the city's international position as a major cultural centre, capitalising on the successful profile generated by the 2002 Commonwealth Games. This came at a moment when the city was being indexed as 'the most creative place in Britain', under the maxim of Richard Florida's 'Creative Class' (Frean, 2003). But also with the city council arguably coming quite late to the idea that it could generate economic investment from deploying and enhancing the city's cultural mythology. Manchester City Council acted as the primary initiator and key public sector funder of the new festival, supplemented by significant investment from Arts

Council England and corporate sponsors. The city council's leadership was driven by a clear civic ambition to utilise high-profile cultural events to promote economic regeneration, attract investment, and enhance the city's international profile. As one city council representative articulated:

> Manchester has heavily invested in cultural capital: Buildings and organisations to attract wealth to the city centre... The intervention point is different if it is physical regeneration we are talking about, or if it is about the iconic infrastructure such as with Manchester International Festival, which is a big economic driver. We want to generate entrepreneurship.
>
> *(Olsen, 2012: 123)*

To achieve this ambition and create a distinctive artistic identity for MIF, the city council appointed Alex Poots as its founding Artistic Director. Poots established a core ambition and brand for the festival, distinguishing it from similar large-scale international festivals by staging exclusively new work. The founding myth of cultural festivals can be very important. In a sense, it is that founding myth which is the repeated, unrepeatable, that plays out over each edition of the festival. With the Edinburgh International Festival, to which the early editions of MIF were consistently compared. The founding myth of the festival in 1947 was as an act of post-war cultural reconciliation and hope for Europe. This is something Poots seemed to intrinsically understand when developing the programme of MIF. He presented a simple and compelling vision for MIF, to create 'the world's first festival of entirely new and original work...[with] 10 major pieces, commissioned from "the world's greatest artists", and performed across Manchester city centre' (Naylor, 2006). This ran against an explicit provincial sensibility – 'MIF is not about Manchester celebrating Manchester, with well-known Mancunians to the fore. Instead, it intends to reflect an intrinsic Mancunian character' (Naylor, 2006). Rather, Poots rooted MIF's grounding mythology in the city's history of innovation in cultural and industrial production. To meet this ambition the city council put significant investment into the first edition (£2m of a £5m overall budget), this would allow the festival to work with resources not far short of the well-established Edinburgh International Festival.

Central to Poots' curatorial ethos was an appetite for risk. He had a track record of creating high impact, boundary-crossing productions. Such as taking the English National Opera to Glastonbury Festival's Pyramid Stage to perform Act III of Wagner's *Die Walküre*. He readily accepted the uncertainty and risk of exposure that came with breaking artistic conventions and uniting seeminly disparate cultural forms. As he put it, 'the minute we put a glass case over it and never allow for failure, it's a dying culture' (Poots in Financial Times, 2007). This ethos deliberately avoided the repertory festival programming model common for other international festivals, centrally positioning MIF with the character of entrepreneurialism and innovation that the city council directly sought. Over the first editions the festival staged a wide range of projects, performances, exhibitions and events, not all of which were entirely new. But there were two key programming forms to generating novelty and innovation that the festival became known for in its early biennial editions. The first was high-profile cross-cultural events, in the model of presenting opera at Glastonbury. Here the process was about re-situating art forms in other cultural domains beyond their conventional field of presentation. In the first edition of the festival in 2007, this included projects such as electronica producer William Orbit's *Orchestral Suite* created with the BBC Philharmonic Orchestra. Or the project *Il Tempo del Postino*, curated by Hans Ulrich Obrist and Philippe Parreno that presented sequential, live performance art in an opera house, featuring time-based works by 15 major contemporary artists (including Matthew Barney and Tino Sehgal). In the 2009 festival electronic music pioneers Kraftwerk performed a concert at the Manchester Velodrome, which included a new commission of minimalist contemporary classical composition Steve Reich. In 2011, Björk premiered her Biophilia project at the festival, a series of multi-media, immersive shows – that used a set of interactive apps that connected musical compositions to natural phenomena and scientific concepts. Here the repositioning of artists and musicians into other cultural domains (or in Björk's case media domains) offered the potential for innovation, but generally on a *single author / co-production* basis – where the novelty for artists is presenting their work in unconventional contexts in a way that is mirrored for the audience. Novelty emerges from the relocation of artistic practice, out of their conventional sites of presentation – but their work itself generally retains its form.

Alongside these cross-cultural projects, MIF also produced large-scale, high-budget, interdisciplinary commissions, which operated through a *co-author / co-production* form of integration. The opening show of the first festival exemplified the approach, while also deploying cross-cultural elements. The experimental opera, or 'rock'n'roll circus' *Monkey: Journey to the West* united theatre director Chen Shi-Zheng with musician Damon Albarn, illustrator Jamie Hewlett (who worked together as Gorillaz) and a group of Chinese circus acrobats (Hickling, 2007a). In the 2009 edition, the site-specific theatre company Punchdrunk, the investigative filmmaker Adam Curtis and Damon Albarn, worked together to stage *It Felt Like A Kiss* within a derelict office building. In 2011 Albarn again contributed to a collaboration with theatre director Rufus Norris and the BBC Philharmonic Orchestra to create the experimental opera *Dr Dee*. As art historian and critic Claire Bishop (2011) observed, all these large-scale cross-cultural and interdisciplinary commissions created an 'energetic flirtation among art, theater, and pop music' a comparison Hans Ulrich Obrist extended to Cedric Price's *Fun Palaces*, in the spirit of building flexible, interdisciplinary arts spaces (Cashdan, 2011).

This focus on complex, integrative commissions served a number of purposes for both the festival and the city council. Such a strategy addressed the city council's desire to attract valuable national and international visitors and develop symbolic cultural capital for the city via high-status, media-generating events. But it was also a mechanism for seeking a form of audience development or audience aggregation, by bringing together collaborators with distinctive appeal from different art forms. This need for a broad appeal generated through such interdisciplinary cultural production could be said to be driven by an accountability logic orientated towards the wider Manchester population, especially given the substantial financial investment of city council resources. The programming of large-scale interdisciplinary collaborations, such as pairing popular artists like Gorillaz with culturally 'high-brow' art forms like opera, was thus a means of satisfying this need for accountability while realising the spectacle of innovation central to the city council's economic mission. The interrelationship was clearly articulated by a member of the Manchester City Council Cultural Strategy Team:

> It has to be a balance between accessible art forms and challenging new audiences. And how you do that is the [crux]. It depends on what you want to do. Manchester International Festival has got Opera as its headline. It is very high brow, but however they use some innovative techniques. It is very spectacular, so it is about educating the audience. So we do have to challenge, but on a different scale it is how you translate that. Any organisation has a responsibility to translate this…Because we want to be cultural[ly] distinctive we have to look at innovative programs. So yes, we take risks, it is that balance between providing an accessible program, and merge that with innovative works.
>
> *(Olsen, 2012: 124)*

The utility of cross- and interdisciplinary cultural production to Manchester City Council and MIF was therefore three-fold: in offering a means to present a distinctive programme that would generate attention and set it apart from competitor festivals; as a means to showcase innovation, something desired by the local authority; and as a means of accountability through the promise of appealing to wide audience demographics and tastes. It is important here to see how these three logics work together in demonstrating why interdisciplinary cultural production was important in the early editions of MIF. Crucially, through the frame of the festival as a cultural form, interdisciplinary cultural production's value here was not just its promise as a means to achieving artistic novelty, but its capacity to simultaneously fulfil the instrumental demands of broad audience engagement and wide media appeal.

Poots articulated a clear and defined programming ethos for the festival, grounding this approach in a high degree of risk-taking that privileged cross-cultural, multi, and interdisciplinary collaborations. This approach and the risk that came with it was simultaneously embedded and within the broader economic and urban context of the host city and diffused to both the city council and the population of the city. As Poots expressed, 'Manchester is probably the only place in Britain that would welcome a festival with this much risk,' thereby aligning the festival's curatorial strategy with the city's historic industrial 'pioneering spirit' (Poots, 2009). Risk is important in the context of a new festival seeking to establish itself and maintain and grow audiences and investment, because risk is a precondition for innovation. Where innovation, so central to policy-led urban cultural investment and the search of cultural distinction, involves introducing something novel by departing from conventions, rather than seeking incremental development. Here risk is treated as something to invest in, rather than a threat to be mitigated. This follows the 'Schumpeterian' view of innovation emerging from new combinations of knowledge and resources that enables commercial gain (Woronkowicz, 2021).

While risk is a term frequently evoked by cultural leaders and producers in relation to interdisciplinary cultural production, it often remains abstract. So, it is worth considering what risk signifies in this context, and how is it distributed across the festival, its funders, and the wider field of interdisciplinary cultural production. We can think about risk as a high probability of failure or as exposure to danger. In the context of the festival, this may point to an interconnected areas of possible failure or danger – this might be financial or commercial, reputation or status, practical or operational, artistic or critical, and audience engagement and response.

From a practical arts production perspective, risk means entering the unknown, working with untested production methods, towards uncertain outcomes. In venues or urban spaces without established practices, protocols or technical facilities to present such work. Poots (2009) described this practical uncertainty in the run-up to the 2009 edition: 'the excitement and the challenge is that you literally don't know what you don't know...my time is taken up with problem-solving across about 20 productions...to find solutions.' This highlights the practical risk inherent in generating new work with collaborators from diverse and unrelated backgrounds, who have not worked together before, on novel commissions, that take their form in the process of their devising, rehearsal and realisation. As he noted, 'as we are a festival of entirely new work, at this stage things need polishing and adapting, even changing...It's like speeded-up evolution' (Poots, 2009). Crucially, many of these risks were mitigated by the MIF possessing one of the largest budgets among UK arts festivals at the time, and as a new festival having little requirement to follow expectations or conventions. But also, in financial and reputational terms by the co-commissioning of many productions with international partners.

Then there is the risk of failure to generate any aesthetic or intellectual value beyond the sum of the components of new commissions. This risk is defined by the possibility of a failure of integration or emergence, where the new work does not achieve synthesis but merely becomes a spectacle of juxtaposition, failing to exceed the sum of its individual parts. The critical reception of early MIF commissions frequently focused the evaluative framework on the degree to which a coherent, emergent synthesis was achieved. Reviews indicate mixed success. The 2007 production *Monkey: Journey to the West*, for instance, was lauded, with one critic noting that while 'each individual contribution was superb, the sum of those parts was superlative' (Mottershead, 2007). Although others felt the elements did not cohere, noting while, 'the stunts can be breathtaking, the musical and dramatic development is fairly inert' (Hickling, 2007a). It is the level of conjunction and the coherence of the conjunction that judgements play out, where they are considered against each other. The 2011 opera *Dr Dee*, was criticised for a 'lack of a clear, over-arching plan' resulting in an 'inadequacy of the final product' and the 'BBC Philharmonic [playing] a distinctly limited role.' This prompted the critic to conclude: 'the time has surely come to say that in the future, if the festival wishes to commission an opera, they should invite an opera composer...' (Mottershead, 2012). This reveals a significant risk: that the new works fail to transgress the established disciplinary boundaries they set out to challenge. Such critical perspectives demonstrate how entrenched disciplinary standards operate when attempts at transgression are undertaken, particularly when the underlying logic is one of accountability. As the critic further articulated, this exemplifies the 'possible pitfalls of the apparently deliberate policy of choosing composers to write works clearly well outside of their comfort zone, merely to curry favour with an audience' (Mottershead, 2012). Something that was similarly alluded to in relation to William Orbit's *Orchestral Suite* in 2007, which prompted another reviewer to argue: 'There is no reason why a leading artist in one field should not have the freedom to experiment in another' but questioned the logic, when the result turned out to be 'so conventional' (Hickling, 2007b).

A similar sentiment was exposed in relation to *It Felt Like a Kiss* (2009), where the components were perceived to interfere, that then cohere . Here Adam Curtis's film 'could easily stand alone.', Albarn assembled an 'eclectic score' and Punchdrunk's 'visual surround' meant 'watching this show is a bit like unwrapping a parcel in which you have to tear off superfluous mounds of brown paper in order to get to the choice present that you really wanted'. Ultimately the result was considered through its components, rather than as single emergent performance – 'When the show is good, it is very, very good: when it is bad, it is excruciating' (Billington, 2009). Or as another writer considered the project, the collaboration pushed the resulting work deep into a space of uncertainty – 'no one really knows what it is...I'm not saying it doesn't make sense; if anything, it forges its own new brand of coherence whether you like it or not' (Brooker, 2009).

There are also many risks associated with encountering such work for the audience, who are asked to embrace a greater degree of uncertainty than they would expect from a conventional presentation. Interdisciplinary commissions can create a challenging encounter for the very audiences and critics they are designed to attract. If the primary appeal rests on only one collaborator (e.g., a well-known musician), the diminished quality of the collaborative output may detract from the audience's encounter with that art form. This places a significant demand on the audience, who are expected to appreciate the presented conjunctions as inherently valuable. In such a case it can be the festival that seeks to hold the risk – and as a result tries to achieve a lower barrier to entry for audiences. On the basis that the potential audience for the festival is perceived to be willing to take their own risks and experience experimental practices or art forms they might not typically seek out or be familiar with, by giving their trust to the organisers based on their reputation to create new work of merit – that does not bear the marks of specific art form or disciplinary alignment.

Overall, we can think about this sense of risk as diffuse and shared. It is distributed among the city council and funders, as reputational and financial risk, MIF as the programming and producing entity, the invited practitioners (creative and reputational risk), and the audience. Reputational risk for the city, the festival, and individual creative practitioners becomes particularly salient for interdisciplinary cultural production when outcomes are judged against conventional disciplinary standards.

Yet some of this risk is also mitigated or diffused by the medium of the festival and its unique spatial and temporal frame. Where lots of work is presented in a short time – for critics and the audience it is impossible to see and make sense of it all. This was the case with MIF and something that Poots acknowledged from the start, in fact failure was expected and built into the plan for the festival, as he set out before the first edition – 'it's impossible that everything we commission will be successful' (Naylor, 2006). The medium of the festival enables some failure to be assimilated without significant damage to the organisation. Essentially because of the scale and concentration of programming, the festival is shielded from individual project failures to a degree. In addition, the organisation benefits by evaluating the commissioning process to refine future programming approaches and production strategies. By commissioning multiple new works that are presented simultaneously, alongside more conventional presentations, the model ensures that not all commissions need to be critically or commercially successful. There is therefore a broad tolerance for failure built into the organisational model, programming strategy and medium of the festival. Such an approach creates a critical mass around the totality of the festival that garners media attention, enabling the risks of interdisciplinary cultural production to be played out at comparatively lower stakes at the individual project level. There is an acceptance that some new works will fail, but in the context of the festival that may have limited consequences if enough new works are commissioned that some will also succeed (where there is sufficient budget to enable this kind of approach). To a point, a festival and a city can still ultimately benefit in this instance, even with multiple critical and commercial failures because of the association to risk taking and innovation and the particular sense of entrepreneurial spirit such an approach generates. Regardless of if the new work does generate genuinely new artistic or intellectual advances, credit is given for innovation based on intent not necessarily results alone. As Tom Bloxham, the Chair of MIF/Factory International from 2005 to 2023 put it, 'MIF is an artistic, entrepreneurial story, one that started with a great idea but before it was fully funded...we've articulated quite a tricky, interesting, and ambitious idea about creating new artworks, about allowing great artists and different art forms to come together' (Bloxham in Walters, 2023).

The growth of contemporary cultural festivals since the 1980s has been fundamentally driven by a shift towards city branding, with a view to enhancing urban competitiveness. This broadens the instrumentalisation of cultural festivals, moving beyond models of cultural reconstruction or social participation, to economic policy instruments. In such processes the strategic embedding of a cultural event into a locality is paramount. Where festivals are designed to drive urban regeneration, enhance city image, attract tourism, and generate symbolic capital, without necessarily engaging deeper structural economic issues. Interdisciplinary cultural production has been strategically adopted in this context because it serves as a primary mechanism to promise innovation and distinction while simultaneously achieving audience aggregation and accountability, through cross-cultural programming. While genuine artistic and intellectual developments may occur in the process, it is clear that the spectacle of innovation, distinction and audience aggregation is also at play in these contexts – as organisations must remain accountable to public funders. For new arts organisations such MIF in 2007, the value of high-risk interdisciplinary and cross-cultural programming was three-fold: achieving distinctiveness, showcasing innovation and novelty, and ensuring broad audience appeal. Irrespective of the critical response to individual projects in the early editions of MIF, the strategy was effective in realising its goals. The high-risk programming ethos developed by Poots was remarkably successful. Poots left MIF in 2015 to become the founding artistic director and CEO of a new $500 million arts centre The Shed in New York, where he deployed a similar large-scale cross-cultural and interdisciplinary approach to programming, enabled by the architectural flexibility of the new venue, set within the contested urban development of Hudson Yards. Similarly, the success of MIF led to major regeneration projects and new property-led investment such in Manchester with the creation of Arriva Studios to present the kind of flexible cross-cultural, interdisciplinary projects championed by Poots (see chapter 3).

4.10 Novelty and innovation in form: Shanghai Project

As MIF shows, biennials and festivals can be important sites for interdisciplinary cultural production as a mode of cultural organising that prioritises a search for innovation, novelty and futurity. Something that is especially the case for new events that may seek to try to stand out in the field. Next, I want to use this framework to examine the founding (and slow demise) of the Shanghai Project as another example of this approach in practice. Launched in 2016, the Shanghai Project emerged as an adjunct programme from the Shanghai Himalayas Museum – a private, non-profit, museum founded in 2005 by businessman Dai Zhikang of the property and investment company Zendai. The Shanghai Himalayas Museum was one of the first private museums to focus on the collection, production and presentation of contemporary art in China (Fei, 2025). While many cultural institutions are located in the western part of Shanghai, the Himalayas Museum was located in Pudong, a developing area in the east of the city with fewer established cultural institutions. The museum was part of a wider development by the Zendai Group, at the time one of the leading property developers in China, and brought together art, entertainment, a hotel, and a department store complex – a vision to 'integrate art, luxury and commerce' (Fei, 2025). A vision replicated unsuccessfully elsewhere in the world by Zendai such as in Johannesburg, South Africa (see Brill and Reboredo 2019).

From 2012 the museum in Pudong was housed in an ambitious, statement building designed by Japanese architect Arata Isozaki to resemble the Himalayan mountain range. The Shanghai Project emerged as the first major international event to be staged by the museum – with the initial idea that it would take place around Pudong rather than the museum itself. It was a concept initiated by Yongwoo Lee, the South Korean art historian and curator who was invited to become the Executive Director of the Shanghai Himalayas Museum. He set out to create a major international event developing global reach for the museum – that would challenge the conventional format of the contemporary art biennial. Having been the founding director of the Gwangju Biennale in 1995 and co-initiator of the International Biennial Association (IBA) in 2012, he was well placed to develop such a new initiative against the backdrop of the global proliferation of international contemporary art biennials in the 1990s and 2000s. The museum and idea of The Shanghai Project in the context of Chinese international contemporary art, 'generated great expectations – both symbolic and economic' (Fei, 2025).

Yongwoo Lee's pitch for the Shanghai Project was given the backing of Dai Zhikang through a commitment to financially support the project. The basis for the new venture was that it would be ambitious, large-scale and multi-year, it would command attention both within Shanghai, China and the wider global art world. To do this, Lee proposed developing something that would bring together multiple disciplines, beyond the frame of contemporary visual art. As well as the support of Dai Zhikang, another private backer also invested in the project –Envision Energy, a Shanghai based, global renewable energy company. This sponsorship came with the condition of titling the event's first edition, which became known as *Envision 2116*.

It was clear from the outset of the Shanghai Project that it would need to differentiate itself within Shanghai, a city with a broad ecology of major and well-established international cultural events focused on specific art form disciplines such as the Shanghai Biennale, founded in 1996 (Brittney, 2015). This informed Lee's early thinking about the shape and form of the event. But it was the biennial as a cultural format that Lee proposed the Shanghai Project, as engaging with or in opposition to and in some sense needing to transcend. As Lee explained, 'The Shanghai Project will experiment with the actual structure of the biennale, developing not only a new "platform" or "laboratory" but also the rules, guidelines and methodology of this "laboratory"' (Lee in Brittney, 2015).

Part of the justification for devising a new form of cultural event was rooted in who the organisation sought to engage at a local level. As Lee set out, this was in response to Shanghai as one of the largest and fastest-growing migrant cities, and to develop that audience the Project would need to engage the 'social matrix of Shanghai' by working through 'different practices, conceptual tools and frames of reference to understand and harness its creative force' (Lee in Kontova, 2016). Or as Kontova (2016) put it, this was an attempt 'to rethink the format of the biennial in order to adapt it to the fluid nature of megacities'. At a local level within Shanghai this led to a focus for the event on 'general audiences' and 'ordinary citizens', for Lee it was important to 'encourage the participation of diverse audiences in Shanghai, including those who have never set foot in a museum before' (Lee in Brittney, 2015). This approach to enabling broad audience appeal as a means to define the distinction of the new event was set against a sense of how international contemporary art in China was primarily aimed at collectors, or academic audiences, both well served by existing cultural institutions (Brittney, 2015).

While such claims to local engagement are nothing new for many contemporary art biennials, Lee also sought to differentiate the Shanghai Project – through its structure, form and mode of cultural commissioning. He defined the new organisation to be 'an important step in this evolution of biennales and other international art events into new hybrid, interdisciplinary and reflexive modes of exhibition making' (Lee in Kontova, 2015). At the launch of the Project, bringing this together, Lee articulated the form of the event as 'a hybridised international art festival…[a] cultural forum in which the civil society of Shanghai [...] can speak, participate, discuss and relate to one another in the name of culture and art' (Lee in Brittney, 2015). This sense of reaching out to new audiences was also one of the primary ideas for the focus on the interdisciplinary nature of the new event:

> One of the principal goals of the Shanghai Project is to help make new and old 'Shanghainese' aware of the artistic and cultural resources that are available and rapidly expanding in their city. We would like to extend the reach (as well as translate the mediums) of current cross-disciplinary dialogues to embrace the multiple publics of Shanghai in ways that are not only accessible to them but can also be taken up by these publics to articulate different outlooks and needs.
>
> *(Lee in Brittney, 2015)*

One of the promises made of interdisciplinary cultural production in this context is that it will in some way meet the scale and complexity of the migrant city population. But the ambitions for the project went beyond Shanghai and its residents, for Lee and funders Dai Zhikang and Envision the potential of large-scale cultural events to reach international audience was also to project this novel format as a 'radical hybridisation of culture' – that in doing so would 'put Shanghai more firmly on the world map', through the international attention such an event might garner (Adam, 2016). For Dai Zhikang this was the most important element, with the means of the interdisciplinary approach perhaps a secondary concern, then the ability of such an event to gather famous international artists and thinkers in Shanghai. But Lee's ambition to innovate the biennial format effectively combined with Dai Zhikang's ambition and that of Envision to extend their brands into an international cultural space (Leam, 2025). The first step to realising this generated the high-status, international profile of the event and work through the proposed alternative format and multi and interdisciplinary Lee invited star-curator and regular interdisciplinarian, Hans Ulrich Obrist to be co-artistic director.

As a new international event seeking to act as an 'antidote to the spectacle of biennials and art fairs', The Shanghai Project was positioned to directly engage with the climate crisis as the most pressing global issue (Jovanovic, 2016). And a focus highly relevant for the lead sponsor Envision. There was a sense that to strategically engage with questions of climate change, an interdisciplinary approach was required by default because of the complex and multifaceted nature of the problem (Leam, 2025). This was expressed by Obrist (in Jovanovic, 2016) at the launch: 'the questions of the 21st century are so complex that it needs different disciplines to solve them'.

The first public element of The Shanghai Project was presented from September to November 2016, under the title *2116*. This title offered the space for a projection 100 years into the future that was connected to

Shanghai through a cautionary statistic cited by Zhang Lei (Envision Energy) that due to rising sea levels, 70% of downtown Shanghai would be submerged by that date (Cheung, 2017). The imperative to engage with the issues was described as a provocation to all creative and scientific disciplines, as well as the people of Shanghai to think critically about sustainability. To achieve this, it was proposed that the Shanghai Project would present interdisciplinary projects 'as a way of engaging audiences that have not previously participated in discourses generated within cultural realms. It is through interdisciplinarity that we attempt to challenge pre-conceptions of what is "culture" and what is "practice"' (e-flux, 2016b). Here the potential of interdisciplinary cultural production was implicated both for its problem-solving capacities, but also its ability to engage new audiences. Although there was no explicit detail here of *how* interdisciplinary cultural production within the Shanghai Project would achieve these aims.

To work our way through the rhetoric, it is valuable to set how in a practical sense the Shanghai Project operated its interdisciplinary model of cultural production. The plan was to develop a structure that would be replicated cyclically over different editions of the Project. As well as Lee and Obrist, there was also a team of four assistant curators, a team of technicians and a group of educators. Due to the international nature of the team and the participants they engaged, the working language of the project was English. The wider curatorial team came up with a structure to enable distinction from the conventional biennial format – where an artistic director or a curatorial team set a theme and select a group of artists, who are commissioned to create new work that relates to the theme. The structure they came up with was a 'a three-way system'. Central to the system were a group of ten or so participants, each from different disciplines – these were called the 'Root Researchers'. Lee and Obrist selected the 'root researchers' with many associated with Obrist's wide network of previous collaborators. Overall, there was a sense that they needed to represent a balanced range of disciplines and across the demographics of the participants. These primary agents came from a range of disciplinary backgrounds, including art, architecture, film, business. They were then given autonomy to form a new interdisciplinary team with whoever they wanted to work with. Each of these teams then created a proposal for what they would like to produce. There were no limits in form or content in relation to what this might be – it could be any kind of material or digital artefact, from a physical building to an interactive computer programme. The idea was that this would produce an 'organic' branching effect – an expanding network of 'researchers' some working together, others in parallel but also others in silo. There was an expectation from the curatorial team that someone in each team should be from Shanghai or China, or engage local residents, such that the project teams were connected to the city.

What the Shanghai Project would be and the form it would take would then emerge from this process of root and branch research and development. The lead curators of Lee and Obrist, the assistant curators, the technicians and educators then worked in between the 'root researcher' teams to mediate the process, such that something coherent across all the themes might emerge. The ambition of this approach was that through this convergence of different disciplinary practices, new thinking and ideas would be generated. And these would speak to the complexity of the population of Shanghai but also the climate, futurity and sustainability (Leam, 2025).

All those invited by the curators to participate were identified as 'researchers' as means to encompass the range of disciplines through a single identifiable and non-hierarchical label. But this also sought to present the Project as a mode of inquiry and knowledge production. Undertaking research in Shanghai was viewed as central to the process of developing a proposal – the ambition was that the curators would work with the participants to develop a local site visit to the city to allow them to develop an understanding of the city in relation to their own disciplinary background, giving them space, experience and time to develop their response and proposal. But emerging budget constraints meant that it wasn't possible to develop this space and time for all participants.

Each individual root researcher responded differently, with some concerned more with their overall visibility within the structure of the project than others. But the curators also found pushing participants to work beyond their disciplines and engage in the local context in Shanghai a challenge at times. One of the Root Researchers invited to contribute was philosopher Bruno Latour – he brought an existing team of interdisciplinary researchers to create *Reset Modernity! Shanghai Perspective* an expansion into Shanghai of his existing reset modernity project. One issue with the research-led approach was that the work undertaken had limited external visibility , and there was a requirement to make Project more spectacular (Leam, 2025). In response to this , Japanese architect Sou Fujimoto was commissioned to construct a pavilion, taking the form of a large scaffold-like structure in front of the museum. This became the *Envision Pavilion* and acted as a central location for public programming and discursive events.

Budget constraints led to the first iteration being split into two parts and the after the initial launch in 2016, and a second presentation was created that became the exhibition *Seeds of Time* began in April 2017 at the museum. Presented in a more conventional exhibition format, the displays featured work from the Root Researcher (Bruno Latour, Sophia Al-Maria, Qiu Anxiong, Otobong Nkanga, and Zhang Haimeng), but there was also a strong emphasis on dialogue and public debate, with many other invited speakers. The exhibition was designed by Hong Kong-based studio COLLECTIVE – who explicitly sought to bring interdisciplinary connections to the forefront of the space through 'points of contact between spheres of interdisciplinary knowledge' organised into zones called, Field, Sequence, and Rooms (COLLECTIVE, 2016).

Over the opening days of *Seeds of Time* there were numerous 'conferences, roundtable discussions, marathon Q&As and presentations unfolded over two full days, marinating curators, journalists, artists and Shanghainese citizens in research-heavy diatribes against the sustainability of our Anthropocene' (Cheung, 2017). Part of the expression of the requirements for all this dialogue between disciplines on the part of the co-curators was that 'disciplines...have in our contemporary age been split or sequestered from each other...[the event was therefore] planting metaphorical seeds for reuniting in a future world.' (Cheung, 2017). As the press release for the *Seeds of Time* put it:

> Exploring the causes and effects of ecological transformation, Shanghai Project participants, address sustainability through the lens of interdisciplinarity. From its initiation in 2016, the Shanghai Project has been an experiment, a laboratory for testing the boundaries of existing assumptions, and for considering how ideas might expand beyond the confines of individual silos of knowledge.
>
> *(Shanghai Project, 2017a)*

The exhibition and discussions around it were as far as the Shanghai Project travelled. The financial support of Dai Zhikang became increasingly strained and the resources required to establish and run the ambitious project were not forthcoming. Dai Zhikang's business had come under scrutiny. As Fei (2025) sets out:

> In 2019 Dai admitted to creating unauthorised capital pools and misappropriating approximately £1 billion in funds from the public, leading to his arrest along with 40 associates. In December 2022 he was sentenced to 19 years in prison, and his assets, including a dilapidated mansion in Shanghai, were auctioned off to repay creditors.

The Shanghai Himalayas Museum turned into what has been labelled, 'zombie museum' – still technically functioning, but slowly dissolving through lack of funding, staffing and wider institutional support (Fei, 2025).

But it was not just in financial terms that the Project struggled to establish itself. The ambitious challenge set out to reinvent the biennial model through interdisciplinary also proposed challenges / while the research structure and inquiry based model offered promise – and was not that dissimilar from other curatorial models of co-inquiry (Triscott, and Santomauro, 2021), it was perhaps in tension with the needs of major new cultural events to offer a scale of visibility, media attention and spectacle. As Fei (2025) notes 'in China's current cultural landscape, it's never the exhibitions that matter anyway. Here, art frequently serves as a decoy for something else'. It is perhaps the case that the necessity for interdisciplinarity was not translated into a coherent form within the structure of the event. This was reflected in some ambiguity over its form and purpose – that was possibily alienating to the audience and participants. the Project was variably described in different places as an: 'ideas platform'; 'hybridized international arts festival'; 'cultural forum'; 'festival of ideas'; 'a culture and knowledge "emporium"', 'a shared time and space for people to gather, procure, and exchange knowledge and culture'; 'a year-long multidisciplinary research platform'; 'an experiment, a laboratory' (e-flux, 2015; Cascone, 2016; Jovanovic, 2016; e-flux, 2016b; e-flux, 2016c). And from the archived version of the defunct project website 'an experiment, a laboratory for testing the boundaries of existing assumptions' (Shanghai Project, 2017b). This kind of rhetorical disorientation points to the wider issue of trying to grapple with the extensive field of practices that the Project sought to bring together – both in terms of content and form, it was reaching very wide, while making attempts to engage at a deep level in Shanghai, with varying results.

Clearly such an approach has potential, but requires clarity of purpose, time and resources to be developed in practice. The risk as emphasised here is that little emerges beyond the individual contributions, and the audience struggle to find ways into the programme. While working through interdisciplinary methods offered a clear route to novelty and an ability to engage with urgent challenges like the climate crisis, beyond denoting the root and branch structure of the teams, how that interdisciplinarity would be rigorously enabled and enacted successfully within the structure was seemingly given limited consideration. Here interdisciplinarity appeared to be considered an end itself, something that would be of instinctive value,rather than a working process that needed to be considered as its own specific methodological approach. As such, the Shanghai Project was deeply infused with the rhetoric and mythic promise of interdisciplinarity. This is also a good example of how ambitious interdisciplinary projects can return to the default disciplinary processes of production and presentation that those creating them emerge from. In this case the team consisted of curators with backgrounds in the visual arts working on a project that ended up being an exhibition in a museum, a form and language that was familiar to them (Leam, 2025).

The Shanghai Project aimed to challenge and transcend the conventional contemporary art biennial format by adopting a hybrid, interdisciplinary, and multi-year structure to achieve global reach and distinction. The project also sought to transcend the conventional biennial format by structurally promoting research across disciplines and focusing on urgent global issues like the climate crisis to attract international attention and engage local, non-traditional museum audiences in Shanghai. This ambition was also closely tied to the financial backers' goals of brand extension, setting up an inherent tension between ambitious innovation and commercial imperatives. Despite its highly articulated rhetoric and its detailed 'Root Researcher' structure, the Shanghai Project ultimately failed to establish a rigorous, sustained interdisciplinary model, eventually defaulting to a conventional museum exhibition format. The project's demise was ultimately caused by the financial collapse of its primary backer underscoring the precariousness of private funding. But was also challenged by structural and conceptual ambiguity, where interdisciplinarity was considered as an end goal rather than a complex methodological process that resulted in a lack of clarity and spectacle, proving insufficient to overcome internal tensions, budget constraints, and the pressures to perform internationally.

4.11 Conclusion

Drawing together the insights from the case studies in this chapter it is possible to articulate a framework defining the central parameters of interdisciplinary cultural production across different institutional contexts. Here the key themes that emerge revolve around the structure and design of interdisciplinary cultural projects, their strategic function in specific institutional contexts, how time, space, place and process are considered, and the institutional logics that underpin these practices. The following define the critical parameters governing how and why interdisciplinary cultural production is mobilised and structured.

Within the institutional structure, design and methodology, the 'frame' of such projects operates most effectively in non-hierarchical forms, where there is space created to put aside, as much as possible, economic demands and constraints, as well predetermined outcomes, rigid disciplinary roles, or external bureaucratic demands. This enables risk to play out in safe spaces for experimental, where the expectation for some failure is acknowledged and built into the structure and working process, such that risk is accommodated. Ultimately this is to treat such interdisciplinary exchange as a privilege, something that requires nurturing and respect. The practical success of interdisciplinarity is contingent upon translating this structural ambition into a rigorous, well-resourced (not just financially, but also temporally) methodological process, rather than treating it merely as an end goal in itself or a spectacle of juxtaposition.

Here the cultural institution and the cultural manager or producer, be it a curator or artistic director etc, play a crucial role as a mediator or facilitator who intentionally structures and manages these key constraints, particularly time and public presentation, to generate a high-risk, low-stakes contexts that enable practitioners to work in new ways together.

The strategic function of interdisciplinary cultural production can also be wider here, as a political and decolonial tool, working towards cultural affirmation to challenge cultural hierarchies and legitimising diverse knowledge forms and cultural practices. Interdisciplinary cultural production can function as a dynamic, adaptive, and place-based mediator, driven by a political and social agenda to build solidarity and challenge dominant narratives. As with AfroAsia, this can be achieved by intentionally intersecting critical historical research with diverse, often non-discursive, contemporary arts practices to bridge isolated social and linguistic communities. Time becomes an essential resource here to develop projects with depth, rigor, and nuanced outcomes by embracing process, iteration, failure, and the integration of situated knowledge.

But we can also see how the cultural production of interdisciplinarity can be strategically instrumentalised as a mechanism for demonstrating innovation – often aligned with wider economic agendas, such as in the contemporary urban festival. The spectacle of high-risk innovation and novelty is used to generate media attention, secure distinction, and achieve broad audience aggregation and accountability to public funders, thereby creating valuable symbolic capital for urban regeneration. This operates in a similar way to how interdisciplinary cultural production can be mobilised to define and mediate the identity of major civic and corporate developments, often driven by a fusion of legislative public art mandates and the commissioning organisation's strategic need to express its corporate/academic values and identity as with the work of Paterson and Zeller & Moye. Finally, taking pleasure in collaboration is something often overlooked as a central parameter of interdisciplinary cultural production – where even when there is friction, if participants meet each other as equals – interdisciplinary cultural production can be treated as a privilege to practice.

Bibliography

Adam, G.(2016) 'A bridge to culture — before the deluge' [Online], *Financial Times*, 25 March. Available at: www.ft.com/content/428e8b0e-f121-11e5-9f20-c3a04 7354386 (Accessed: 23 July 2025).

Apple. (2023) *Apple Event — September 12, 2023.* [Online]. Available at: www.yout ube.com/watch?v=ZiP1l7jlIIA (Accessed: 11 June 2025).

APRB. (n. d.) *About Us.* [Online]. Available at: https://aprb.co.uk/about/ (Accessed: 16 June 2025).

Apter, A. (2021) 'Festac 77: A black world's fair', in *Oxford Research Encyclopedia of African History.* Oxford: Oxford University Press. Available at: https://doi.org/ 10.1093/acrefore/9780190277734.013.798 (Accessed: 23 May 2025).

Arts Council of Great Britain. (1991) *Percent for Art: A Review.* London: Arts Council of Great Britain.

Aterianus-Owanga, A. (2020) 'A Pan-African space in Cape Town? The Chimurenga archive of Pan-African festivals', *Journal of African Cultural Studies*, 32(3), pp. 251–269.

Ball, P. (2019) 'Artist of deep time', *Nature*, 568, p. 457. https://doi.org/10.1038/ d41586-019-01240-4.

BBC. (2016) *What Do Artists Do All Day? Katie Paterson.* BBC Four, 7 May.

Bewley, J. and Tarbuck, J. (eds.) (2016) *Katie Paterson.* Cologne: Kerber Verlag.

Bianchini, F. (1999) 'The relationship between cultural resources and urban tourism policies: Issues from European debates', in Dodd, D. and van Hemel, A. (eds.) *Planning Cultural Tourism in Europe: a Presentation of Theories and Cases.* Amsterdam: Boekman Studies.

Billington, M. (2009) 'It felt like a kiss', [Online] *The Guardian*, 3 July. Available at: www.theguardian.com/culture/2009/jul/03/manchester-international-festi val (Accessed: 27 March 2025).

Bishop, C. (2006) 'The social turn: Collaboration and its discontents', *Artforum*, 44(6), pp. 178–183.

Bishop, C. (2011) 'Rooms for improvement: Claire Bishop around the manchester international festival', *Artforum*. [Online]. Available at: www.artforum.com/columns/claire-bishop-around-the-manchester-international-festival-198012/ (Accessed: 14 June 2025).

Bishop, C. (2023) 'Information overload: On the superabundance of research-based art', *Artforum*, 1 April. Available at: www.artforum.com/features/claire-bishop-on-the-superabundance-of-research-based-art-252571/ (Accessed: 27 May 2025).

Brill, F. and Reboredo, R. (2019) 'Failed fantasies in a South African context: The case of Modderfontein, Johannesburg', *Urban Forum*, 30, pp. 171–189. https://doi.org/10.1007/s12132-018-9348-1.

Brittney (2015) 'The Shanghai Project 2016: Yongwoo Lee – interview', [Online] *ArtRadarJournal*, 6 December. Available at: https://web.archive.org/web/20210615100523/https://artradarjournal.com/2015/12/06/the-shanghai-project-2016-yongwoo-lee-interview/ (Accessed: 23 July 2025).

Brooker, C. (2009) 'The Untied States of America', [Online] *The Guardian*, 20 June. Available at: www.theguardian.com/culture/2009/jun/20/it-felt-like-a-kiss (Accessed: 27 March 2025).

Cascone, S. (2016) 'Hans Ulrich Obrist to Helm First Edition of Mysterious Shanghai Project', [Online] *Artnet News*, 28 March. Available at: https://news.artnet.com/art-world/hans-ulrich-obrist-yongwoo-lee-helm-first-edition-mysterious-shanghai-project-460199 (Accessed: 23 July 2025).

Cashdan, M. (2011) 'Live from manchester', *T-Magazine, New York Times*, 13 July. Available at: https://archive.nytimes.com/tmagazine.blogs.nytimes.com/2011/07/13/live-from-manchester/ (Accessed: 14 June 2025).

Chayka, K. (2011) 'Seven artists meet seven technologists, but who's who?', *Hyperallergic*, 17 May. Available at: https://hyperallergic.com/24685/seven-on-seven-rhizome-review/ (Accessed: 27 May 2025).

Che, O. (2015) *My Utopia*. [Film]. KADIST. Available at: https://kadist.org/work/my-utopia/

Che, O. (2022) *International Friendship: The Gifts from Africa.* Heidelberg: Kehrer Verlag.

Che, O. (2025) Interview with Che Onejoon and Sun A Moon, AfroAsia. Interviewed by Peter Merrington [Zoom], 18 May.

Cheung, Y. (2017) 'Field Trip: Shanghai Project Chapter 2', [Online] *ArtAsiaPacific*, 26 April. Available at: https://www.artasiapacific.com/ideas/field-trip-shanghai-project-chapter-2/ (Accessed: 23 July 2025).

Chimurenga (ed.) (2019) *Festac '77: The 2nd World Black and African Festival of Arts and Culture.* Cologne: Walther & Franz König.

City of Cupertino. (2025) *Chapter 19.148: Required Artwork In Public and Private Developments.* [Online]. Available at: https://codehub.gridics.com/us/ca/cupert ino (Accessed: 11 June 2025).

Cohan, N. (2014) 'Preprofessional development: Rhizome's seven on seven', *Art in America*. Available at: www.artnews.com/art-in-america/features/preprofessional-development-rhizomes-seven-on-seven-59746/ (Accessed: 27 May 2025).

COLLECTIVE (2016) '#014 "SEEDS OF TIME" SHANGHAI PROJECT, HIMALAYAS MUSEUM SHANGHAI', [Online], *Collective Studio*, Available at: www.collective-studio.co/shanghai-project (Accessed: 20 July 2025).

Connor, M. (2014) 'Seven on seven 2014: Frances Stark & David Kravitz', [Online]. *Rhizome*. Available at: https://rhizome.org/editorial/2014/may/03/seven-on-seven-2014/ (Accessed: 27 May 2025).

Connor, M. (2015) 'Eight big ideas from seven on seven', [Online]. *Rhizome*. Available at: https://rhizome.org/editorial/2015/may/4/seven-seven-2015/ (Accessed: 27 May 2025).

Cornell, L. (2011) 'Seven on seven 2011 - opening remarks', [Online]. *Rhizome*. Available at: https://rhizome.org/editorial/2011/may/14/seven-on-seven-2011/ (Accessed: 27 May 2025).

Council. (2022) *About*. [Online]. Available at: www.council.art/about (Accessed: 20 May 2025).

Crary, J. (2013) *24/7 Late Capitalism and the Ends of Sleep*. London: Verso.

Delanty, G., Sassatelli, M. and Young, L. (eds.) (2011) *Festivals and the Cultural Public Sphere*. Abingdon: Taylor & Francis.

Dougan, L. D. (2014) 'Boxing lesson', *Africa Is a Country*, 8 April. Available at: https://africasacountry.com/2014/04/africa-is-a-country-video-george-khosis-boxing-club (Accessed: 16 June 2025).

e-flux (2015) 'Nihao, Shanghai!', [Online], *e-flux*, December 2. Available at: https://www.e-flux.com/announcements/3734/nihao-shanghai (Accessed: 23 July 2025).

e-flux. (2016a) *Art and Technology Events - New Museum*. [Online]. 14 December 2015. Available at: www.e-flux.com/announcements/35623/seven-on-seven-a-conference-bridging-contemporary-art-and-technology (Accessed: 5 May 2025).

e-flux (2016b) 'Yongwoo Lee & Hans Ulrich Obrist announced as Co-Artistic Directors of inaugural edition', [Online], *e-flux*, 26 March. Available at: www.e-flux.com/announcements/44484/yongwoo-lee-hans-ulrich-obrist-announced-as-co-artistic-directors-of-inaugural-edition (Accessed: 23 July 2025).

e-flux (2016c) 'Envision 2116', [Online], *e-flux*, 23 August. Available at: www.e-flux.com/announcements/44978/envision-2116 (Accessed: 23 July 2025).

Ellis-Petersen, H. (2014) 'The extinction marathon: The art world's bid to save the human race', [Online]. *The Guardian*, 20 October. Available at: www.theguardian.com/artanddesign/2014/oct/20/serpentine-extinction-marathon-yoko-ono-gilbert-george (Accessed: 8 April 2025).

Eshun, K., Gordon, A.F. and Pethick, E. (2017) 'Navigating pan-Africanisms', *Afterall: A Journal of Art, Context and Enquiry*, 43 (Spring/Summer), pp. 80–87.

Falassi, A. (1987) *Time Out of Time: Essays on the Festival*. Albuquerque: University of New Mexico Press.

Financial Times. (2007) 'Manchester man on a mission', *The Financial Times*, [Online]. 19 March. Available at: www.ft.com/content/8a85e3b0-d63e-11db-99b7-000b5df10621 (Accessed: 14 June 2025).

Fino-Radin, C. (2022) 'Episode 037 Lauren Cornell', *Art and Obsolescence* [Podcast], 5 October. Available at: www.artandobsolescence.com/episodes/037-lauren-cornell (Accessed: 5 May 2025).

Foster, H. (2015) 'Exhibitionists', *London Review of Books*, 37(11), 4 June.

Foster, N. (2017) 'The designer of Apple's new headquarters explains how he brought Steve Jobs's vision to life', [Online]. *Inc.* Available at: www.inc.com/kevin-j-ryan/apple-park-norman-foster-steve-jobs-vision.html (Accessed: 11 June 2025).

Frean, A. (2003) 'Manchester's bohemian rhapsody to wealth', *The Times*, [Online]. 26 May. Available at: www.thetimes.com/travel/destinations/uk-travel/england/manchester/manchesters-bohemian-rhapsody-to-wealth-9qqg679sjcj (Accessed: 26 March 2025).

Gallardo, F and Lastra, C. (2016) *Talking Dirty: Tongue First! Recipes from the Mouth of the Thames*. London: Arts Catalysts.

Garcia, B. (2005) 'Deconstructing the city of culture: The long-term cultural legacies of Glasgow 1990', *Urban Studies*, 42(5-6), pp. 841–868.

Garlake, M. (1998) *New Art New World: British Art in Postwar Society*. New Haven, CT: Yale University Press.

Gregory, J.J. (2015) 'Creative industries and urban regeneration – The Maboneng precinct, Johannesburg', *Local Economy*, 31(1-2), pp. 158–171. https://doi.org/10.1177/0269094215618597.

Haraway, D. (1988) 'Situated knowledges: The science question in feminism and the privilege of partial perspective', *Feminist Studies*, 14(3), pp. 575–599.

Harvey, D. (1988) 'Voodoo cities', *New Statesman and Society*, 30 September, pp. 33–35.

Hawthorne, C. (2011) 'Critic's notebook: Apple's new campus will be a retrograde cocoon', [Online]. *LA Times*. Available at: www.latimes.com/business/la-xpm-2011-sep-10-la-ca-applehq-20110911-story.html (Accessed: 11 June 2025).

Hickling, A. (2007a) 'Monkey: Journey to the West', [Online]. *The Guardian*, 29 June. Available at: www.theguardian.com/music/2007/jun/29/classicalmusicandopera.manchesterfestival2007 (Accessed: 27 March 2025).

Hickling, A. (2007b) 'William Orbit', [Online] *The Guardian*, 10 July. Available at: www.theguardian.com/music/2007/jul/10/manchesterfestival2007.manchesterfestival (Accessed: 27 March 2025).

Hill, K. (2011) 'Names you need to know: Rhizome', *Forbes*, 18 May. Available at: www.forbes.com/sites/kashmirhill/2011/05/18/names-you-need-to-know-rhizome/ (Accessed: 27 May 2025).

Hobsbawm, E. (2013) *Fractured Times: Culture and Society in the Twentieth Century*. London: Little, Brown.

Jacobs, S. (2024) 'Chop-chop spirit', *London Review of Books*, [Online] 46(9), 9 May. Available at: www.lrb.co.uk/the-paper/v46/n09/sean-jacobs/chop-chop-spirit (Accessed: 23 June 2025).

Jobs, S. (2011) *Steve Jobs Presents to the Cupertino City Council (6/7/11)*. [Online Video]. City of Cupertino. Available at: www.youtube.com/watch?v=gtuz5OmOh_M (Accessed: 11 June 2025).

Jobs, S. (2021) *Apple Event, March 2011* [Podcast], Apple. 2 March. Available at: https://podcasts.apple.com/gb/podcast/apple-events-video/id275834665?i=1000100978751 (Accessed: 18 June 2025).

Jovanovic, R. (2016) 'The Shanghai Project Offers Sustainability With Little Spectacle', [Online] *Artnet News*, 7 November. Available at: https://news.artnet.com/art-world/on-spectacle-and-sustainability-at-the-shanghai-project-738206 (Accessed: 23 July 2025).

Kentridge, W. (2014) *Six Drawing Lessons*. Cambridge, MA: Harvard University Press.
Kentridge, W. (2023) *William Kentridge Lecture: Finding the Less Good Idea*. [Online Video]. Granoff Center for the Creative Arts, Brown University. Available at: www.youtube.com/watch?v=JbQ89KGJg70 (Accessed: 10 March 2025).
Kentridge, W. (2024) *Self-Portrait as a Coffee Pot* [Film]. Mubi.
Kim, J. E. (2024). 'Rethinking the "Arts of the Contact Zone" after thirty years: Korea between the Cold War and decolonization'. *Inter-Asia Cultural Studies*, 25(2), 157–160.
Kontova, H. (2016) 'Yongwoo Lee on the Shanghai Project', [Online] *Flash Art*, 4 January. Available at: https://flash---art.com/2016/01/yongwoo-lee-on-the-shanghai-project/ (Accessed: 23 July 2025).
Krauss, R. (2000) *A Voyage on the North Sea: Art in the Age of the Post-Medium Condition*. London: Thames & Hudson.
Krauss, R. (ed.) (2017) *William Kentridge*. Cambridge, MA: MIT Press.
Kućma, A. (2022) 'North Korean sculptures shaping the African horizon | Interview with Che Onejoon', [Online]. ZAM. Available at: www.zammagazine.com/arts/1510-north-korean-sculptures-shaping-the-african-horizon-interview-with-che-onejoon (Accessed: 9 July 2025).
Kwon, M. (2002) *One Place after Another: Site-specific Art and Locational Identity*. Cambridge, MA: MIT Press.
Lace, B. (2025) *Interview with Bronwyn Lace, Co-founder & Director, The Centre for the Less Good Idea*. Interviewed by Peter Merrington [Zoom], 18 March.
Lai Fei. (2025) 'A eulogy to China's art museums', *ArtReview*, 11 July. Available at: https://artreview.com/a-eulogy-to-chinas-art-museums-opinion-lai-fei/ (Accessed: 23 July 2025).
Larsen, L.B. (2014) '1000 words: Katie Paterson and Margaret Atwood', *Artforum*, 53(3). Available at: www.artforum.com/features/1000-words-katie-paterson-and-margaret-atwood-221827/ (Accessed: 12 June 2025).
Lastra, C. and Santomauro, A. (2025) *Interview with Claudia Lastra, CEO and Anna Santomauro, Head of Programme, Arts Catalyst*. Interviewed by Peter Merrington [In person], 6 February.
Lau, M. (2013) 'Taryn Simon and Aaron Swartz's experiment with images', *The New York Times (The 6th Floor blog)*, 19 January. Available at: https://archive.nytimes.com/6thfloor.blogs.nytimes.com/2013/01/19/taryn-simon-and-aaron-swartzs-experiment-with-images/ (Accessed: 27 May 2025).
Leam, S. (2025) Interview with Sooyoung Leam. Interviewed by Peter Merrington [Zoom], 7 April.
Lee, H. and Lee, H. (2025) 'Mountain residents clash with US military over better access to village', *Korea Times*. Available at: www.koreatimes.co.kr/southkorea/society/20250428/mountain-residents-clash-with-us-military-over-better-access-to-village (Accessed: 8 July 2025).
Levene, R and Clinch, M. (2021) *Towards A Common Waters Policy*. Sheffield: Arts Catalyst.
Mann, D. (2023) *Reflecting on Seven Years of the Less Good Idea*. Available at: https://lessgoodidea.com/reflecting-on-seven-years-of-the-less-good-idea (Accessed: 22 June 2025).
Martin, F. (2007) 'Science marathon at the Serpentine', [Online]. *The Guardian*, 22 August. Available at: www.theguardian.com/artanddesign/2007/aug/22/art1 (Accessed: 8 April 2025).

Mashile, L. (2019) 'Venus Hottentot vs. Modernity In conversation with Lebogang Mashile', *Esclavages & Post-esclavages.* https://doi.org/10.4000/slaveries.360.

Moon, S, A. (2025) Interview with Che Onejoon and Sun A Moon, AfroAsia. Interviewed by Peter Merrington [Zoom], 18 May.

Morison, G.I. and Rottenburg, J. (2024) 'Infrastructures for a Black/African renaissance: Cultural institution building and organisational frameworks in selected postcolonial Pan-African festivals', in Leonhardt, N. and Balme, C.B. (eds.) *Developing Theatre in the Global South: Institutions, Networks, Experts.* London: UCL Press, pp. 33–51.

Moscardo, G. (2007) 'Analyzing the role of festivals and events in regional development'. *Event Management*, 11 (1-2). pp. 23-32.

Mottershead, T. (2007) 'Manchester International Festival', *Tempo*, 61(242), pp. 39–44.

Mottershead, T. (2012) 'Manchester International Festival, 2011', *Tempo*, 66(259), pp. 68–72.

Mountford, S.J. (2021) *Oral History Interview with S. Joy Mountford.* Interviewed by Jeffrey R. Yost, Charles Babbage Institute, [Online]. 25 March. Available at: https://conservancy.umn.edu/server/api/core/bitstreams/12140608-503c-4138-8a89-25972994ea59/content (Accessed: 18 June 2025).

Mozingo, L.A. (2014) *Pastoral Capitalism: A History of Suburban Corporate Landscapes.* Cambridge, MA: MIT Press.

Murphy, D. (2018) 'Performing global African culture and citizenship: Major Pan-African cultural festivals from Dakar 1966 to FESTAC 1977', *Tate Papers*, 30. Available at: www.tate.org.uk/research/tate-papers/30/performing-global-african-culture-and-citizenship

Murphy, D. (ed.) (2021) *The First World Festival of Negro Arts, Dakar 1966: Contexts and Legacies.* Liverpool: Liverpool University Press.

Naylor, T. (2006) 'The holy grail of art', *The Guardian*, 24 August. Available at: www.theguardian.com/culture/2006/aug/24/manchesterfestival2007.manchesterfestival (Accessed: 26 March 2025).

New Museum. (2018) 'Exhibitions real artists ship: Recent projects from seven on seven', [Online]. *New Museum.* Available at: https://archive.newmuseum.org/exhibitions/2530 (Accessed: 27 May 2025).

Olsen, C.S. (2012) *Re-thinking Festivals: A Comparative Study of the Integration/Marginalization of Art Festivals in the Urban Regimes of Manchester, Copenhagen and Vienna.* PhD thesis. Available at: www.4cities.eu/wp-content/uploads/2016/06/MAthesis_4CITIES_SACHS_OLSEN_CECILIE_Cohort2.pdf.

Otieno, A. (2023) 'Interview with Katie Paterson and Zeller & Moye', *Mirage Apple Inc.* [Online]. Available at: https://mirage.place/information/ (Accessed: 17 June 2025).

Palankasova, B. and Cook, S. (2024) 'Historicising media arts: The role of documentation and records of festivals', *MAP - Media | Archive | Performance*, 14(1), pp. 1–10. https://doi.org/10.25969/mediarep/23006.

Pasmore, V. (1969) *Apollo Pavilion.* Peterlee, County Durham, UK.

Pasternack, A. (2010) 'Seven on seven: A 24-hour particle accelerator for art and technology', [Online] *Vice*, 20 April. Available at: www.vice.com/en/article/rhizome-s-seven-on-seven-a-large-hadron-tech-art-idea-collider/ (Accessed: 27 May 2025).

Paterson, K. (2008) *Earth-Moon-Earth 4'33".* Available at: https://katiepaterson.org/artwork/earth-moon-earth/ (Accessed: 16 March 2026).

Petherbridge, D. (ed.) (1987) *Art for Architecture: A Handbook on Commissioning*. London: H.M. Stationery Office.

Pittwood, L. (2023) 'Around you the landscape lies transfigured: Arts Catalyst's home and garden in Sheffield'. [Online]. *Corridor8*. Available at https://corridor8.co.uk/article/around-you-the-landscape-lies-transfigured-arts-catalysts-home-and-garden-in-sheffield/ (Accessed: 16 March 2026).

Pollock, V.L. and Paddison, R. (2010) 'Embedding public art: Practice, policy and problems', *Journal of Urban Design*, 15(3), pp. 335–356.

Poots, A. (2009) 'My week: Alex Poots', [Online] *The Observer*. 28 June. Available at:https://www.theguardian.com/theobserver/2009/jun/28/my-week-alex-poots-manchester (Accessed: 27 March 2025).

Pratt, M. L. (1992) *Imperial eyes: travel writing and transculturation*. London: Routledge.

Quin, J. (2022) 'A handful of dust: An interview with Katie Paterson'. [Online]. *The Quietus*. Available at: https://thequietus.com/culture/art/katie-paterson-requiem-ingelby-gallery-interview/ (Accessed: 14 June 2025).

Quinn, B. (2005) 'Arts festivals and the city', [Online] *Urban Studies*, 42(5), pp. 927–943.

Rhizome. (2010) *Seven on Seven 2010: Trailer*. [Online Video]. Rhizome. Available at: https://video.rhizome.org/w/p/vEG845TxjbsrYznSsqRXGj (Accessed: 27 May 2025).

Rosenberg, E. and Cork, R. (1992) *Architect's Choice: Art in Architecture in Great Britain since 1945*. London: Thames and Hudson.

Rybczynski, W. (2018) *The Untold Story of Apple Park*. [Online]. Architect. Available at: www.architectmagazine.com/Design/the-untold-story-of-apple-park_o (Accessed: 11 June 2025).

Sang-Hun, C. and Chung, J. (2023) 'A brutal sex trade built for American soldiers', *The New York Times - International Edition*, 5 May. Available at: www.nytimes.com/2023/05/02/world/asia/korea-us-comfort-women-sexual-slavery.html.

Sassatelli, M. (2011) 'Urban festivals and the cultural public sphere: Cosmopolitanism between ethics and aesthetics', in Delanty, G., Sassatelli, M. and Young, L. (eds.) *Festivals and the Cultural Public Sphere*. Abingdon: Routledge, pp. 11–28.

SAIC. (2021) *Katie Paterson: Visiting Artists Program Lecture (in conversation with Mary Jane Jacob)*. [Online Video]. Available at: www.youtube.com/watch?v=O-rdSR8lwEE (Accessed: 12 June 2025).

Schwedel, H. (2017) 'Why doesn't Apple's state-of-the-art new campus include a day care?', *Slate Magazine*. Available at: https://slate.com/human-interest/2017/05/apple-s-new-headquarters-apple-park-has-no-child-care-center-despite-costing-5-billion.html (Accessed: 25 June 2025).

Shanghai Project (2017a) 'Press Release: Opening of Shanghai Project, Chapter 2', [Online], *Biennial Association*, available at: https://www.biennialassociation.org/article/opening-of-shanghai-project-chapter-2/ (Accessed: 22 June 2025).

Shanghai Project (2017b) 'About Shanghai Project', [Online], *Shanghai Project*, available at https://web.archive.org/web/20170521150214/http://www.shanghai-project.org/about (Accessed: 22 July 2025).

Sheppard Robson. (2025) *University of Bristol Life Sciences Building*. [Online] Available at: www.sheppardrobson.com/projects/university-of-bristol-life-sciences-building (Accessed: 16 June 2025).

Simon, T. and Swartz, A. (2012) *Image Atlas.* [Online]. Available at: https://anthology.rhizome.org/image-atlas (Accessed: 27 May 2025).

Situations. (2015) *Katie Paterson: Artist Talk at Arnolfini* [Podcast]. Available at: https://soundcloud.com/situationsuk/katie-paterson-artist-talk-at-arnolfini (Accessed: 16 June 2025).

Sneed, G. (2011) '7 on 7: Rhizome, AOL, New Museum', *Art in America.* Available at: www.artnews.com/art-in-america/features/7-on-7-rhizome-aol-new-museum-58275/ (Accessed: 27 May 2025).

Southern, J. (1977) 'FESTAC '77', *The Black Perspective in Music*, 5(1), pp. 104–117.

Stevens, P. (2017) *Interview with Architects Christoph Zeller and Ingrid Moye of Zeller & Moye. Designboom*, Available at: www.designboom.com/architecture/zeller-and-moye-interview-christoph-zeller-ingrid-moye-03-14-2017/ (Accessed: 18 June 2025).

Sullivan, M. (2011) 'Seven on seven 2011: Opening remarks', [Online] *Rhizome.* Available at: https://rhizome.org/editorial/2011/may/14/seven-on-seven-2011/ (Accessed: 27 May 2025).

Swartz, A. and Simon, T. (2012) 'Aaron Swartz & Taryn Simon in conversation', *Rhizome Seven on Seven Conference*, New Museum of Contemporary Art, New York, 14 April. Available at: https://tarynsimon.com/essays-videos/docs/Aaron%20Swartz%20%26%20Taryn%20Simon%20in%20conversation.pdf (Accessed: 27 May 2025).

Symons, J. (2016) 'Untangling creativity and art for policy purposes: Ethnographic insights on Manchester International Festival and Manchester Day Parade', *International Journal of Cultural Policy*, 24(2), pp. 205–219. https://doi.org/10.1080/10286632.2016.1150268.

Tibken, S. (2017) 'Apple's Spaceship campus doesn't have daycare', *CNET.* Available at: www.cnet.com/tech/tech-industry/apples-campus-apple-park-spaceship-has-just-about-everything-except-daycare/ (Accessed: 25 June 2025).

Toledo, A. (2021) 'Cupertino: Apple unveils plans for sculpture using sand from the world's 58 deserts', *Bay Area News Group, The Mercury News.* Available at: www.mercurynews.com/2021/06/16/cupertino-apple-unveils-plans-for-sculpture-using-sand-from-the-worlds-58-deserts/ (Accessed: 17 June 2025).

Triscott, N. (ed.) (1996) *Body Visual.* London: The Arts Catalyst.

Triscott, N. and Santomauro, A. (2021) 'Transdisciplinary co-inquiry as curatorial methodology: From the Canadian Arctic to the Calder Valley, Yorkshire', in Rogers, H.S., Halpern, M.K. and de Ridder-Vignone, K. (eds.) *Routledge Handbook of Art, Science, and Technology Studies.* Abingdon: Routledge.

University of Bristol. (2016) *George Hare Leonard Memorial Event: Katie Paterson Zeller & Moye, Dr Jon Bridle in Conversation* [Podcast], 9 May. Available at: https://soundcloud.com/university-of-bristol/hollow-a-new-public-artwork-with-the-artist-katie-paterson (Accessed: 10 June 2025).

University of Bristol. (2025) *Commissioning and Partnerships.* [Online] Available at: https://public-art.bristol.ac.uk/about-us/commissioning-and-partnerships/ (Accessed: 20 June 2025).

Walters, S. (eds) (2023) *Everything That Happened: Manchester International Festival.* Lewes: Unicorn.

Waterman, S. (1998) 'Carnivals for elites? The cultural politics of arts festivals', *Progress in Human Geography*, 22(1), pp. 54–74.

Winograd, T. (1996) *Bringing Design to Software*. New York, NY: ACM Press.
Woronkowicz, J. (2021) 'Arts, entrepreneurship, and innovation', *Journal of Cultural Economics*, 45, pp. 519–526.
Yeoman, I. (ed.) (2004) *Festival and Events Management: An International Arts and Culture Perspective*. London: Routledge.
YoHa. (2015) *Collecting Lost Species*. [Online] Available at: http://yoha.co.uk/lost (Accessed: 27 May 2025).
Fuller, M. (2010) 'Pits to Bits: Mattew Fuller - Interview with Graham Harwood', [Online]. YoHa. Available at: http://yoha.co.uk/pitstobits (accesed: 16 March 2025)

5

UN-DISCIPLINED AUDIENCES

5.1 Introduction

By bringing together concepts and practices from different disciplines to create new work, interdisciplinary cultural projects often offer audiences something rooted in a sense of the unknown. Working beyond the conventions of specific disciplines may challenge audiences' expectations, action and behaviour. While in some cases this is the logic behind why arts organisations develop interdisciplinary cultural productions, in other cases the audience or any specific idea of public engagement can also be a secondary or irrelevant concern. This chapter considers who interdisciplinary cultural projects are created for and examines how the organisations creating those projects conceive of their work in relation to their conception of the audiences, participants or publics who are likely to encounter or engage with them. To set the scene, we can turn to a short text written by composer John Cage (1967) titled, *Diary: Audience 1966*:

> Are we, so to speak, going south in the way we experience art? Audience participation? (Having nothing to do, we do it nonetheless; our biggest problem is finding scraps of time in which to get it done. Discovery. Awareness.) "Leave the beaten track. You'll see something never seen before." After the first performance of my piece for twelve radios, Virgil Thomson said, "You can't do that sort of thing and expect people to pay for it."...An audience can sit quietly or make noises. People can whisper, talk and even shout. An audience can sit still or it can get up and move around. People are people, not plants. "Do you love the audience?" Certainly we do. We show it by getting out of their way.

DOI: 10.4324/9781003514947-5

If interdisciplinary cultural production is the process of attempting to leave the beaten track, and ultimately benefiting by getting lost somewhere unknown, then this may be very uncomfortable for those participants or audiences involved. Perhaps akin to trying to communicate in a foreign language for the first time. How is this audience imagined by those that seek to communicate interdisciplinary cultural production to a public, however conceived, quantitatively or qualitatively? Does this kind of work demand anything from its audience, is that demand as high as Cage alludes? Are there ways those demands are mitigated by producers? Or is the spectacle of conjunction enough in its own right to pique the interest of the public. Do arts organisations think of audiences as plural complex people as Cage notes, or as 'disciplined' in their taste, knowledge and experience of the formalities of experiencing particular art forms. As sociologist Howard Becker (1982: 30) defines it, these are the conventions that shape how audiences understand and respond to creative work – 'the possibility of artistic experience arises from the existence of a body of conventions that an artist and an audience can refer to in making sense of the work'. The risk then is that if the work is not constructed and understood according to existing conventions – the audience may, in some way, be alienated.

What Cage also points to is the ambiguity about what we mean by the term 'audience'. Is this the quantitative, paying audience, those bodies in the room, or an imagined audience, conceived in terms of their relation to the art or knowledge form, an obstruction or abstract idea to be set aside? Or is the audience a feeling aesthetic subject? In the context of creating an interdisciplinary cultural project, how is the aesthetic and physical experience of the audience conceived as Cage notes, the breathing, moving living body of the audience. This slippage about what is understood as the audience in the context of interdisciplinary cultural production means it is worth critically considering the claims made in relation to the audience for this work by curators, producers and those running arts organisations that focus on interdisciplinary cultural production.

This chapter draws on insights from case studies already encountered in the book to understand how such organisations conceived of, imagined and sought to engage an audience in the process of creating interdisciplinary cultural projects. The aim is to set out a framework for considering the role, significance and promise of the audience in interdisciplinary cultural production more generally.

Here we will examine how the audience is implicated and imagined in the process of creating interdisciplinary cultural projects. This does not consider how audiences themselves interpret, understand and respond to such work. For the purpose of this chapter, we are paying attention to how arts organisations conceive their audiences, rather than how audiences themselves respond to such work. That would need to be the subject of further study as a means to respond to the 'invisibility' of audience responses for the researcher (Barker,

2021). But the base assumption here is that audiences are active and plural in how they interpret and respond (Livingstone, 2013).

It is worth noting from the outset that there have been attempts to classify the audience for interdisciplinary arts, or innovative practices that seek to challenge disciplinary conventions. If we look in the UK, where arts audience 'segmentation' approaches are common, and encouraged by public funders, such research shows audiences are not necessarily strongly defined by singular art form preferences, with many other factors shaping their engagement, with tastes crosscutting art forms. But this also shows that for 'innovative creative partnerships between artists of contrasting styles and backgrounds' – this is only likely an appeal to a narrow, elite group of cultural consumers. In the UK context this group is said to make up 5% of the UK population, those that are: 'prosperous, liberal, highly-educated urbanites, passionately interested in a very wide cultural spectrum, concentrated in large metropolitan areas' (Audience Agency, n.d.). This group might align with what Becker (1982: 28) calls 'adventurous... audiences' – those who are willing to embrace the ambiguity and discomfort of encounters outside of convention. For whom, the experience of convention breaking is an exciting and engaging end in itself. This may be a group who relish the risk and unconformity or breaking of conventions through conjunction that interdisciplinary cultural production may bring. This sets up a particularly problematic tension, as we saw in Chapter 3 and with examples like Manchester International Festival, public funders privilege innovation through such forms of 'innovative creative partnerships', but at the same time are required to be accountable by demonstrating how their investment reaches a broad spectrum of the population as a whole.

5.2 The audience as liability in interdisciplinary cultural production

If we assume introducing the public to a project involving unfamiliar disciplinary assemblages could be akin to working in a foreign language. Then it is clear that for cultural managers – this task may be nuanced and complex. As others have noted, 'interdisciplinary works often demand a high degree of openness to unfamiliarity from their audiences...bring them into a foreign territory where the traffic signs are unfamiliar and the road ahead potentially treacherous' (Cecchetto, 2008:xv). As a starting point it is worth setting out what the likely risks are for the audience in encountering interdisciplinary work. There are three specific liabilities that stand out. These liabilities represent potential critical points of failure in audience reception and engagement, each posing a distinct threat to the work's perceived value, and a challenge for cultural producers.

Firstly, that an audience is alienated by the seeming complexity, peculiarity, oddness or pointlessness of the conjunction. This initial friction arises when the audience struggles to identify the work's established genre or interpretive rules. If we follow Becker (1982), for the audiences to make sense of creative work, they must understand the specific disciplinary or art form conventions associated with it. When a work synthesises two or more unfamiliar or specialised fields, it effectively breaches this conventional contract, leaving the audience without a usable interpretive map. The risk then is that if the work is not constructed and understood according to existing conventions – the audience may, in some way, be alienated by uncertainty, lost in the unknown. This feeling of being lost results in reframing attention to the nature of the conjunction rather than the result; rather than engaging with the content, the audience is caught or stuck trying to understand the basic premise of the work. The ambiguous identity of the work makes it difficult for audiences to understand, and ultimately rather than perceive it as something innovative and valuable, it becomes devalued and difficult to engage with. This devaluation can manifest as outright rejection or a quiet dismissal of the work as 'pretentious' or 'inaccessible', where the audience projects the perceived failure of communication onto individual collaborators, or the commissioning organisation. The work's radical unfamiliarity thus undermines its potential for serious consideration, forcing audiences to want to retreat to familiar ground.

At the other end of that spectrum, is an audience patronised – where the conjunction is perceived as superficial, without sufficient disciplinary specificity or complexity, where an audience is assumed not to understand disciplinary conventions. This liability is a particular danger when interdisciplinary work seeks to be broadly accessible but sacrifices intellectual rigour in the process. The audience, especially those members who have more knowledge rooted in one of the contributing disciplines, recognise that the disciplinary elements are merely used subordinately, or as metaphorical or aesthetic decoration, rather than being deeply integrated into the work's structure or methodology. The consequence is that the work is dismissed as 'disciplinary tourism', with style over substance, failing to convince the informed audience of its seriousness or its innovative value, thereby collapsing the potential for critical engagement.

But there is also a third risk, an audience presented with interdisciplinarity as spectacle where conflict, connection or synthesis is presented as novelty or an end-in-itself in a superficial way. In this scenario, the work successfully grabs attention, but it does so for the wrong reasons. Here the conjunction itself is held up as the 'hook' for the audience, the element that should gain attention. The friction between disciplines is placed at the forefront of the work overshadowing the content it was meant to convey. As well as potentially reinforcing disciplinary distinctions in the process, rather than challenging them. Here the meaning or value, or innovation of a project for an audience might be overtaken by the spectacle of bringing disciplines into connection or conflict, where the bright glow of novelty overwhelms any detailed engagement with the work (Cecchetto, 2008). This can be driven by a desire to bring together 'distant' disciplines with a strong sense of juxtaposition. Where the unlikeliness of the pairings is foregrounded in the presentation and marketing of the work. This focus on novelty creates a short-term, sensational engagement that can fail to foster sustained critical dialogue. Once the initial surprise of the unusual combination wears off, the work has little inherent substance left to hold attention, limiting its capacity to contribute meaningful insight or innovation.

5.3 The significance of the audience to interdisciplinary cultural producers

Given these inherent complexities and the associated liabilities involved in engaging audiences with interdisciplinary cultural projects, what level of significance do arts organisations actually place on the audience? The case studies in this book clearly demonstrate a spectrum of importance placed on the audience in the creation and presentation of new work.

At one end, this spectrum ranges from the audience being viewed as entirely insignificant or an intentional afterthought. In the latter, there is either no or very limited consideration of the audience during the primary stages of development and production of new work. This distancing from the audience is often emphasised by organisations that privilege working in highly experimental or research-based contexts. In these 'residency,' 'seeding,' or 'incubating' models, the focus is entirely on the generation of new work, new ideas, new approaches, or on developing the knowledge and skills of individual practitioners. Presenting this to an audience is considered a secondary concern. Even factoring in an audience and their potential response is sometimes viewed as a distraction or a form of instrumentalisation that might, in some way, compromise or impinge upon the freedom of the creative collaborative process.

Organisations such as the Centre for The Less Good Idea in Johannesburg, prioritised the collaborative process in the studio, rather than in front of an audience. Where if work emerged from this that had a life beyond, that was a welcome but additional benefit to the activity undertaken in the studio. The Centre deployed a 'lightness of being' towards the final creation and its presentation in front of an audience (Lace, 2025). However, even when presenting new, untested work, these organisations are keenly aware of the audience's liabilities – the challenges and risks they face in encountering novel, potentially incomplete productions. This awareness is sometimes directly communicated to the audience as a means to mitigate these liabilities and reframe the audience's relationship to the work. At the Centre for The Less Good Idea, this communication specifically conveyed that what the audience was encountering was 'raw,' 'uncooked,' and 'still being assembled'. Importantly, this reframing positioned the audience as being in a privileged position of seeing a work for the first time. Yet, with that privilege came a responsibility: to understand and appreciate the vulnerability of those presenting new work. To enable this, the audience needed to be 'reset' to understand that the work was being tested, and that their normal modes of critical judgement and evaluation could be suspended in this context. The aim was for the audience to contribute to a safe atmosphere of energy and space, playing a role in creating a safe space for experimentation to play out. This required the audience to engage in a particular kind of active work: not 'sitting back' expecting to be entertained, but 'sitting forward' – to see themselves as part of the process of generating this new work (Lace, 2025).

Mediale, based in the UK, was another organisation that focused on artists developing their practices in relation to other disciplines, primarily new technology. In these contexts, the audience was not necessarily an insignificant consideration, but rather they are often considered only after the development of new practices has been established with artists and their collaborators. Such organisations, which function as 'incubators' for new work, do not take authorship of the resulting projects. The work created belongs to those who developed it, who are then free to take that work out into the world, grow it further, and present it to new audiences as they wish.

Then there are specific contexts where the audience is viewed as a meaningful, practical component of an interdisciplinary cultural project – a shaping factor in the working process. This can manifest through a service-based mode of interdisciplinarity, where the combination of disciplinary practices is deployed to solve specific problems related to how audience experience, knowledge, or understanding is conceived. In this model, one discipline works with or co-opts the skills, knowledge and experience of another discipline to realise a project or solve a specific problem in relation to the audience. But it can also operate in a more open and non-hierarchical way, through *co-author/co-production* dynamics. This was exemplified by the collaborations between artist Katie Paterson and architectural practice Zeller & Moye. In their co-authored projects, they worked together to create spatial and conceptual environments that sought to offer a specific and determined experience for an imagined audience. Working through what this aesthetic and sensorial experience would be for the audience was central to the collaboration between the different practitioners.

At the opposite end of the spectrum are contexts where participation from those outside the project (though not necessarily always conceived as an 'audience') is fundamental to the deployed process of interdisciplinary cultural production. This model begins with engagement or collaboration with specific social groups, communities, or places, and working with them becomes the justification or rationale for the project. For AfroAsia working in the South Korean city of Dongducheon, the specific driving impetus for their work was the intersection of three specific social groups: immigrant African communities, the local Korean population and US service personnel stationed in the city. While these interconnecting local communities defined the core activity of AfroAsia, the organisation also sought to connect their work and present it within the international art world. The creation of such projects can also be about demonstrating the importance of their subject, serving as a mode of advocacy for a particular type of practice, a specific social issue or group. For AfroAsia, while rooted in a specific urban context, a wider strategic desire was fundamental to their working ethos which was to seek to challenge attitudes towards immigration in South Korea.

For Arts Catalyst, based in the UK, this commitment to placing specific social groups at the centre of their interdisciplinary work also meant seeking to work with a particular type of artist or collaborator who understood their ethos towards developing and responding to this situated knowledge. Their approach dictated that 'the audience, the engagement, the participation is not... an afterthought or something that [the artist] needs to figure out once they've developed the project... that has [to be] taken into consideration from day one'. This approach, particularly in long-term projects, also allowed for openness and growth, where relationships and strong ties could be established over time between participants and those working for the organisation itself (Lastra and Santomauro, 2025).

In a different context, an imaginary of the 'quantitative audience' can dominate and fundamentally shape how projects are produced. This is often the case where funders or the organisations they support want to engage the audience at scale because this scale offers accountability for their investment. This is supported by an evaluative framework where the return on investment is measured by the number of people who encounter it (regardless of how deep that encounter is). This framework can influence what work is commissioned and how it is presented, often prioritising projects that can be seen or encountered by the largest number of people. This, in turn, is seen to offer a strong sense of accountability or value for money, regardless of the qualitative experience of the audience.

We can also place the audience as a central material component in interdisciplinary projects. Consider artist Miranda July and writer and coder Paul Ford's contribution to Rhizome's *Seven on Seven* in 2016. After their 24-hour period of collaboration, they presented a fictional narrative performance during the conference, featuring user-generated visuals and screenshots drawn from social media and the internet. The story unfolded in the second person, with July and Ford taking turns to pronounce new details in the form, 'you did' etc. As the performance developed, the audience realised that the material being presented was not fabricated but rather drawn directly from the digital world of those sitting in the room. The story was a personal chronology of the attendees' lives, featuring materials connected to their birth, right through to themes of death and goodbyes.

The material was all pulled from their social media presence after July requested the guest list from Rhizome in advance. Ford built an aggregating search tool, and he and July worked with journalist Starlee Kine to identify and sort material for the narrative from the mass of data they could extract. The work focused on the story that could be told from publicly available data, exploring themes of visibility, vanity, and narrative construction through juxtaposition, while implicitly raising open questions about the ethics of aggregating and using personal data in the creation of the performance. However, this ethical question did not seem to unduly trouble the audience. As one reviewer present in the room put it, 'based on the appreciative murmurs of recognition, it seemed that people were happy to be interpellated back to themselves, unperturbed by the secret scrutinizing' (Goodman, 2016).

Central to all of these modes is how an idea of an audience as a social group is imagined and established through production processes. To follow cultural theorist Raymond Williams' (2015: 132-3) adage 'there are in fact no masses; there are only ways of seeing people as masses'. From this perspective it is important that we consider how the audience is imagined and utilised for specific means. Doing so will not only help us understand the logic driving interdisciplinary cultural production in relation to the audience, but also help us understand the promises these formulas make in seeking to engage, influence, and in some cases, exploit those audiences.

It is also important to remember that, in this context, imagining audiences is a form of 'boundary work' (Rogers et al, 2021). Thinking about who might be included as a possible audience or set of participants for a project is also, by its very nature, a latent process of imagining who might be excluded. The imagined audiences for interdisciplinary cultural production come into play because audiences and the public offer legitimacy to such activities, and this conceptualisation is part of the process of how the boundaries and narratives around particular art forms are formed and maintained.

When considering how these narratives are constructed and how such groups are conceived, it is also worth acknowledging, as Livingstone (2005) does, that there can be a tendency in such discourses for the concept of the 'audience' to be trivialised as passive and individualised, while notions of 'publics' are more actively valued, seen as critically engaged and of political significance. The key distinction here is between the idea of a public, that is knowing, thinking and influential, and the mass or crowd, something more fluid that experiences, watches and shares, but at some form of distance. Beyond these are mass consumers who are individualised, and driven by tastes, preferences and base motivations.

In relation to how the potential audience is imagined for interdisciplinary cultural projects, there are three underpinning logics or, as I will define them here, 'promises' that characterise this practice that are important to highlight. These promises may not always be entirely distinct and may overlap to different degrees in individual projects. The purpose here is not only to set out how audiences are conceived by those creating interdisciplinary cultural projects, but also how an imagined audience is implicated in that creative process. Defining these approaches as promises is done to emphasise the unknown or speculative nature of this kind of work, but also to acknowledge the risks or dangers inherent in working through these approaches. The novelty or spectacle of conjunction, or the rhetoric of integration, can make promises that are rarely kept or fully realised in practice. These promises can very broadly be defined into three categories, the promise of eliminating, educating and developing the audience.

5.4 The promise of eliminating the audience

The first promise is that by working through an interdisciplinary method, modes of cultural production can break down barriers, or erode the conventional separation between artists and audiences in cultural production. Here we can borrow a provocation from artist Allan Kaprow. In the outline of principles for his happenings and assemblages, he articulated the ultimate objective was the complete elimination of the audience itself (Kaprow in Bishop, 2006: 103). This was not merely a means to minimise distance, but to dissolve the very categories that define the relationship. Interdisciplinary production has historically served as a critical pathway toward achieving this kind of dissolution, the breakdown of the asymmetric power relations that typically govern the dynamic between producers and consumers. The adoption of interdisciplinary approaches, however, often motivates and facilitates the creation of cultural practices that deliberately seek to challenge this. This might be through work that is participatory or interactive, demanding physical or intellectual contributions from participants. It might be multi and intermedia contexts, where the assemblages of mediums necessitate diverse contributions. It might be in contexts that are socially engaged, where the interdisciplinary cultural work is embedded in and responsive to specific communities. It might be in new media, cybernetic or networked contexts where technology is used to create feedback loops and decentralised structures. In all these forms, the emphasis is placed on two-way interchanges and interconnections over one-way transmission. The fundamental promise of these practices lies in their capacity for the narrowing or outright eradication of distance between the conventional audience member and the performer/artist.

There is a correlation between such art and cultural practices and the adoption of interdisciplinary methods. This link stems from a core shared motivation: the innate impulse in both to challenge the authority of singular authorship. This is the case in models of interdisciplinary cultural production that privilege *co-author / co-production* dynamics. The notion of a sole, authoritative creator, can be contested within interdisciplinary projects. This collaborative structure directly contests the authority of the singular voice, replacing it with a collective, shared process of discovery and making.

One promise made in these contexts is that in dissolving the (assumed passive receiving) audience, greater agency is given to the role of participant or collaborator. This is frequently operationalised as a designated community (quite often problematically unified) that is invited to contribute to or engage with the interdisciplinary project. This process involves actively recruiting a group that is typically considered outside the specific cultural production practices being deployed, a group conventionally held at a distance, and inviting them to collaborate directly in the creation of the project or artwork. Their very 'outsideness' or external perspective to the specific disciplines involved is often the source of their value to the project. This is particularly salient in a political sense, as many such projects explicitly seek to engage marginalised or disenfranchised groups. By centring the perspectives and contributions of those traditionally excluded from cultural authority, the interdisciplinary work attempts to inject new forms of knowledge and challenge established conventions.

It is, however, important to approach these participatory claims with critical caution. As art historian and curator Miwon Kwon (2002: 6) showed, such practices, despite their transformative aims, carry inherent risks. Without careful practical consideration, they can inadvertently exacerbate or entrench uneven power relations (and disciplinary distinctions), where the artist/institution still dictates the terms of engagement. They can remarginalise or even colonise already disenfranchised groups, by using their stories or experiences without yielding power or authorship. They can mythify artistic or creative processes, making collaboration seem inherently progressive when its outcomes may be superficial, especially if the collaboration fails to generate lasting, substantive change beyond the life of the project. Therefore, while interdisciplinary cultural production promises shared authorship through the elevation of the audience/community to a collaborator, the actual dismantling of power asymmetry depends on the ethical and structural integrity of the project's design.

For interdisciplinary cultural organisations that operate within this mode of shared authorship and social engagement, achieving their goals requires moving beyond superficial collaboration. These organisations must commit to nuanced and skilful engagement, dialogue and interaction throughout the entire process of co-production. The inherent complexity and nuance of integrating non-conventional voices, particularly those from external communities, must be explicitly acknowledged and managed. Consequently, successful efforts often necessitate the formation of long-term relationships rather than short-term, project-based interventions. This sustained commitment is important to establishing the trust and deep understanding required to genuinely contest power dynamics and avoid tokenism and re-marginalisation. This is something that was clearly playing out in practice in work of both Arts Catalyst and AfroAsia. Where the organisations operated as intermediaries between both disciplines and geographic communities. Seeking to understand and work with those communities over long periods of time, allowed them to move beyond a reductionist view of those communities as singular entities, into more complex internally diverse formations, fractured by class, ethnicity, geopolitics and gender.

A distinct challenge arises for agency or portfolio interdisciplinary producers, working under a project-to-project basis. In this context, the audience/community does not necessarily maintain a direct, continuous relationship with the central organisation itself, but rather connects solely through the specific, episodic projects the organisation produces. In effect, a distinct audience/community must be built anew for each venture. While this functional ephemerality provides a degree of organisational freedom, as there are fewer expectations or market demands connected to their past activity, it simultaneously creates significant challenges. It necessitates the continuous creation of new relationships through project-specific communication strategies and unique modes of dissemination for each output to be effective and achieve its intended objectives.

5.5 The promise of educating the audience

The second promise of interdisciplinary cultural production relates to its educational or pedagogical value in relation to a particular public. This value is fundamentally rooted in the promise of utility, where interdisciplinary work is mobilised as a functional instrument for knowledge transfer. This educational drive can manifest as a highly instrumentalised and often asymmetrical process (or, in more ideal scenarios, a reciprocal one).

In this instrumentalised model, a discipline with resources (Discipline X) adopts or utilises practices from a less-resourced discipline (Discipline Y) as a communicative medium. The goal is to teach an audience, typically one already familiar with Discipline Y, about the concepts, findings, or importance of Discipline X. The foundation of this approach is often a perceived knowledge deficit or a desire for broader reach within the participating disciplines in relation to a public audience. This dynamic is visible in the 'art-science complex' (Salter, 2021), where scientific bodies use the arts to bridge a perceived gap between specialised knowledge and public understanding. This conceptualisation of the audience echoes Kwon's (2002: 81) critique, where a specific community is 'conceived as an inadequately prepared audience' and is therefore deemed to be in need of engagement. A need that an interdisciplinary mode of cultural production can be tasked with fulfilling.

As Barry and Born (2013) have demonstrated through their analysis of Wellcome Trust-funded interdisciplinary cultural projects in the UK, specifically those linked to 'public understanding of science', art and science collaborations have been frequently and explicitly designed as a pragmatic instrument for communicating scientific findings and complex concepts. Here the stated objective is to successfully engage a 'new,' 'non-science' audience. Operating as a mode of broadcasting scientific knowledge, these projects exist as a deliberate addition to more conventional means of media communication, television, radio and publications, and have been seen to function essentially as another communication tool.

Crucially, these collaborations are generally one-sided in their operation. They typically function through a subordination-service mode under the logic of accountability (Barry and Born, 2013). This dynamic is often mirrored by the funding relationship, where the project is underwritten by the discipline, such as a science, that seeks to educate the audience primarily associated with the other discipline, an art form. The asymmetry of power inherent in this model risks reducing the artistic practice to a mere delivery mechanism, prioritising the educational mandate over genuine disciplinary exchange.

In practice, this focus on audience engagement, education and communication through interdisciplinary cultural production may inadvertently exacerbate existing disciplinary distinctions rather than challenge them. This tension is often rooted in the contrasting epistemologies and priorities of the participating fields. Where artistic and cultural production may focus on intuition, and practitioners are comfortable with forms of meaning rooted in ambiguity, uncertainty and complexity, and prioritise emotional resonance, aesthetic experience, individual expression and the unspoken. Compared to normative science communication, which more fundamentally seeks clarity, definitive evidenced-based positions and the systematic reduction of uncertainty (Nowotny, 2003).

Complicating this further is a situation as Salter (2021) notes, where the arts are simultaneously under significant external pressure to appear 'useful' – socially, economically, and environmentally – to public funders, policy makers and the wider society. This internal and external demand for accountability also drives this promise, creating a context where interdisciplinary relations are valued precisely for their capacity to connect with other disciplines. This may involve connecting with groups within the arts that already have strong audience relationships, but also, in a wider sense, with powerful external partners who can validate the broader social relevance of the arts.

In practice, the operational realities of many interdisciplinary arts organisations in contexts like the UK suggest a strategic manoeuvring through these funding pressures. As observed with agency or portfolio producers and adjunct projects, these organisations often utilise instrumentalised funding to their own ends. They may use such resources to facilitate experimentation in a safe, adjunct space separate from their core work (as seen with organisations like the Royal Shakespeare Company or the Serpentine Gallery). Alternatively, organisations like Arts Catalyst demonstrate a strategy of clustering funding from different sources into a single large-scale project. This approach dilutes the requirements of any single funding stream, enabling the organisation to fulfil external objectives while simultaneously pursuing the artistic experimentation and core creative agenda they may be more fundamentally interested in.

It is valuable to recognise that the parameters of specific collaborations can qualify these dynamics. Longer-term, sustained collaboration that shares resources and commits to greater depth of engagement is less likely to be narrowly focused on short-term, quantitative audience engagement metrics. Such relationships are more likely to enable deeper reflection on the qualitative experiences of those who encounter the work, moving beyond a simple transfer of facts. While the inherent pedagogical value of interdisciplinary collaboration should not be discounted, in a practical sense, the design and development of interdisciplinary cultural projects should actively strive to create space for modes of knowledge exchange that are 'mutually enhancing' (Muller et al, 2020). This requires a foundational commitment to curiosity and a genuine openness to exchanging, challenging and contesting the disciplinary thinking and practices brought to the collaboration by all partners.

5.6 The promise of developing the audience

The final promise highlighted here moves beyond audience agency and audience knowledge and understanding to focus on audience composition. In this context, interdisciplinary cultural production is strategically deployed, guided by the logic of audience development. This means interdisciplinary methods are used as tools to create new audiences or to intentionally change the composition of existing ones in terms of demographics, behaviours, attitudes and motivations. More simply, the creative output seeks to develop new audiences, transform the existing audience, or deepen their engagement. Crucially, considering audience development in this context is not merely a practice of arts or culture marketing; rather, it engages a much wider set of strategic questions regarding how arts and cultural organisations orient themselves toward the public, often underpinned by mandates related to cultural policy and cultural democracy (Hadley, 2021).

The motivation for arts and cultural organisations to actively seek audience change often stems from two primary sources. First, there may be internal or external criticism leveled against their narrow focus on single disciplines or art forms. This narrowness is often perpetuated by rigid institutional structures that emphasise excessive specialisation or niche activity, resulting in an isolated, narrow audience group, often perceived as elite or privileged. Second, the motivation may be based on an observable stagnation or decline in the audiences associated with specific disciplines. Regardless of whether the criticism is internal or external, the creation of interdisciplinary projects frequently emerges as a necessary response to these pressures, a strategy to reach or connect with new audiences.

Arts organisations typically employ four core variables to define and segment existing and potential audiences: taste and art form preferences; demographic groupings (e.g., age, geography, education level, socio-economic status); behaviour (e.g., attendance or engagement frequency) and attitudes and motivations (the primary driving forces behind participation). Leveraging interdisciplinary methods serves as a strategic route to attempt to alter any of these established relationships with potential audiences.

Similarly, audience development can drive the curatorial framing of interdisciplinary projects themselves, particularly in situations where audiences and art forms are perceived to be in a bounded alignment. Curator Hans Ulrich Obrist (2015: 148) illustrates this problem: 'Normally, when you invite somebody from the architecture world to give a talk, it's mostly the architecture crowd that attends; when you invite somebody from the art world, the art-world types attend. Each speaker attracts a particular audience to his or her field of interest, yet there's little crossover.'

Obrist offered this observation as justification for creating discursive platforms that feature multiple divergent disciplinary speakers such as his Marathons at the Serpentine Gallery and the talks programmes of the Shanghai Project. The underlying rationale is that such platforms lower the barrier to entry, allowing audiences to encounter ideas from other disciplines through chance rather than necessarily conscious choice. This approach circumvents the conventional expectations associated with specific disciplines, creating a level platform for various fields and their respective audiences to meet. This mechanism aims for a form of audience aggregation, bringing together individuals with divergent interests. However, this model ultimately places the emphasis and demand on the audience to perform the interdisciplinary labour – the cognitive synthesis required to bring disparate disciplines together and construct meaning. Furthermore, such approaches may prove to be reductive rather than cumulative (merely combining one art form's audience with another). As they may in actuality only appeal to a narrow subset of these groups: the adventurous audiences, who are themselves directly interested in interdisciplinarity or comfortable with the confluence of different disciplinary knowledge forms in unusual settings.

There are generally considered three routes to expanding the audience (McCarthy and Jinnett, 2001). Increasing the existing audience, which involves an organisation seeking to attract a greater number of their normative audience, the group that already is most likely to engage with their work, sharing similar demographics, tastes, behaviours and motivations. Deepening engagement with the existing or normative audience by increasing their level or frequency of participation. And diversifying the audience, which means attracting entirely new groups outside of the existing, normative audience in terms of demographics, tastes, behaviours and motivations.

Interdisciplinary cultural production is most often located within this third route, the desire or need to diversify. However, all three modes of audience development carry inherent risks for interdisciplinary cultural production, particularly concerning the maintenance of the relationship with the existing or normative audience. This tension is most pronounced when interdisciplinary work challenges the very conventions and aesthetic rules that make the normative audience's experience understandable and meaningful.

It is this third mode of audience development, oriented toward diversification, where the logic and promise of innovation most clearly intersects with audience development goals. This form of audience development has itself been formally considered a type of innovation for arts and cultural organisations (Bakhshi and Throsby, 2013: 75). The relationship between innovation, audience development and interdisciplinary cultural production was central to the early programming of the Manchester International Festival (MIF). From 2007 MIF deployed large-scale collaborations between high-profile, contrasting cultural institutions (encompassing both high art and popular forms) as a dual mechanism: a means to achieve artistic innovation, and a means to engage a diverse audience whose cultural interests spanned multiple art forms. This strategy, in turn, supported the festival's accountability to the city council, as it demonstrably sought to offer something to a broad demographic of the city's population without succumbing to the siloing of perceived groups within cultural hierarchies.

Audience development manifests differently depending on how it relates to an organisation's core activities. For organisations with adjunct interdisciplinary projects,audience development is often a central motivator, a way of testing or building new audience relationships beyond those normally associated with the organisation. This allows the organisation to keep the experimental practice at a safe distance, ensuring the conventional audience is not confused or alienated. Agency or portfolio interdisciplinary producers do not generally possess their 'own' audience. They are tasked with constantly reinventing relationships with new audiences for every project, making audience development a task of continuous reinvention within new contexts. This is something that they must become expert at, as they cannot rely on an established audience engaging with their work. Organisations where interdisciplinarity is a core programming or curatorial concern are likely already engaged with the aforementioned 'adventurous audience'. However, their legitimacy often requires a constant appeal to innovation, which makes organisational growth, maturation, and change a significant challenge. The inherent risk is that if they become too conventional, this adventurous audience may disengage. Conversely, because this audience group is relatively niche, such organisations may face perpetual pressure from public funders to diversify their audience and make their work more relevant to wider groups, which creates a fundamental tension in how they operate in practice.

5.7 Conclusion

The very nature of interdisciplinary cultural production, which inherently seeks to venture into the unknown and challenge established art form conventions, creates a core tension: the potential discomfort and alienation this causes for the audience, set against the organisation's crucial need to justify and value that public engagement. This process is inherently risky for organisations, as audiences may receive interdisciplinary productions in ways that result in their alienation due to perceived complexity, their feeling of being patronised by superficial execution, or the reduction of their encounter to mere spectacle.

The case studies examined in this book reveal that producers' consideration of the audience spans a wide spectrum, influencing the work's development and presentation. This range extends from treating the audience as insignificant or a purposeful afterthought, particularly in highly experimental practices, to viewing them as a meaningful component of the interdisciplinary process in service or co-production models. At the far end of the spectrum, the audience, or a specific social group, becomes fundamental and the core justification for the interdisciplinary conjunction itself. Across this spectrum, the connection between audience and interdisciplinary cultural production is characterised by the conceptual promises of eliminating, educating, or developing that audience.

As was considered in relation to the UK, operating in contexts where public accountability is central, the actual audience for innovative creative partnerships is often a narrow, elite group: the adventurous audience who embraces ambiguity and convention-breaking for its own sake. This reality creates a problematic tension for publicly funded organisations, which must balance the pursuit of innovation with the mandate to demonstrate broad public relevance.

To successfully meet the promises of interdisciplinary cultural production and overcome its risks, producers must approach the audience as an active and heterogeneous construct. Organisations must acknowledge that audiences are plural and constantly changing over time. There must be a continual critical awareness of the potential to perceive certain groups as inadequately prepared, coupled with a genuine recognition of individuals' diverse backgrounds and capacity. As Cage (1967) reminded us, 'People are people, not plants'. Furthermore, it is important to recognise that some audiences actively seek the experience of entering a 'foreign territory' and are excited by the possibility of innovation, confluence or friction in these modes. A key role for arts organisations, therefore, is to expand this sense of open curiosity, ensuring audiences feel empowered rather than alienated when encountering the unconventional, while still avoiding the unrealistic expectation that the audience should be endlessly curious, and dismissing them when they are not.

Bibliography

Audience Agency. (n. d.) *Audience Spectrum: Metro-Culturals*. Available at: https://audiencespectrum.org/en/segments/metroculturals?tab=sectors (Accessed: 29 August 2025).

Augsburg, T. (2017) 'Interdisciplinary arts', in Frodeman, R., Klein, J.T. and Pacheco, R.C.S. (eds.) *The Oxford Handbook of Interdisciplinarity*. 2nd edn. Oxford: Oxford University Press, pp. 131–143.

Bakhshi, H. and Throsby, D. (2013) *A Manifesto for the Creative Economy*. London: Nesta Operating Company.

Barker, M. (2021) 'The concept of "engagement": A cautious manifesto', *Participations: Journal of Audience & Reception Studies*, 18(1), pp. 177–205.

Barry, A. and Born, G. (eds.) (2013) *Interdisciplinarity: Reconfigurations of the Social and Natural Sciences*. Abingdon: Routledge.

Becker, H. (1982) *Art Worlds*. Berkeley: University of California Press.

Bishop, C. (2006) 'The social turn: Collaboration and its discontents', *Artforum*, 44(6), pp. 178–183.

Bishop, C. (2012) *Artificial Hells: Participatory Art and the Politics of Spectatorship*. London: Verso.

Cage, J. (1967) *A Year from Monday: New Lectures and Writings*. Middletown, CT: Wesleyan University Press.

Cecchetto, D., Cuthbert, N., Lassonde, J. and Robinson, D. (eds.) (2008) *Collision: Interarts Practice and Research*. Cambridge: Cambridge Scholars Publishing.

Goodman, M.S. (2016) 'Seven on seven', *Frieze*, 24 May. Available at: www.frieze.com/article/seven-seven (Accessed: 27 May 2025).

Hadley, S. (2021) *Audience Development and Cultural Policy*. Dordrecht: Springer International Publishing AG. Available at: http://ebookcentral.proquest.com/lib/york-ebooks/detail.action?docID=6522069 (Accessed: 2 November 2025).

Kaprow, A. (1966) 'Notes on the elimination of the audience', in Bishop, C. (ed.) (2006) *Participation*. London: Whitechapel, pp. 101–104.

Kwon, M. (2002) *One Place after Another: Site-Specific Art and Locational Identity*. Cambridge, MA: The MIT Press.

Lace, B. (2025) *Interview with Bronwyn Lace, Co-founder & Director, The Centre for the Less Good Idea*. Interviewed by Peter Merrington [Zoom], 18 March.

Lastra, C. and Santomauro, A. (2025) *Interview with Claudia Lastra, CEO and Anna Santomauro, Head of Programme, Arts Catalyst*. Interviewed by Peter Merrington [In person], 6 February.

Livingstone, S. (2005) 'On the relation between audiences and publics', in Livingstone, S. (ed.) *Audiences and Publics: When Cultural Engagement Matters for the Public Sphere*. Bristol: Intellect Books, pp. 17–41.

Livingstone, S. (2013) 'The participation paradigm in audience research', *Communications Review*, 16(1–2), pp. 21–30. https://doi.org/10.1080/10714421.2013.757174.

McCarthy, K.F. and Jinnett, K. (2001) *A New Framework for Building Participation in the Arts.* Santa Monica, CA: Rand Corporation. Available at: www.rand.org/content/dam/rand/pubs/monograph_reports/2005/MR1323.pdf (Accessed: 2 November 2025).

Muller, L., Froggett, L. and Bennett, J. (2020) 'Emergent knowledge in the third space of art-science', *Leonardo*, 53(3), pp. 321–326.

Nowotny, H. (2003) 'Wish fulfillment and its discontents', *EMBO Reports*, 4(10), pp. 917–920.https://doi.org/10.1038/sj.embor.embor954.

Obrist, H.U. (2015) *Ways of Curating.* London: Penguin.

Packer, R. and Jordan, K. (eds.) (2001) *Multimedia: From Wagner to Virtual Reality.* New York: Norton.

Salter, C. (2021) 'The art–science complex', in Rogers, H.S., Halpern, M.K., Hannah, D. and de Ridder-Vignone, K. (eds.) *Routledge Handbook of Art, Science, and Technology Studies.* Abingdon: Routledge, pp. 204–233.

Santos, L. (2018) *Multidisciplinarity: Projects for Social Change in Art and Culture.* London: Routledge.

Thompson Klein, J. and Philipp, T. (2023) 'Interdisciplinarity', in Philipp, T. and Schmohl, T. (eds.) *Handbook Transdisciplinary Learning.* Bielefeld: transcript Verlag. https://doi.org/10.1515/9783839463475.

Triscott, N. and Santomauro, A. (2021) 'Transdisciplinary co-inquiry as curatorial methodology: From the Canadian Arctic to the Calder Valley, Yorkshire', in Rogers, H.S., Halpern, M.K., Hannah, D. and de Ridder-Vignone, K. (eds.) *Routledge Handbook of Art, Science, and Technology Studies.* Abingdon: Routledge.

Williams, R. (2015) *Culture and Society: Coleridge to Orwell.* London: Vintage Digital.

6

CONCLUSION

Creating and holding space

Hopefully one of the clear messages of this book is that interdisciplinary cultural production can be more complex than it might perhaps appear. Or require greater dexterity and skill from cultural managers and producers to realise in practice than is often acknowledged or understood. There is a necessary rigour to the practice that can often be taken for granted. But the other message of this book is that such rigour can be developed through understanding examples and practice – through action, through experimentation and trying it out. Yet given the inherent risks, the challenges, pitfalls and the persistent threat of failure that overhangs interdisciplinary cultural production as I have set out in the preceding chapters, it is also perhaps worth asking the question why undertake it at all when greater specialisation and disciplinary entrenchment offers its own kind of security.

The cover image for this book is a photograph of an artwork by the London-based Argentine artist Amalia Pica. It is titled *Venn Diagrams (under the spotlight)* and was first exhibited at the 54th Venice Biennale in 2011. The work is created by two spotlights, each with different colour gels that shine bright, well-defined circles onto the opposing wall. But the work is interactive: in addition to the spotlights, there are motion sensors (MoMA, 2025). The spotlights are only illuminated as visitors approach, such that two or more people are required to approach the light to illuminate them both and create the interaction of the beams of light on the opposite wall, defining the pattern of a typical Venn diagram, with the synthesis of the two original colours generating a new colour between them on the wall. Beyond the obvious visual metaphor, the work also points to something more fundamental in how it is contextualised by the arts as it is presented in the gallery. Pica situates the work against action undertaken during the military dictatorship of Argentina

DOI: 10.4324/9781003514947-6

(1976–83) to repress collective organisation and political resistance. Notably, she presents the work alongside a textual description which sets out a memory that Venn diagrams were not taught in schools during this repressive period because of their association with models of collaboration (Fiske, 2013). While the work is a mediation of the relationship between textual historical meaning and objectives and forms, it powerfully illustrates that conjunction and collaboration that seeks to challenge and transgress inclusions and exclusions is not a neutral practice, nor can it be taken for granted as a mode of experimentation that needs support to be enabled. Where interdisciplinarity enters into and challenges modes of cultural production, it highlights, either implicitly or explicitly, that cultural production is always political.

For arts and cultural managers entering the territory of interdisciplinary cultural production there are several key considerations to take from this book. Acknowledging disciplinarity and working through interdisciplinarity is often conditional on understanding disciplinarity more generally. Cultural production that seeks to be interdisciplinary must in some sense be critically committed to engaging with and understanding the forms which it seeks to bring into confluence or conflict. Fundamental to this is seeking to understand the promise that interdisciplinary methods offer in the context or situation in which they are being presented or promoted. Here the policy and funding context can significantly shape the promise and form of interdisciplinary cultural projects. As was clear in the two public artworks created by artist Katie Paterson and architects Zeller & Moye, interdisciplinary collaboration in major public art commissions can function as a powerful strategic tool for the expression of organisational and civic identity, driven by external legislative and financial requirements, as much as artistic and creative desires to create inspirational and thought-provoking forms. These promises are multifaceted and entangled but range from the radical transformation of conventional forms to the promise of utility, that can also be derived from a logic of accountability (Barry and Born, 2013) – where interdisciplinarity is strategically deployed to particular ends – be they social, political, or economic. The challenge for cultural managers and producers is to acknowledge this and understand how to work within or against these constraints to navigate the risks of instrumentalisation driven by clear asymmetric power relations. Then there is the promise of innovation. The promise of innovation offers to yield new possibilities, often by applying the artist's seemingly unique way of 'seeing differently' to technological or social contexts. Such a promise is often overestimated, and innovation is frequently entwined with questions of accountability, as public funding pressures arts organisations to seek new income streams and audience growth or diversification. Attention also needs to be paid to the way interdisciplinary cultural projects are framed and described. In practice, such promises are also shaped by how interdisciplinary cultural projects are conceived in terms of scale, metaphor and form. Critically considering these frames aims to help producers assess and understand a project's underlying assumptions and desired outcome. Doing so can avoid an oversimplification of practical realities, creating or reinforcing oppositional binaries, or generating spectacle. Part of the challenge is recognising fields are already fragmented. While metaphors are beneficial for creating a shared, accessible vocabulary for collaborators and audiences, over-reliance can obscure, oversimplify, or sensationalise the genuine complexity, conflict and promise of the work. Understanding the modes of interdisciplinarity as integrative, subordinate and antagonistic (Barry and Born, 2013), as well as the authorship/production dynamics at play within interdisciplinary cultural production, enables a valuable set of insights into the practical and operational reality of such projects.

While I have identified three key organisational modes of interdisciplinary cultural projects in the UK, they are likely to be more widely applicable. Interdisciplinarity, when adopted as a central programming or curatorial concern by arts organisations, festivals and arts centres, involves deliberately placing the integration of various disciplines and art forms at the core of operations. This approach is characterised by commissioning, presenting and supporting new, experimental, collaborative work that challenges conventional disciplinary boundaries but requires specific and determined organisational and artistic leadership to overcome the default tendency towards conventional, siloed programming structures. Institutional structures and architectural design play an important role as a means to encourage innovation, collaboration and public engagement outside of established cultural norms, though its implementation can be complex, costly and financially risky – particularly with regard to audience demands. By contrast, interdisciplinarity as an adjunct practice offers some protection from these risks. This is where arts organisations, primarily rooted in a single discipline, engage in time-limited, project-based experimentation that runs alongside their core programming. This approach serves multiple strategic goals, including exploring innovation, diversifying participation, meeting social objectives and raising funds from non-traditional academic or corporate sources. By treating interdisciplinary work as a peripheral activity, or one of proximity rather than organisational synthesis, organisations create a low-stakes environment to test convention-breaking ideas, effectively mitigating the potential risks to their core reputation while still allowing them to foster institutional connections and credit for successful ventures. The agency or portfolio interdisciplinary producer is an organisation, often a small, non-profit specialist, that does not run a venue or festival but focuses on developing and facilitating complex interdisciplinary projects by working with both arts and non-arts partners. Their primary value is their expertise as a mediator or broker, able to translate artistic ideas into the language of different disciplines, funders and partners to ensure a project's intellectual, aesthetic, financial, or logistical success. These agencies pride themselves on a specific kind of rigour in managing the nuances of collaboration, understanding the needs of diverse artists, and expertly navigating the financial precarity of project-by-project funding, often around thematic specialisms such as science, ecology, or technology.

The book has also sought to show how festivals as a mode of cultural organisation are particularly important sites for the creation and presentation of interdisciplinary cultural production. As a temporary, high-intensity cultural format, festivals can make interconnected promises in relation to innovation, subversion and symbolic capital. The festival's inherent appeal to novelty and the 'here and now' offers a signal of futurity. As with the post-independence Pan-African cultural festivals (FESMAN, PANAF, Festac '77), the festivals were leveraged by their post-colonial host states and communities as critical, interdisciplinary legislative platforms to affirm and legitimise marginalised cultural forms while simultaneously subverting established international hierarchies and projecting possible collective political futurity.

Festivals can also introduce potentially high-risk, disruptive interdisciplinary practices within a safe, low-stakes environment, a structure that validates new practices and simultaneously generates powerful economic and symbolic value associated with host cities or locations. As with the founding programme of the Manchester International Festival, and to a certain extent the Shanghai Project, interdisciplinary cultural production can be strategically adopted as a powerful tool to simultaneously fulfil civic, economic and artistic demands. MIF's success was rooted in its high-risk commissioning of exclusively new and interdisciplinary works which served three critical and entwined logics: generating unique distinction to elevate the city's international brand; showcasing innovation as demanded by public and corporate funders; and ensuring broad audience appeal/accountability by aggregating audiences from across art forms. This approach strategically leveraged the spectacle of creative risk to acquire symbolic and financial capital for the city.

All of these organisational forms, from those more closely aligned with interdisciplinarity at their core, to festivals as platforms for experiments, are about managing and mediating a set of parameters that shape the space created for interdisciplinary production. In the interviews, several curators and producers talked about how they sought to control or shape these parameters, and in doing so sought to create or 'hold space'. What this meant in practice, was an articulation of how they understood these shaping parameters impacted upon those involved in collaborative projects. Holding space meant defining these parameters, both by what they enabled to happen in the context of interdisciplinary collaboration, but also what it allowed them to keep out of that space as well. Holding space was about offering a protective role, a caring role, a role that kept certain demands that might taint those working processes, be they institutional, instrumental, financial, practical, or logistical, at bay. This was about working out what the genuine borders and boundaries were vs the percieved borders and boundaries – as it was only by testing them in practice that they became evident. While holding space meant setting some parameters, it also meant getting out of the way as required to let things take their course, to play out, to flow. That required trust. And through all the discussions with curators and producers there was a continual articulation that trust was essential. Trust in the process and method, trust in people. This is also a reminder that it is hard to achieve anything by oneself, and there is great privilege in collaboration with others who know things you do not and are willing to share that openly and reciprocally.

Even if we look at extreme examples of parameters such as the 24 hours of Rhizome's *Seven on Seven* – the constraints and public performativity can be intentionally leveraged by cultural institutions to create a high-risk, low-expectation environment that nonetheless strategically benefits the organisation, the participants and yields occasional, stark intellectual and aesthetic insights, innovations, and generates valuable critical discourse. Yet it is also clear that from the long durations of interdisciplinary cultural production, exemplified by Arts Catalyst's mode of 'co-inquiry' (Triscott and Santomauro, 2021), that time is an essential, non-negotiable resource required to achieve depth, rigour and transformative change at a local level. Such working processes allow cultural organisations and their partners to move beyond superficial collaboration to facilitate a deep, iterative and reciprocal transfer of disciplinary and situated knowledge. This slow, patient process is crucial for building the necessary trust, navigating complex bureaucratic and ecological constraints, allowing for failure, and ultimately enabling nuanced outcomes by aligning a project's pace with complex systems and the lived temporalities of the issues being addressed.

We can see how parameters and constraints function most clearly by their absence in the approach developed by The Centre for the Less Good Idea. Here, financial and artistic autonomy can enable an egalitarian space that prioritises process, emergent discovery and non-hierarchical exchange over external pressure for pre-determined outcomes, financial accountability, or rigid disciplinary adherence. By operating in a 'responsive mode' and eschewing conventional, bureaucratic structures, The Centre is able to create an incubator studio environment where practitioners from diverse fields can embrace the mess of many things coming together to ensure that interdisciplinary collaboration is a creative privilege for practitioners that might otherwise not get the opportunity (Lace, 2025).

As with AfroAsia, successful place-based interdisciplinary arts management can be defined by the organisation's capacity for constant, pragmatic adaptation to complex social and geopolitical realities to build solidarity between distinct, isolated communities. But this takes time, resources and a willingness to become embedded and part of those localities; there is no quick fix. Operating in a 'contact zone' (Kim, 2024) like Dongducheon in South Korea, AfroAsia demonstrated that bridging significant cultural, linguistic and historical divides (between Korean locals, African migrants and US military personnel) can require organisations to function as active social mediators to effectively generate meaningful interaction, challenge historical stigmas and foster newly co-created local narratives.

Audiences, participants, users, and so on, are all implicated in different ways through processes of interdisciplinary cultural production. But the relationships between these groups and the cultural organisations that facilitate interdisciplinary projects are characterised by a central tension: while the work's novelty or innovation is highly valued, its departure from disciplinary conventions makes the audience a significant liability that must be carefully considered. Arts and cultural organisations that work through interdisciplinary methods conceive of the audience across a spectrum, from a purposeful afterthought, prioritising the working process, to a meaningful, practical component. This potential of interdisciplinarity in relation to the audiences and publics is three-fold: there is the promise to eliminate the audience by turning them into active co-authors (risking tokenism if engagement is superficial), there is the promise of education by serving as an instrumental tool for knowledge transfer (risking subordination), and there is the promise of audience development and diversification through aggregation (risking the alienation of established or conventional audiences or appealing only to a narrow adventurous group). Consequently, producers must strategically reframe the audience relationship where possible to mitigate these core risks to ensure the perceived value of the work is realised. In doing so interdisciplinary cultural production requires a conscious commitment to risk the security of specialisation in exchange for imagining and creating space to engage with a more complex and critical understanding of the world.

Bibliography

Barry, A. and Born, G. (eds.) (2013) *Interdisciplinarity: Reconfigurations of the Social and Natural Sciences*. Abingdon: Routledge.

Fiske, C. (2013) 'Playing telephone': An interview with Amalia Pica', *Art in America*, 10 April. Available at: www.artnews.com/art-in-america/interviews/playing-telephone-an-interview-with-amalia-pica-56318/ (Accessed: 14 August 2025).

Kim, J. E. (2024). 'Rethinking the "Arts of the Contact Zone" after thirty years: Korea between the Cold War and decolonization'. *Inter-Asia Cultural Studies*, 25(2), 157–160.

Lace, B. (2025) Interview with Bronwyn Lace, Co-founder & Director, The Centre for the Less Good Idea. Interviewed by Peter Merrington [Zoom], 18 March.

MoMA. (2025) *Amalia Pica: Venn Diagrams (Under the Spotlight), 2011*. The Museum of Modern Art. Available at: www.moma.org/collection/works/220342 (Accessed: 14 August 2025).

Triscott, N. and Santomauro, A. (2021) 'Transdisciplinary co-inquiry as curatorial methodology: From the Canadian Arctic to the Calder Valley, Yorkshire', in Rogers, H.S., Halpern, M.K. and de Ridder-Vignone, K. (eds.) *Routledge Handbook of Art, Science, and Technology Studies*. Abingdon: Routledge.

INDEX

For Product Safety Concerns and Information please contact our
EU representative GPSR@taylorandfrancis.com Taylor & Francis
Verlag GmbH, Kaufingerstraße 24, 80331 München, Germany